NAJIB MAHFUZ

Najib Mahfuz 1987

NAJIB MAHFUZ

The Novelist-Philosopher of Cairo

Menahem Milson

St. Martin's Press, New York

The Magnes Press, The Hebrew University, Jerusalem

© The Magnes Press, The Hebrew University, Jerusalem 1998

St. Martin's Press, Scholarly and Reference Division, 175 Fifth Avenue, New York, N.Y. 10010

First published in the United States of America in 1998

Printed in Israel
Typesetting and Layout: Daatz, Jerusalem
ISBN 0-312-21518-5

Library of Congress Cataloging-in-Publication Data

Milson, Menahem.
        Najib Mahfuz: the novelist-philosopher of Cairo / Menahem Milson.
p. cm.
Includes bibliographical references and index.
ISBN 0-312-21518-5 (cloth)
1. Mahfuz, Najib, 1911- -- Criticism and interpretation.
I. Title.
PJ7846.A46Z7125   1998   98-14267
892'.736--dc21   CIP

To Arnona

Contents

Preface

I have been a faithful reader of Najīb Maḥfūẓ's works for many years. I discovered him in 1963, when, as a newly appointed lecturer at the Hebrew University of Jerusalem, I was looking for novels to use as material for a course on contemporary Arabic literature. As my background was principally in medieval Arabic, and my knowledge of modern writers stopped with the generation of Taha Husayn, I started to read contemporary Arab authors with whom I was unfamiliar. The first Egyptian novelist I tried was Najib Mahfuz, and before I was half-way through *Bidaya wa-nihaya* ("The Beginning and the End," 1949) I told myself with satisfaction: "This is really a good novelist." I was impressed by the narrative power of the novel, by the realistic descriptions of Cairo and its people, and, above all, by the humane spirit which pervaded the book. Much to my regret, this book was too long for my first-year students, and my continued search brought me to the much shorter *al-Liss wa'l-kilab* ("The Thief and the Dogs") published twelve years later, which I loved and which I have never ceased to admire. From this point on, I tried to get hold of as many of Mahfuz's books as I could. At the time – that is, before 1967 – books printed in Arab countries could be obtained in Israel only through Blackwell, Brill or Luzac, the famous Oriental book-dealers of Europe. I have tried to read everything Mahfuz has published and have used many of his novels and short stories in courses I have taught.

Mahfuz's stories awoke in me an immediate sense of recognition and shared values, even friendship. Here was a person I wanted very much to meet and talk to, but at the time there was little prospect of our ever meeting. At the end of 1970, I sent a copy of my first published article on Mahfuz to the author himself. Because of the political circumstances and the absence of direct postal services between Israel and Egypt, I sent the letter via an Israeli colleague on sabbatical in England. Together with the article I enclosed three lines of medieval Arabic poetry:

> Tell a friend whom God has not allowed me to meet
>   that although I have not met him, I do meet him
> And that my gaze is turned upon him
>   though his abode is far from mine
> God knows, I do not recall him to mind
>   for how can I recall him, if I have never forgotten him.

A couple of months later I received Najib Mahfuz's generous reply, which he concluded as follows:

> I was profoundly moved by the verse you chose with such sincerity and affection, and I can find no better response than this verse by [the medieval poet] Mihyar:

> Remember us, as we remember the days of our friendship
>   how often memory brings the departed near.

In 1979, on my first visit to Cairo, I finally met Najib Mahfuz and was able to enjoy his hospitality.

Since 1932, when the twenty-one-year-old Mahfuz published his first short story, he has produced more than fifty volumes of novels, short stories and plays, in addition to many screenplays and articles. This is virtually a library, within which there is a great variety not only of genre and theme, but also of literary style. Mahfuz has moved from classical nineteenth-century realism to more modern forms of narrative. He has been the subject of a multitude of book-length studies and innumerable articles in both Arabic and Western languages. Three of the books which have appeared in English deserve special mention. The earliest and best known of these is Sasson Somekh's *Changing Rhythm* (1973), which presents a systematic study of Mahfuz's novels up to 1966, and includes a postscript reviewing his publications between 1967 and 1971. The two most recent books on Mahfuz in English are Rasheed El-Enany's *Naguib Mahfouz* (1993), a comprehensive and perceptive study which includes chapters on Mahfuz's works in the 1970s and 1980s, and Michael Beard and Adnan Haydar's valuable collection of articles, *Naguib Mahfouz: From Regional Fame to Global Recognition* (1993).

Why then another book? Great writers can be read in many ways which are not mutually exclusive. In this book I present my own reading, and attempt to illuminate some areas of Mahfuz's work and personality which have so far been overlooked. My approach is one of close reading of the text – a product, no doubt, of my philological training in classical Arabic and my study of medieval Islamic texts. This book is based primarily on analysis of Mahfuz's works in terms of their linguistic and literary sources. His writings are not only the subject of my research, but also my main interpretative instrument: Mahfuz's works cast light upon one another. Mahfuz's biography and the historical and social background, interesting and important as they are, take second place here. I do not regard literary works as symptoms of an author's psychological development, nor do I view biography, as such, as an explanation of art. A writer's biography is, however, always of interest to his readers as context and support for interpretation, and I have therefore included a fairly long and detailed biography of Mahfuz in Part One of this book.

It is remarkable that knowledge of Mahfuz's life remains limited. Students of Mahfuz are obliged to rely primarily on the interviews he has given, in which he has very carefully protected parts of his biography and concealed his more personal feelings, insisting that a writer should reveal himself only through his art. Thus, all those who have written about Mahfuz, including myself, must rely essentially on the same published sources. There are, therefore, no major differences between my description of Mahfuz's life and those which have appeared in earlier books. Close scrutiny of Mahfuz's interviews, including some of the less well known among them, has, however, enabled me to cast light on a number of previously obscure points. I have attempted to emphasize those aspects of Mahfuz's biography which are particularly relevant to his writing, and have specifically dwelt on those details which I believe to be at the root of certain distinctive traits in his art (such as his unadmitted hostility towards his father and his attitude to his own name).

Part One opens with a brief chapter on the emergence of the Egyptian novel and Mahfuz's literary forerunners. Its third chapter, "The Works of Mahfuz," surveys the writer's literary output from its earliest beginnings to his most recently published works. I have paid particular attention to Mahfuz's early stories; though far less accomplished than the later novels for which he is famous, these stories help us understand the moral and intellectual attitudes which underlie everything he wrote.

Mahfuz, like other great novelists, creates his own universe. Many of those who have written about him refer, indeed, to "the world of Najib Mahfuz," but the contents of this world have not been sufficiently defined. Over the years, Mahfuz has developed a unique imaginative vocabulary and a Mahfuzian iconography which, once identified and interpreted, leads to a better understanding of his works. Some basic terms in his fictional topography – ḥāra ("neighborhood") and khalāʾ ("wilderness") – have been explained by Rasheed El-Enany, but, on the whole, his vocabulary of images has been insufficiently explored. Part Two of the book, "Recurrent Images, Persistent Ideas," is devoted to this topic.

I found it helpful to pursue recurrent themes in Mahfuz's works; one such theme which attracted my attention was his consistently critical portrayal of fathers. As it turns out, this motif in Mahfuz's fiction has its roots in his personal experience, a fact he has tried hard to conceal in his interviews. At various points throughout the book, I indicate how Mahfuz's criticism of the father extends beyond specific fictional cases and, through his use of allegory, assumes political and religious dimensions.

Politics are of great interest to Mahfuz. This has been recognized by most of his critics, and openly admitted by Mahfuz himself. Yet one of the most conspicuous of his political concerns – his attitude to Nasser – was ignored by researchers for many years. Part Three, "Mahfuz as Political Critic" – a revised version of an article I published in 1989 – addresses this issue and examines the various forms of allegory which Mahfuz uses to express his political views. Besides political sensitivities, which may have deterred scholars from delving into Mahfuz's political allegories, there may have been an additional factor at work: the low esteem in which allegory has long been held by many literary scholars. This attitude is a legacy of the Coleridgian romantic view, which regards symbolism as artistic and exalted, and allegory as inferior and mechanical – and thus, unworthy of a major writer. For Najib Mahfuz, however, allegory is an extremely important literary mode. To overlook allegory is to shut oneself off from an essential dimension of Mahfuz's work.

The most idiosyncratic expression of Mahfuz's predilection for allegory is his use of allegorical names. This aspect of Mahfuz's work, which has been largely ignored, has its roots in the writer's personal experience. When I first read Mahfuz's stories I was struck by the care with which he selected names for his characters. The author's special attention to names is to be found everywhere in his work, but, while its presence is unmistakable, its meaning and intent are neither clear nor uniform. This phenomenon aroused my interest in the names of Mahfuz's characters in general. I found that in many cases where there seemed to be no obvious analogy between name and character, further inquiry revealed that Mahfuz, with meticulous care, had loaded the name with a hidden message, to be decoded by the attentive reader. I realized that Mahfuz's choice of meaningful names was more than just a literary device: it was related on the one hand to his experience with his own name, and on the other to his philosophy of language. In Part Four of this book, "What's in a Name," I offer an interpretation of Mahfuz's use of names in six of his major works and two of his early stories.

When I put together the textual findings and the biographical data, the fragments combined to form a clear, intelligible picture. In Part Five, I summarize and tie up my main themes and arguments: Mahfuz's special interest in names and naming, the peculiar story of his own name, his attitude to his father and to the patriarchal order, his allegorical approach, and his philosophy of life.

My exploration of Najib Mahfuz's world continues; nevertheless, I feel I have reached a stage at which I want to share my understanding of Mahfuz's works and the pleasure I took in interpreting them with both the specialist and the general reader.

Acknowledgements

I should like to thank those who have helped me with this book. I wrote the first draft in 1989–90, when I was a visiting scholar at the Woodrow Wilson International Center for Scholars in Washington, D.C. I am indebted to the Center and its staff, and in particular to Heather Sharkey and Bill S. Mikhail who, as interns, undertook invaluable bibliographic research. Heather Sharkey also typed the whole first draft of the manuscript, offering many stylistic suggestions. Their assistance was rendered particularly enjoyable by their enthusiasm.

A number of my colleagues have read the book and contributed both approval and criticism. My thanks are due to Etan Kohlberg, Aryeh Levin, Shmuel Moreh, Shlomith Rimmon-Kenan and Shaul Shaked of the Hebrew University of Jerusalem, and to Mahmoud Manzalaoui of the University of British Columbia.

I should like to take this opportunity to thank the Hebrew University's Research and Development Authority for contributing a special grant toward the publication of this book.

Four chapters of this book are revised versions of two articles which I published originally in *Asian and African Studies*. Chapter four, "Rational Man, Rebellious Devil" and chapter seven, "One Vision, Three Narrative Modes" are based on my article, "Reality, Allegory and Myth in the Work of Najib Mahfuz," which appeared in *Asian and African Studies*, vol. 11, no. 2 (Autumn 1976); both chapters of Part Three, "Mahfuz as Political Critic," are adapted from "Najib Mahfuz and Jamal 'Abd al-Nasir: the Writer as Political Critic," *Asian and African Studies* 23 (1989). My thanks are due to the editors for their permission to make use of this material.

I should also like to thank all those at the Magnes Press who were directly concerned with the production of this book. Dan Benovici, the director of the press, showed an interest and understanding far beyond the requirements of his official position. Doron Narkis, style editor for the Magnes Press, supplied valuable suggestions and corrections. I am also grateful to Joan Hooper, Fern Zeckbach and Susan Fogg who read the proofs, and to Carol Sutherland and Fern Zeckbach who helped me to prepare the index.

Daniel Spitzer generously volunteered his advice on all matters concerning the book's format, and gave unstintingly of his time and his vast store of experience in book production.

A special debt of gratitude is due to Carol Sutherland who, as language editor, has followed this book from its first draft to completion, offering innumerable suggestions on matters of style. Her help was indispensable.

Note on Transliteration and Translations

For transliteration of Arabic words and names I have used a simple system resembling that of the *International Journal of Middle East Studies*. However, I have generally omitted diacritical marks, and have added them only where necessary to ensure correct identification of the Arabic form or to prevent confusion between words which appear identical in English spelling. All transliteration reflects the literary Arabic form and pronunciation, i.e., the Arabic consonant *jim* is always transliterated as *j* (e.g., Najib) and not as the Cairene *g* (e.g., Naguib). Arabic words and place names which have a standard English spelling have not been changed.

All the translations from Arabic which appear in this book are my own, unless otherwise stated.

PART ONE

THE NOVELIST, HIS WORLD
AND HIS WORKS

CHAPTER I

The Emergence of the Modern Egyptian Novel

When the Nobel Prize in literature was awarded to the Egyptian novelist Najīb Maḥfūz in October 1988, a wave of joy swept through the whole Arab world. The fact that an Arab writer had won the Nobel Prize for the first time was a cause for exceptionally great joy in Arab countries, because of the special value and prestige which Arabic literature has in Arab tradition, and the large role it has played in the emergence of modern national consciousness. Naturally, the Egyptians in particular were elated; it was an Egyptian writer who had won for all Arabs this much-coveted token of literary recognition.

Literature is *the* Arab art. Other forms of artistic expression – architecture, painting, music – are not distinctively Arab. The great medieval architectural monuments in Arab countries are Islamic in nature, but not necessarily Arab in origin, attesting rather to a variety of influences, especially Byzantine and Persian. The exquisite miniatures which appear in Arabic manuscripts are mostly Persian in origin. Arab music, which is widely loved and enjoyed by Arabs, has always been viewed with some ambivalence because music is morally suspect in Islam. Its rather dubious standing prevents it from being considered a national art.

It is literature which is distinctively Arab because its medium is, of course, the Arabic language – itself the object of admiration and the source of national pride for all Arabs. (The Egyptians, fifty-seven million in number, constitute one third of all Arabs.) Arabic – chosen by Allah to reveal the Qur'an, the religious truth in its final, consummate form – is considered by Arabs to be the richest and most perfect of all languages. Its sanctity confers special status on the literature written in this revered medium. The popularly-held prestige of Arabic literature would be otherwise hard to understand since illiteracy still runs high in the Arab countries and since the reading of literature is not particularly widespread.[1]

Arabic literature is much older than any of the European literatures, having its origins in the end of the sixth century (a few decades before the advent of Islam) when tribal bards in the Arabian peninsula developed a poetic idiom with an elaborate system of meter and rhyme. For the Arabs, the odes of those ancient poets have remained throughout the ages the model of lyric perfection. Arabic literature flourished in the lands of Islam from Baghdad to Cordova for some six centuries, until the middle of the thirteenth century, when the Mongols devastated the cultural centers of the eastern domains of Islam, and Christian princes pushed the Moors out of most of Spain. A long period of cultural stagnation set in, yielding relatively little in Arabic literary output that was innovative or inspiring. It was only when the Arab world began to modernize under the impact of the West in the nineteenth century that modern Arabic literature began to develop, influenced heavily in content and form by European models.

Thus, although traditional Arabic literature began some fourteen centuries ago, modern Arabic literature is younger and much less self-confident than European literature. In 1932, in a public lecture entitled "Arabic Literature and Its Position among the Great World Literatures," Taha Husayn, the most prominent Egyptian writer of the period, said: "We would be doing injustice to ourselves and to our modern literature if we compared it with the great European literatures, just as it would be unfair to those European literatures if we compared them with our emerging modern literature which is just learning to stand on its own feet."[2]

The Arabs have long awaited admission to "the club" of Western

[1] The rate of illiteracy in Egypt is 52%, in Syria 36%, in Morocco 51%, and in the Arab Republic of Yemen 62%, according to the *World Bank Atlas* (1996).
[2] Taha Husayn, *Min hadith al-shi'r wa'l-nathr* (Cairo, 1932), p. 3.

literature, and it is Najib Mahfuz who has provided the key for Egypt and the rest of the Arab world; hence the gratitude and admiration felt towards him.

In poetry, Western influence was felt mostly in the realm of ideas; in matters of form, the Arab poets of the late nineteenth and early twentieth century found their models in classical Arabic poetry. Much as the poets of the eighth, the ninth and the tenth centuries applied the poetic idiom of the tribal poets of pre-Islamic Arabia to the milieu of the caliphal courts of Damascus and Baghdad, the modern poets during the first half of this century applied the same revered and powerful poetic idiom to new subjects.[3]

But in the field of prose things were different. Those modern writers who wished to create narrative literature dealing with the new reality found no models in their own tradition. It is not that Arabic literature lacked genres of artistic prose, but those that existed were unsuitable as models for fictional narrative.[4]

Arabic possessed, indeed, an esteemed prose literature known as *adab*. This term, understood nowadays simply as "literature," originally referred to the total stock of knowledge that a cultivated person was expected to master.[5] The famous medieval compilations of *adab* were multi-volume encyclopedic works that included countless bits of information from a great variety of sources on a multitude of topics, such as philology, history and religion, the ways of government, the qualities of women, etc. An invaluable source of learning, *adab* did not, however, offer an appropriate model for modern fiction.

A unique genre called *maqama*, which contains a narrative ele-

---

[3] With few exceptions, classical poetic forms held sway until the end of the 1940s. In 1947 free verse (*al-shi'r al-hurr*) was adopted, and has since become the dominant poetic mode. See Pierre Cachia, *An Overview of Modern Arabic Literature* (Edinburgh, 1990), pp. 179–200 ("Tradition, Imitation and Originality in Poetry"). For further information see S. Moreh, *Modern Arabic Poetry 1800–1970* (Leiden, 1976).

[4] Discussing this problem in his pioneer work on the emergence of modern Arabic literature, H. A. R. Gibb noted (1929): "Classical Arabic literature offered practically no models for prose works of entertainment in the modern style." Gibb's "Studies in Contemporary Arabic Literature" originally appeared (in four parts) in *BSOAS* in 1928–1933; it is included in his *Studies on the Civilization of Islam* (Boston, 1962), pp. 245–319, whence it is cited here (p. 261).

[5] On *adab* see H. A. R. Gibb, *Arabic Literature* (Oxford, 1963), pp. 52, 78; for further information see *EI*², s.v. "Adab."

ment of sorts, was developed in the tenth and eleventh centuries. Each of the famous collections of *maqamat* by the two medieval masters of this genre is a series of chapters, composed in highly ornate rhymed prose, describing the adventures of a witty, erudite rogue.[6] A series of episodes, the chapters are only loosely connected through the personalities of the narrator and the hero-rogue. The main artistic quality of the *maqama* is its linguistic virtuosity.[7] Among the attempts by Egyptian writers to adapt the *maqama* to modern use at the beginning of the century, the most successful was *Hadith 'Isa ibn Hisham* ("The Story of 'Isa ibn Hisham") by the journalist and author Muhammad al-Muwaylihi (1858–1930).[8] (Mahfuz mentions that al-Muwaylihi was a friend of his father's and that his *Hadith 'Isa ibn Hisham* was the only work of literature his father possessed.)[9] However, the *maqama* did not become a model for emulation. Its reliance on rhymed prose and recondite vocabulary – the very qualities that had endeared it to sophisticated readers in previous centuries – made it unacceptable to the modern writer.[10]

To a Western reader familiar with the enchanting tales of the *Arabian Nights*, it may seem curious that Arab writers should turn to Western models of fiction rather than to their own literary legacy. Yet, for complex reasons, Arabs have never considered the *Arabian Nights* "high" literature. It has had a somewhat dubious reputation

---

[6] The two celebrated masters of the *maqama* were Badi' al-Zaman al-Hamadhani (968–1008) and Abu Muhammad al-Qasim al-Hariri (1054–1122).

[7] On the *maqama*, see Gibb, *Arabic Literature*, pp. 100–102, 103–25. For further information see *EI*[2], s.v. "Makama."

[8] See Gibb, *Studies*, pp. 289–91, and Roger Allen, *The Arabic Novel* (Syracuse, 1982), pp. 28–30. Al-Muwaylihi first serialized this work in his father's newspaper under the title *Fatra min al-zaman* ("A Period of Time"), but in 1907, when he published it as a book, he entitled it *Hadith 'Isa ibn Hisham* and the original title became a subtitle.

[9] Jamal al-Ghitani, *Najib Mahfuz yatadhakkar* (Beirut, 1980), p. 25.

[10] Al-Muwaylihi's *Hadith 'Isa ibn Hisham* is typically described (in the above-cited article on the *maqama* in *EI*[2]) as "both the first major achievement of 20th century Arabic literature and the swan-song of classical [Arabic] literature." In his study of the emergence of the modern Arabic novel, Moreh demonstrates that al-Muwaylihi's *Hadith 'Isa ibn Hisham* was influenced by al-Ma'arri's *Risalat al-ghufran* much more than by al-Hamadhani's *Maqamat*. Moreh suggests that al-Muwaylihi called his narrator 'Isa ibn Hisham (the name of the narrator in al-Hamadhani's *Maqamat*) in order to associate his composition with the esteemed classical genre of the *maqama*, and thus lend it respectability. See Moreh, *Studies in Modern Arabic Prose and Poetry* (Leiden, 1988), pp. 103–15.

both linguistically (its language is not the sublime classical Arabic but rather "Middle Arabic," influenced heavily by the colloquial language of the Arab Middle Ages) and morally (its characters, men and women alike, are described as seeking and unabashedly enjoying the pleasures of sex).[11] It has, of course, been widely enjoyed in the Arab world but was usually read privately and secretly; young men would hide it from their fathers or teachers.[12] Above all, the *Arabian Nights* was not "modern." With its stories of demons, sorcerers, giants, and magic carpets, it represented the very opposite of what the modern Arab writers wanted their works to be.[13]

Another narrative tradition was that of the popular romances recounting the heroic feats of the Arabian tribe of Banu Hilal, or the adventures of the pre-Islamic Arabian legendary poet-hero 'Antar (colloquial for 'Antara).[14] Professional storytellers, popularly called poets, had been recounting these stories for generations in cafés and teahouses in every Arab country, to the accompaniment of a one-stringed instrument called a *rababa*. Regarded as both vulgar in language (using the vernacular), and unmodern in spirit, this epic tradition, too, was rejected by the modern writers. Significantly, one such *rababa*-wielding "poet" figures as a minor character in one of Najib Mahfuz's novels, *Zuqaq al-midaqq* ("Midaqq Alley," 1947).[15] This professional storyteller is forced to give up his place in the café when his form of entertainment becomes obsolete with the advent of radio. This is one of the signs of the passing of the old customs.[16]

---

[11] On Arab scholars' contempt for this literature, see Moreh, *Studies*, pp. 90–91.

[12] In his autobiographical novel *al-Ayyam*, Taha Husayn relates: "They would pore over [the books they brought home to read during the school vacation] all day and a part of the night. Their aging father approved of this and praised them. But often, on those occasions when they immersed themselves in stories such as the *Arabian Nights* or the romance of 'Antar or Sayf ibn Dhi Yazan, he would become annoyed and reproach them." Taha Husayn, *al-Ayyam*, part 2 (Cairo: Dar al-ma'arif, 1966), p. 175.

[13] On the *Arabian Nights* see EI[2], s.v. "Alf layla wa-layla." That the *Arabian Nights* did not play a role in the emergence of the modern Arabic novel has been noted by many scholars; see Allen, *The Arabic Novel*, p. 16, and Cachia, *An Overview of Modern Arabic Literature*, p. 104.

[14] On these romances see "The Saga of Banu Hilal," EI[2], s.v. "Hilal" and ibid., s.v. "'Antar."

[15] Translated by Trevor Le Gassick as *Midaq Alley* (Beirut, 1966).

[16] *Zuqaq al-midaqq*, pp. 7–10.

Asked in an interview about the role of cafés in his life, Mahfuz recalled that he first entered one as a child to listen to the stories of the "poet": "The first type of narrative I ever encountered came from the *rababa*-playing poet in the café. . . . "[17]

So, in the realm of fiction, the genres of the short story, the novel and the play were borrowed from the West.[18] As an Egyptian scholar puts it: "[Narrative fiction] turned completely to the way followed by Western writers, emulating Western artistic models in the short story and the novel, and turning its back on those experiments which attempted to draw on the classical heritage, such as Muwaylihi's *Hadith 'Isa ibn Hisham*."[19] Najib Mahfuz has stated his view clearly: "The modern literary genres are imported. Some of them may have roots in our [literary] heritage, but in their current form they are imported. . . . The novel in particular is a genre which is almost unknown [in our heritage]."[20]

Here, as in other cultural areas, Egypt led the way in the Arab world. In the last generation of the nineteenth century, writers in Egypt, including Christian immigrants from Lebanon, began experimenting with the imported genre; they translated novels from European languages, mostly French, and imitated their form in writing original works.[21]

This period of experimentation produced various historical novels on subjects taken from Islamic history, as well as novels with modern subjects that were mostly didactic, draping a very tenuous plot with

---

[17] *Al-Musawwar*, Cairo, 21 October 1988, p. 18.

[18] This is generally recognized by Arab and Western scholars alike. See Shawqi Dayf, *al-Adab al-'arabi al-mu'asir fi misr* (Cairo, 1961), pp. 203–17; see also Cachia, *An Overview of Modern Arabic Literature*, pp. 104–22. In his chapter on the modern Arabic novel (s.v. "Kissa" in *EI*²), Charles Vial states: "The modern [Arabic] *kissa* [i.e., novel] owes nothing to Arab tradition. It is linked neither with the folklore of the *Thousand and One Nights* nor with the tales of chivalry nor with narrarives of *adab*."

[19] Ahmad Haykal, *al-Adab al-qasasi wa'l-masrahi fi misr*, 3rd ed. (Cairo, 1979), p. 25; cf. also Gibb, *Studies*, pp. 291–92.

[20] *Hiwar*, 3 (March-April 1963), p. 71.

[21] French authors whose books appeared in Arabic in the latter part of the nineteenth century and at the beginning of the twentieth century include Chateaubriand, Jules Verne, Fénelon, Alexandre Dumas (père), Bernardin de Saint-Pierre and Victor Hugo. See Muhammad Yusuf Najm, *al-Qissa fi 'l-adab al-'arabi al-hadith – 1870–1914*, 2nd ed. (Beirut, 1961), pp. 13–21.

moral advice and edifying information.[22] It was not until the 1920s that truly Egyptian realistic novels began to appear, heralded in 1913 by Muhammad Husayn Haykal's *Zaynab*.[23]

Set in an Egyptian village, *Zaynab* is a story of romantic love which ends tragically with the death of the heroine. This celebrated "first realistic Egyptian novel" is pervaded with romantic spirit. Its lengthy descriptions of the beauty of nature and its idyllic tableaux of work in the fields seem to have been inspired not only by the author's nostalgic mood (Haykal wrote this novel while a student in Paris), but also by his fascination with the teachings of Rousseau.[24]

After World War I, the call for independence became more insistent, and the question of Egypt's national identity a hotly debated subject among intellectuals and politicians. In this climate, some Egyptian literati regarded the development of indigenous fiction as a matter of national importance.[25]

Mahmud Taymur (1894–1973), one of the early masters of the Arabic short story, wrote that realistic fiction is one of the signs of a healthy national life. He declared emphatically: "It is a shame for us, at the beginning of our [national] renascence, to have no Egyptian literature speaking our language, expressing our ethos and emotions and drawing a true picture of our customs and milieu. This is the sort of literature we should be concerned with . . . because it is the mirror which faithfully reflects our true image. Nay, it is more than that – it alone represents us, body and soul; in a word, it is us."[26] Realistic fic-

[22] The champion of the Arabic historical novel was Jurji Zaydan (1861–1914), a Lebanese immigrant to Egypt, who between 1891 and 1914 published 23 historical novels. On Zaydan and his work see Thomas Philipp, *Ǧurǧī Zaidān: His Life and Thought* (Wiesbaden, 1979).

[23] On Haykal (1888–1956) see Charles D. Smith, *Islam and the Search for Social Order: A Biography of Muhammad Husayn Haykal* (Albany, 1983). On *Zaynab* see Gibb, *Studies*, pp. 291–98. See also Hilary Kilpatrick, *The Modern Egyptian Novel* (London, 1974), pp. 20–25; Allen, *The Arabic Novel*, pp. 31–34, and Smith, pp. 47–53.

[24] The influence of Rousseau's *La Nouvelle Héloïse* on Haykal's *Zaynab* is clear. A few years later, Haykal wrote a two-volume study of Rousseau. In his introduction to the third edition of *Zaynab* (published in 1932), Haykal notes that when he wrote the novel he was under the spell of French literature.

[25] See Israel Gershoni and James P. Jankowski, *Egypt, Islam and the Arabs* (New York, 1986), pp. 191, 209–10.

[26] Mahmud Taymur, *al-Shaykh jum'a wa-aqasis ukhra*, 2nd ed. (Cairo, 1927), p. 10.

tion was viewed as both an instrument for bringing the people to modernity and civilization, and as the proof of having achieved that status.

In the years following World War I, a number of other Egyptian authors wrote novels or fictionalized autobiographies. The most notable of these was Taha Husayn (1889–1973), the blind genius who came to be known throughout the Arab world as "the dean of modern Arabic literature." The story of his childhood, al-Ayyam ("The Days," 1929), first serialized in 1926–1927, was regarded as a landmark in the development of modern Arabic literature.[27] The book made a deep impression on the young Najib Mahfuz, who was fifteen at the time it was published. In an interview with Fu'ad Dawwara, Mahfuz mentioned that he tried his hand at describing his own childhood, much in the style of Taha Husayn. This work, al-A'wam ("The Years"), has never been published.[28] In the same interview he recalled another early novel, Ahlam al-qarya ("Village Dreams"), which Salama Musa read and found unfit for publication.[29]

Other eminent Egyptian men of letters wrote novels, among them Tawfiq al-Hakim whose 'Awdat al-ruh ("The Return of the Spirit," 1933), a two-volume, largely autobiographical story, is set at the time of the Egyptian nationalist upheaval of 1919. In spite of its structural faults, this work held a special place in the development of Egyptian literature, mainly because its subject matter (the birth of Egyptian nationalism) had a strong appeal to readers, but also because of its realistic approach and the extensive use of colloquial Egyptian in the dialogue.[30] Al-'Aqqad (1889–1964), known mainly as a poet, literary

---

[27] Pierre Cachia, Taha Husayn: His Place in the Egyptian Literary Renaissance (London, 1956). See also Albert Hourani, Arabic Thought in the Liberal Age (London, 1962), pp. 324–40.

[28] In an interview with Fu'ad Dawwara, al-Katib, 22 (January 1963), reprinted in Dawwara's Najib Mahfuz min al-qawmiyya ila al-'alamiyya (Cairo, 1989). Mahfuz's remark on al-A'wam is to be found on pp. 220–21 of Dawwara's book.

[29] Dawwara, ibid., p. 223. Mahfuz speaks of this book with some irony: "From its title you can imagine what its subject was." Set in an Egyptian village, the novel was probably inspired by Haykal's Zaynab. In another interview, Mahfuz remarks: "It was an isolated experiment which I never repeated." Mahmud Fawzi, Najib Mahfuz – za'im al-harafish (Beirut, 1989), p. 74.

[30] Hilary Kilpatrick, The Modern Egyptian Novel, pp. 41–44.

critic and thinker, also dabbled in this genre. In 1938 he published *Sara*, a tedious, inept account of the ambivalent relationship between the narrator and the eponymous heroine, in what is more of a psychological inquiry than a story.[31] His fame rests, however, on his other literary activities; as a thinker, he influenced a whole generation of younger Egyptian intellectuals, Mahfuz among them.[32]

These three Egyptian intellectuals – Taha Husayn, Tawfiq al-Hakim and al-'Aqqad – are the ones Najib Mahfuz with true modesty mentioned as having deserved the Nobel Prize before him. As Mahfuz put it, "There is no doubt that my winning the prize is partly a matter of luck, because I was preceded by writers at whose feet I sat; the last great one of them [was] Tawfiq al-Hakim."[33]

Haykal, Taha Husayn, Tawfiq al-Hakim, al-'Aqqad and others of their generation were not primarily novelists. They engaged in various cultural and, in some cases, political pursuits, to which writing novels was only peripheral. Narrative fiction had not yet been acknowledged as serious literary art.[34] However, the late thirties and forties saw the emergence of a new generation of writers who devoted themselves to fiction – short stories and novels. Najib Mahfuz was among them.

It would appear that the disdain with which educated Arabs had traditionally viewed the widely popular *Arabian Nights* and the orally transmitted epics of Banu Hilal and of 'Antar was carried over to the new narrative fiction. It was Najib Mahfuz who, in December 1945, published an apologia for the novel in the literary magazine *al-Risala*.[35] This came as a response to no less a literary personality than al-'Aqqad, who a few months earlier had made some disparaging remarks on the novel in his book *Fi bayti* ("At Home").[36] Al-'Aqqad claimed that the novel's lesser value was apparent in the fact that one

[31] Al-'Aqqad, *Sara*, translated into English by Mustafa Badawi (Cairo, 1978). On *Sara* see Kilpatrick, pp. 30–35.

[32] On al-'Aqqad as a critic, see David Semah, *Four Egyptian Literary Critics* (Leiden, 1974), pp. 3–65; on his political thought, see Nadav Safran, *Egypt in Search of Political Community* (Cambridge, 1961), passim.

[33] Interview in *al-Musawwar*, 21 October 1988, p. 11.

[34] See below, p. 29, and interview with Mahfuz, Ghitani, pp. 26–27

[35] "Al-Qissa 'ind al-'Aqqad," *al-Risala*, 3 December 1945, pp. 952–54.

[36] The book was published in Cairo in August 1945.

line of poetry could convey an idea or an experience in a way that a novel could hardly accomplish in fifty pages. He also claimed that the popularity of the novel among a certain "social class" (supposedly low or poorly educated) was in itself proof of its inferiority. Through detailed argument, Mahfuz pointed out the absurdity of al-'Aqqad's judgment. The article demonstrates not only Mahfuz's fine understanding of the distinctive qualities of the art of the novel, but also his readiness to take on the famous al-'Aqqad in its defense. Mahfuz concludes, "The novel is the poetry of the modern world."

A fundamental problem facing modern Egyptian writers was the choice of language for their realistic fiction. Egyptians, like all Arabs, use two kinds of language: the spoken, which is a particular colloquial Arabic dialect, and the written, or literary Arabic, "the eloquent language" (al-fuṣḥā), the language of the Qur'an, of classical Arabic poetry and of all serious literature. Arabic dialects vary greatly from one region to another, and they all differ from literary Arabic, which is however the same throughout the Arab world.

To appreciate the dilemma this poses for Arab authors, one must bear in mind the sharp dichotomy between literary Arabic with its high prestige, as the most important part of the cultural heritage shared by Arabs; and the colloquial dialects, called al-'ammiyya, "the vulgar idiom," regarded as a corrupt form of the literary language.

Thus, certain practices regarding the use of the literary and the colloquial have evolved in modern times. Today, newspapers, magazines and news broadcasts are all in literary Arabic. The only parts in newspapers using the colloquial are cartoon captions and jokes. Most serious drama is in literary Arabic, comedies are in colloquial. Movies, too, are in colloquial, unless they are films on historical subjects.

Literary Arabic was the language used in the novels and stories written at the end of the nineteenth and the beginning of the twentieth century. But when true representation of reality became the literary ideal, the problem of language had to be considered in the light of this powerful new concept. It has remained a deeply perplexing problem for Arab writers to this day. How could literary language convey mundane conversations between people who in reality speak a colloquial dialect? It would be contrary to the notion of realism for characters who were illiterate to use the lofty, literary language which they would not even know. In *Zaynab*, Muhammad Husayn Haykal chose to write the narrative parts of the story in the literary language and the dialogue in the Egyptian colloquial. But the same characters whose words Haykal rendered in the colloquial when they spoke with other people, he presented as using literary Arabic when they were "speaking in their mind" (in interior monologues).

Tawfiq al-Hakim in his novel *'Awdat al-ruh* (1933) followed the same procedure. Other writers, such as Taha Husayn, chose to write in the literary ("eloquent") Arabic exclusively – narrative, dialogue and all. Mahmud Taymur, who, in his programmatic introductions to his short stories in the 1920s, proclaimed the need to create realistic literature that would authentically mirror Egyptian life, started by using colloquial Arabic in dialogue in his short stories. But later, in the 1930s and 1940s, he switched to writing only in literary Arabic and even published new editions of his earlier stories, in which he translated into literary Arabic the dialogue originally written in the colloquial.[37]

Many of the writers of Najib Mahfuz's generation and of the younger generation continue in the tradition begun by Haykal: narrative in literary Arabic and dialogue in colloquial. Mahfuz, however, has followed the line of Taha Husayn, using only literary Arabic. He was often asked why he made this choice. In 1957 he stated in an interview: "I recognize only literary Arabic as a language fit for the writing of literature. The colloquial language is not a language in its own right. . . . It is one of the maladies which afflict our people, from which they will surely be delivered as they progress, as they will be from ignorance, poverty and disease. The writer should aim to create a new Arabic language by taking that which is alive and useful

[37] In the introduction to the second edition of *al-Shaykh jum'a wa-aqasis ukhra* (pp. 14–15), Taymur explains this change: "At first I was convinced that the language of dialogue, that is the conversations, should be written in the colloquial language, because this is closer to actual reality, and, in fact, I wrote the dialogue in many of my stories in that language. But I renounced this view, after repeated experiment showed me that it was an error. There is a wide gulf between these two languages [the literary and the colloquial], and if we use them side by side, one for description and the other for dialogue, it creates palpable incongruity."

from both the literary language and the colloquial. There is also a political consideration: Arab nationalism can be based only on one language, which is naturally the literary Arabic."[38]

When asked a similar question several years later, Mahfuz still insisted on referring to colloquial Arabic as "a malady." But he added: "Nevertheless, I do not want this opinion, to which I am deeply committed . . . to become a missionary doctrine. Every writer is free to use the language he chooses. I read the works of those who write in colloquial, and I enjoy them."[39]

In 1980 he described how he came to create his literary idiom: "The most difficult battle in which I was engaged was my struggle with language. When I began [to be a writer] I regarded the [Arabic] language – as we were taught it in school – as [consisting of] sacred molds which had to be invariably applied to all subjects. Thus you find me, in my historical novels, influenced by the style of the Qur'an, while writing about the Pharaohs. . . . This did not result from any artistic need, but from my desire to express myself in a beautiful style, because I believed, as we had been taught in school, that style is a value in itself. . . . When I started to write realistic novels, I came up against reality. I found myself subconsciously engaged in a struggle: how could I develop this [classical] language so that it would fit the subject."[40] He has been eminently successful in representing in literary Arabic the speech of his characters, educated and illiterate alike. This is, indeed, a unique achievement.[41]

Mahfuz's consistent use of literary Arabic enhanced the popularity of his works throughout the Arab world, whereas Egyptian writers who use the colloquial limit their potential audience in other countries. Outside of Egypt, readers find novels using Egyptian colloquial in dialogue somewhat difficult to follow, although the Egyptian dialect, through Egyptian movies and television, is now understood by many Arabs outside Egypt.

---

[38] 'Abd al-Tawwab 'Abd al-Hayy, *'Asir hayati* (Cairo, 1966), p. 133.

[39] Dawwara, p. 231. Cf. Mahfuz's interview with the critic Ghali Shukri, *Hiwar* 3 (March–April 1963), p. 67.

[40] Interview in *October*, 22 June 1980, p. 22.

[41] It should be noted, however, that Mahfuz is no classical purist, and that he has introduced occasional colloquial usages into his prose. See Sasson Somekh, *The Changing Rhythm: A Study of Najib Mahfuz's Novels* (Leiden, 1973), pp. 134, 152–53 and 190.

According to one bibliographer, seventy novels were published in Egypt between the end of World War I and 1952; no fewer than six of these were by Najib Mahfuz.[42] He published his first short story in 1932, before he was twenty-one years old. His first novel went to press in 1939, while the older masters of the earlier generation were still active and publishing their works and while the novels of others of his generation were also making their debut. Mahfuz was clearly regarded as a promising writer: in 1941 he was one of three novelists to receive an award from the Egyptian Academy of the Arabic Language for a novel. Yet, despite the rather favorable reception which his novels had during the 1940s, Mahfuz would appear to have suffered from a feeling that he was not sufficiently appreciated.[43]

While the flow of novels increased in the decades following World War I – especially in the thirties and forties – it was generally felt that the literary standard of those works, on the whole, fell short of European and American standards. It was only when Najib Mahfuz published his famous Cairene trilogy in 1956–57 that Arab critics felt confident that Arabic literature had finally produced its Dickens, its Balzac, or its Dostoevsky. An Egyptian critic wrote at the time: "I don't know what the writer felt when he completed this great work. But I can tell you what I felt. I felt a great joy and relief that we had finally produced a truly great novel."[44]

The Cairene trilogy established Mahfuz incontestably as the foremost Egyptian – indeed, the foremost Arab – novelist. Once it was published, the acclaim was universal. At long last Egypt and the Arabic language had a great modern novel. Taha Husayn, "the dean of modern Arabic literature," greeted the work as "the greatest accomplishment in the field of the novel in the Arabic language in modern times." He affirmed, "This novel stands up well in comparison with any one of the great novels in world literature."[45]

---

[42] Taha Wadi, *Dirasat fi naqd al-riwaya* (Cairo, 1989), pp. 137–51; also Muhammad Yusuf Najm, "*Faharis al-adab al-'arabi al-hadith*," *al-Abhath* (March 1963), p. 133.

[43] See Dawwara, ibid., p. 223. On the reception accorded to Mahfuz's early novels see 'Ali Shalash, *Najib Mahfuz: al-tariq wa'l-sada* (Beirut, 1990) pp. 100–105.

[44] 'Ali al-Ra'i, "*Thulathiyyat bayn al-qasrayn*," in *Dirasat fi 'l-riwaya al-misriyya* (Cairo, 1964), p. 245; see also in Ghali Shukri (ed.), *Najib Mahfuz: Ibda' nisf qarn* (Cairo, 1989), p. 63.

[45] Taha Husayn, "*Bayn al-qasrayn*," *Min adabina al-mu'asir* (Cairo, 1959), p. 80. This

Mahfuz's road to recognition and popularity was not easy. Luwis 'Awad, one of Egypt's most eminent critics, wrote in 1962, "I don't know any writer who, like Najib Mahfuz, was unknown, wronged and neglected throughout his literary life for no good reason, only to have all the roads to glory open before him in the last five years, again for no good reason."[46] Although Luwis 'Awad was not particularly kind to Mahfuz, he did affirm that "Mahfuz has become a popular institution about whom people speak of their free choice in cafés, at home, and wherever literate people meet."

For the Arab public, the fact that thirty-one years after the appearance of the trilogy it was Najib Mahfuz who was chosen by the Swedish Academy as the first Arab writer to be awarded the Nobel Prize was a reaffirmation of something they already knew; it was a fully warranted decision which had been long overdue. Celebrating this event, a leading Egyptian critic entitled an article he wrote at the time, "Nobel Wins the Najib Mahfuz Prize."[47] By the time Mahfuz received the prize, he was already established as the most widely admired writer of fiction in the Arab world. His name had become familiar to Arabs who did not even read literature, by virtue of the many films based on his novels and stories, shown in cinemas and on television throughout the Arab world. The Egyptian public in particular sees him as one of themselves, as the writer who describes their lives and their problems with deep empathy. Their attitude toward him is one of wholehearted admiration.

---

was high praise indeed, if we recall that it was Taha Husayn who, in 1932, maintained that modern Arabic literature had not yet developed to the point where it could be compared with the great European literatures.

[46] Luwis 'Awad, "al-Liss wa'l-kilab," in Ghali Shukri (ed.), ibid., p. 101. It is, indeed, only after the appearance of the trilogy that Mahfuz was acclaimed as Egypt's leading novelist, but, as was demonstrated by 'Ali Shalash, he had been quite favorably received even before that, and was neither "unknown" nor "neglected." See Shalash, ibid.

[47] Ghali Shukri, "Nobel yafuz bi-ja'izat Najib Mahfuz," in al-Ahram, 19 October 1988, p. 12. Other articles in the Egyptian press express the same sentiment. A list of some two hundred articles published in Egyptian papers in the weeks following Mahfuz's winning the prize includes the following titles: "He Deserved It Before Many Others," al-Masa', 19 October 1988, p. 3; "Najib Mahfuz Has Given a Certificate of Credibility to the Nobel Committee," al-Jumhuriyya, 20 October 1988, p. 9; "Finally, the Nobel Prize Has Redeemed Itself," ibid., 31 October 1988, p. 5. See 'Alam al-kitab 25 (1990), pp. 172–78.

CHAPTER 2

Najib Mahfuz and His Cairo

Najib Mahfuz was born on 11 December 1911 in Cairo, the city which is the setting for all but one of his novels. Mahfuz has never vacationed, let alone lived, outside of Egypt, except for two short trips he made as a member of official delegations to Yugoslavia and to Yemen. (He went to Yugoslavia in 1956 for a writers' conference, and to Yemen in 1966, with a group of Egyptian writers and journalists sent by the Government as observers and apologists for Egypt's war there.)[1] Indeed, he has hardly left his native city except for summer trips to Alexandria. For Mahfuz, Cairo is the universe.

His life covers a period in which many changes – political, social and cultural – have taken place in Egypt and in Cairo. At the time of his birth, Egypt, though still, formally, under the supreme sovereignty of the Ottoman sultan, was, in fact, a separate entity, having become virtually independent of Ottoman rule in the early nineteenth century under Muhammad 'Ali. Muhammad 'Ali's rise to power was occasioned by a crucial event in the history of the region: Napoleon's invasion of Egypt in 1798 which, though short-lived, left its indelible mark on the region, heralding the beginning of Westernization and shaking the very foundations of Ottoman rule. After a chaotic interregnum lasting a number of years, Muhammad 'Ali, an Albanian officer in the service of the Ottoman sultan, eventually seized power, then engineered his official nomination by the sultan as viceroy of

---

[1] Jamal al-Ghitani, *Najib Mahfuz yatadhakkar* (Beirut, 1980), p. 93.

Egypt in 1805. He established a dynasty which was to rule Egypt for a century and a half, until it was brought down by the 1952 revolution.

The British occupied Egypt in 1882 and ruled the country, without changing its nominal status as an Ottoman province, until the outbreak of World War I, when it was formally declared a British protectorate. By the end of the war, Egyptian nationalists, under the charismatic leadership of Sa'd Zaghlul, were clamoring for independence. When the British deported Sa'd Zaghlul, in February 1919, a rebellion broke out. Riots and large-scale demonstrations forced the British to allow his return and eventually to grant Egypt partial independence. Subsequently, in 1922, the Egyptian Sultan Fu'ad (great-grandson of Muhammad 'Ali) declared himself king.

The British continued, however, to exert great influence on Egyptian affairs and continued to maintain troops along the Suez Canal, a situation which the Egyptians bitterly resented. As a character in Mahfuz's Cairene trilogy expresses it, "We are now in 1935, eight years since the death of Sa'd Zaghlul, fifteen years since the [1919] rebellion, but the English are still everywhere – in [their] barracks, in [command of] the police, in [command of] the army, and in all the ministries. And the foreign concessions are still in force, making every [foreign] son of a bitch into a revered lord."[2] This residue of British domination was finally removed by Nasser in 1956, when he nationalized the Canal and ordered the British out.

For Mahfuz, who was only a child at the time, the 1919 rebellion has remained the most crucial event in Egypt's modern history, and Sa'd Zaghlul has remained its hero. Fifty years later, Mahfuz told an interviewer, "To tell you the truth, I did not distinguish between the two [my love for Sa'd Zaghlul and my love for Egypt], I loved them together, it was difficult for me to separate the two. . . ."[3] A faithful supporter of Sa'd Zaghlul's party, the Wafd, Mahfuz would not forgive Nasser for banning this and all other parties, for suspending parliamentary life and for attempting to obliterate Sa'd Zaghlul's memory.[4]

---

[2] *Al-Sukkariyya*, p. 50

[3] "*Najib Mahfuz wa-thawrat 1919*," an interview with Samih Karim, *al-Katib* (Cairo, April 1969), p. 22.

[4] Mahfuz mentions that when, in 1977, the newly resurrected Wafd held a memorial for Sa'd Zaghlul and for his successor, Mustafa Nahhas, these names were new to his daughter. "This was a great shock to me," says Mahfuz. Ghitani, p. 79.

Egypt had been opened up to Western influence more than a century before Mahfuz's birth, in the aftermath of Napoleon's invasion in 1798. Muhammad 'Ali and his successors wanted to build a strong army as protection against the encroaching European powers as well as against the Ottoman sultan, Egypt's nominal suzerain. To achieve their purpose, they had to acquire the military technologies of the West, a quest that paved the way for other cultural imports.

European cultural influence became especially conspicuous under Muhammad 'Ali's Francophile grandson Isma'il, who ruled from 1863 to 1879. Isma'il tried to turn Egypt into a part of Europe, and Cairo into another Paris. (His reckless spending, presumably to achieve this goal, brought instead financial ruin and eventually British occupation.) The Cairo Opera House, modeled on the Paris Opera, was for a century a monument not only to his relentless Westernizing zeal but also to the appalling gap between the Westernized upper class and the masses.[5]

Demographic change in Mahfuz's lifetime has been equally dramatic. Before World War I, the population of Cairo was about three quarters of a million and the total population of Egypt about eleven million. By the time Mahfuz was working on his Cairene trilogy around 1950, Cairo's population had tripled to two and a quarter million, while Egypt's population approached twenty million. Cairo has grown constantly since then, due largely to a massive influx from the countryside, and is today an exploding megalopolis of eleven million people (out of Egypt's total population of fifty-seven million).

Mahfuz was born in a quarter of Cairo called Jamaliyya, which is part of the old section of the city built by the Shi'ite Fatimid caliph who captured Egypt in 969.[6] This caliph founded it as a garrison town for his army and named it *al-Qahira*, "the victorious" (whence Cairo); it quickly overshadowed the older garrison city established more than three centuries before by the Muslim Arab army which had conquered Byzantine Egypt. Surrounded by an old wall and full

[5] The opera house was built in 1869 and was inaugurated in November of that year as part of the celebrations for the opening of the Suez Canal. This vestige of European culture was destroyed by fire in 1971.

[6] See *EI*[2], s.v. "Fāṭimids."

of mosques and *madrasa*s (religious colleges) built, generation after generation, by the rich and powerful seeking prestige in this life and reward in the next, this part of Cairo has a very distinctive traditional character. The revered shrine of al-Husayn, to which worshippers flock from all over Cairo, and the famous bazaar of Khan al-Khalili are also part of the Jamaliyya quarter. Adjacent to it is al-Azhar, to this day the most famous center of Islamic learning, built by the same Fatimid caliph who founded Cairo. History and tradition have remained palpable in Mahfuz's native neighborhood, more than in any other part of Cairo, in spite of modernization.

The mixture of the old and the new, the indigenous and the imported has been present in Cairo in all aspects of life ever since the beginning of modernization. When Mahfuz was born, Cairenes were already using a tram system built at the end of the nineteenth century by a Belgian company, but horse- and donkey-drawn carts and carriages were still the most common means of transportation. Even today, when all types of modern vehicles congest the streets of Cairo, one regularly sees donkey-drawn carts in the midst of early-morning traffic, carrying vegetables from the farms to the city markets. Donkey-drawn garbage carts are a common sight in every section of the city. Then as today, one would see men in *galabiya*s next to men in Western suits, women dressed according to European fashion alongside women in the traditional black *milaya*s which cover them from head to toe. In Cairo, the old does not disappear; it continues to exist alongside the new. With the constant influx of immigrants from the rural areas, which have always been less affected by the imported new ways, Cairo continually absorbs masses of people who maintain the old traditional ways for another generation or so.

When Mahfuz was a child, a middle-class woman would not appear in public without veiling her face. But the veil has disappeared gradually since the mid-1920s. (In 1930, the university opened its doors to women, signifying another major step toward emancipation.) During the last decade, under the impact of the growing fundamentalist movement, more and more women appear in public with their hair covered with a head-scarf; the face veil, however, has not returned.

Information on the personal life of Mahfuz is rather scanty. This may seem an odd comment to make about the most famous twentieth-century Arab writer, about whose work so much has been written (Mahfuz and his works have generated more than fifty volumes of studies, reviews and interviews, in addition to chapters devoted to him in dozens of books dealing with modern Arabic literature, thousands of articles in newspapers and journals and scores of unpublished Ph.D. dissertations all over the Arab world). But Mahfuz is an extremely private person; he has always kept his personal life away from the public.[7] Even his literary friends and colleagues did not find out that he was married until several years after the marriage had taken place.

The two main sources of information about Mahfuz are the interviews which he has given over the years and his works, particularly the Cairene trilogy. In this novel, the character of Kamal comes very close to being the author's alter ego, as a child aged ten to twelve in the first volume of the trilogy, as a student of seventeen to nineteen in the second volume, and as a bachelor in his late thirties in the third volume. Kamal represents the psychology and intellectual quandaries of Mahfuz. In an interview with Ghali Shukri, he said: "Kamal reflects my intellectual crisis. It was, I believe, the crisis of a whole generation; otherwise I would not have emphasized it as much as I did."[8] Mahfuz has frequently declared that Kamal is the only character in whom, as he puts it, "I deposited directly a portion of myself."[9] In another interview Mahfuz has said that he sometimes regrets having created a character so closely similar to himself. Although Mahfuz did not explain the reason for his regret, one may conjecture that he came to feel that through Kamal he had allowed the public to

---

[7] Fatma Moussa-Mahmoud, a well-known Egyptian literary scholar, notes: "Fans of long standing and critics who have interviewed him were never invited to his home." "Depth of Vision: the Fiction of Naguib Mahfouz," *Third World Quarterly* I, n. 2 (April 1989), p. 156.

[8] *Hiwar* 3 (March–April 1963), p. 67.

[9] E.g., interview in *October* (22 June 1980), p. 22; *al-Musawwar* (October 1988), p. 15. In both of these interviews Mahfuz stresses that Kamal represents his intellectual and psychological crises. He adds, however (in the interview in *October*), "This does not necessarily mean that I am him." See also his interview with Ghali Shukri, *Hiwar* 3 (March–April 1963).

scrutinize his own private life too closely. Mahfuz has rejected suggestions that Kamal's parents were closely modeled on his own. But his childhood friend, Dr. Adham Rajab, recalls Mahfuz's father as so strict that Mahfuz's friends never visited him at home, and he believes that this is reflected in the portrayal of the stern patriarch in the trilogy.[10] Mahfuz, however, while admitting that there is something of his own mother in Kamal's mother, Amina, has consistently denied that Kamal's despotic father in any way resembles his own.[11] This denial, however, is not fully convincing; the literary evidence to the contrary is overwhelming: many of Mahfuz's works portray fathers as selfish autocrats.[12]

His many interviews are a somewhat problematic source of information. Sabri Hafiz, who edited a collection of ten interviews with Mahfuz, says: "In most of the interviews with the great novelist Najib Mahfuz, he speaks like a cunning diplomat, hinting rather than speaking frankly and resorting to silence when confronted with questions to which he does not want to give a final answer or when he enjoys the disputes of those who argue about them."[13] He seems happy to supply information about his reading, literary preferences and views on language and art. When he is required to explain his controversial political opinions – a recurrent subject for many years now – his answers tend to be ambiguous. He has told his interviewers very little about his relations with friends and colleagues and hardly anything about his many years as a civil servant. When it comes to his family history, he is reticent; the information he gives about his parents and his brothers and sisters is minimal, and he refuses to talk about his marriage.[14]

---

[10] Adham Rajab, "*Safahat majhula min hayat Najib Mahfuz*," al-Hilal (Cairo, February 1970), p. 99.

[11] Ghitani, p. 116.

[12] One of the most revealing examples of this is the short story "*al-Qarar al-akhir*" ("The Final Decision"), in which the violent and despotic father suffers a sudden stroke while quarrelling with his son, the narrator. See "*al-Qarar al-akhir*," published in 1996, in the collection of the same name.

[13] *Atahaddath ilaykum* (Beirut, 1977), p. 75. The editor, Sabri Hafiz, provides a bibliography of 129 interviews with Mahfuz published between 1956 and 1972.

[14] 'Abd al-Muhsin Taha Badr correctly remarks on the problematic nature of Mahfuz's interviews in *al-Ru'ya wa'l-ada: Najib Mahfuz* (Cairo, 1984), pp. 10 and 66.

In an interview he gave in October 1957 (when he was forty-six years old), Mahfuz was asked why he had never married. He told the interviewer Jadhibiyya Sidqi (herself a novelist of some repute) that he had been compelled to give up his marriage plans, because after his father's death (twenty years before) he had had to support his mother and his widowed sister. The interviewer commented, "But now, surely, this impediment no longer exists." To this Mahfuz replied that he had missed the right age for marriage. "Marriage," said Mahfuz, "requires flexibility and compromise on both sides; I have got used to being a bachelor and I refuse to change my habits."[15] The interview appeared under the headline "Najib Mahfuz Explains Why He Has Not Married." At the time, Mahfuz had already been married for three years. Technically speaking, Mahfuz did not lie; he did not actually tell his interviewer that he was a bachelor, but he certainly misled her and the readers into believing that he was.

Why did Mahfuz do this? Why was it so difficult for him to say he was married? Did he want to play a joke on the interviewer in retaliation for her attempt to pry into his private life? Was it part of a game of hide-and-seek he has been playing with the public? Whatever the explanation of this puzzling incident, it demonstrates Mahfuz's insistence on protecting his privacy. Mahfuz has often been asked why he has not written an autobiography. He has given all sorts of evasive answers, sometimes saying that he intended to write one, when he had the time, and sometimes – more recently – reminding the interviewer that his *al-Maraya* ("Mirrors," 1972) and *Hikayat haretna* ("Stories of our Neighborhood," 1975)[16] include many autobiographical elements.[17] In an interview in *al-Musawwar* in 1990 he revealed his strong aversion to this kind of literature. He maintains that there is nothing to be gained from the autobiographies

---

[15] *Sabah al-khayr* (Cairo, 31 October 1957), p. 35.

[16] *Al-Maraya* was translated by Roger Allen as *Mirrors* (Minneapolis, 1977); Soad Sobhy, Essam Fattouh and James Kenneson translated *Hikayat haretna* as *Fountain and Tomb* (Washington, 1988).

[17] Researchers and critics have identified some of the characters in *al-Maraya*. See Rasheed El-Enany, *Naguib Mahfouz: The Pursuit of Meaning* (London and New York, 1993), p. 132, n. 8. For a study of *al-Maraya* see Roger Allen, "*Mirrors* by Najib Mahfuz," in Trevor Le Gassick (ed.), *Critical Perspectives on Naguib Mahfouz* (Washington, 1991), pp. 131–50.

of famous writers beyond the cheap satisfaction of reading about scandal. According to Mahfuz, only biographies or autobiographies of politicians and military men, which reveal unknown facts about significant public matters, are of interest. As for the others, says Mahfuz: "I truly suffer when I read such autobiographies or hear about them, and I ask myself, 'What have the writer's father and mother done to deserve this? The writer is a public figure but his father and mother and children are not. Should every family that has a famous son be destined to be shamelessly exposed?'"[18] Mahfuz's belief that the writer has no right to reveal family secrets may explain his insistence that the character of the father in the trilogy bears no resemblance to his own father.

In response to the interviewer's question, Mahfuz harshly criticizes the famous Egyptian writer Luwis 'Awad for having exposed the private life of his parents in his autobiography, published the previous year.[19] Mahfuz says:

> The writer should present his experience in his artistic work, and it would then be above scandal-mongering. It would become a general human experience through which the writer transcends the personal. This has been my conviction ever since I read Jean Jacques Rousseau's *Confessions*. If my life deserved to be written or were beneficial to anyone, I would immediately write [my autobiography]. . . . A writer who at a ripe age still has an abundance of human experiences which need to be told in an autobiography has surely never written anything of value. . . . There may be some exceptions, for example, Taha Husayn who overcame unimaginable obstacles; that is why I respect his autobiography.[20]

A small collection of personal letters, written by Mahfuz to his friend Dr. Adham Rajab in the 1940s and made public by the latter in 1988, gives us a rare opportunity to see something of the private Najib Mahfuz. Regrettably, however, the number of these letters is small,

---

[18] *Al-Musawwar* (Cairo, 19 October 1990).

[19] Luwis 'Awad's autobiography, *Awraq al-'umr* ("Leaves of Life") came out in 1989.

[20] Mahfuz is referring here to the autobiographical novel *al-Ayyam* (1929) by the blind Egyptian writer Taha Husayn. See above, p. 10.

and the period they cover is quite limited (from the end of 1943 to 1947).[21]

Born to a middle-class traditional Muslim family, Mahfuz was the youngest of seven children, by ten years.[22] His father 'Abd al-'Aziz was a government official who upon retirement became an accountant in a store belonging to one of his friends.[23] His name, Najib Mahfuz, was given to him in honor of the obstetrician who delivered him after a very difficult labor.[24] His mother's account of this experience seems to have had a profound influence on Mahfuz, and, indeed, difficult births are described in a number of his stories.[25] In one of them, "Walīd al-'anā'" ("The Child of Suffering"), a short story published in 1970, the difficult birth allegorically represents the suffering of Egypt (the mother) at the time of the war of attrition in 1969–70.[26]

Mahfuz's memories of his early years in school are not very happy. When he was five years old, he was sent to the local kuttab (Qur'an school), where he discovered that he was "the weakest of all the children"; the others used to snatch the food his mother gave him for lunch and eat it.[27] This experience would eventually be described in one of Mahfuz's early stories, "Thaman al-du'f" ("The Price of

[21] These letters were given by Dr. Rajab to Diya' al-Din Baybars, who published them in the Cairo weekly October (11 December 1988), pp. 39–46. The correspondence is incomplete: we have Mahfuz's letters to Dr. Rajab but not the latter's to Mahfuz. The letters are not dated, and their dates must be conjectured on the basis of internal evidence.

[22] Interview, al-Musawwar (21 October 1988), p. 17.

[23] Ghitani, pp. 14–15, 116. Mahfuz's father died in 1937.

[24] In a postscript appended by the publisher to the new edition of some of Mahfuz's novels after he won the Nobel Prize, Sa'id Jawda al-Sahhar, the publisher, writes: "My brother 'Abd al-Hamid told me the following: Najib Mahfuz's mother had a very difficult labor – she was delivered by the famous physician Dr. Najib Mahfuz and she named her newborn son after him" (from the publisher's postscript to Kifah Tiba).

[25] The difficult labor suffered by Kamal's sister 'A'isha is described in the trilogy (Bayn al-qasrayn, chap. 68, pp. 544–52), as is that of her daughter Na'ima who dies in childbirth (al-Sukkariyya, chap. 24, pp. 181–89). It is also the theme of a short story called "al-Samt" ("Silence"), in the collection Bayt sayyi' al-sum'a ("A House of Ill Repute," 1965).

[26] See Menahem Milson, "An Allegory on the Social and Cultural Crisis in Egypt: 'Walīd al-'Anā'" by Najib Mahfuz," IJMES 3 (1972), pp. 324–47.

[27] 'Abd al-Tawwab 'Abd al-Hayy, 'Asir hayati (Cairo, 1966), p. 128. This interview originally appeared in al-Idha'a (21 December 1957).

Weakness").[28] In primary school, Mahfuz remembers, the Arabic teacher used to spend hours telling stories about demons (*'afarit*), and he would warn the children that if they failed to do their homework or did not behave themselves, the demons would come all the way from their abode in hell to punish them.[29] He remembers his years in elementary school for the harsh physical punishments: "I did not read about the [Spanish] Inquisition until after I had finished elementary school, but later I would remember that school with every line I read about the Inquisition. I would remember the ruler hitting my finger joints in the cold of winter and myself almost bursting with pain and tears."[30]

When Mahfuz was ten years old he suffered from a neurological disease which was diagnosed at the time as epilepsy. Apart from missing one year of school, he overcame this illness without any lasting damage. Apparently it did not affect his mental or physical faculties.[31]

In 1924, when he was about thirteen, the family moved from the old Jamaliyya quarter to the then fashionable 'Abbasiyya quarter. Mahfuz was to live in this neighborhood for about thirty years (until his marriage), and the friends he made in secondary school there remained his friends for life. The new neighborhood made the young Najib Mahfuz aware of class differences. The residents of 'Abbasiyya were of two kinds: upper-class and middle-class, those who lived in villas surrounded by gardens and those who lived in modest homes and apartment buildings. The class difference corresponded to a difference in political allegiance: the middle-class supported the Wafd, the aristocracy and upper bourgeoisie the Liberal Constitutionalist Party. Mahfuz recounts: "During lunch break we used to stand in the school yard, the Wafdists talking about battles, principles, goals, strikes and the greatness of the leader [Sa'd Zaghlul]; the Liberal Constitutionalists talking about the plays of Yusuf Wahba, evening parties and the weather of Europe in summer."[32]

---

[28] *Al-Majalla al-jadida* (3 August 1934). See below, p. 60.
[29] *'Asir hayati*, p. 129.
[30] Ibid.
[31] Interview with Sabri Hafiz, *Atahaddath ilaykum* (Beirut, 1977), p. 81.
[32] Ibid.

Mahfuz was an outstanding student both in scientific subjects and in Arabic composition, but he did not do so well in English and other humanistic studies. He was also an excellent soccer player and one of the champions of the school team. Many years later one of his classmates said that he was the fastest player he had ever seen, and that "if he had chosen a career in football instead of in writing, he would have become a national champion."[33]

In his teens, he underwent two crises which deeply affected him for life: a crisis of unrequited love and a religious crisis. When he was about thirteen years old, he became infatuated with a girl – the daughter of one of 'Abbasiyya's wealthy families – who was a few years older than him. In an interview Mahfuz reflected, "It was an experience devoid of any contact, due to the differences in age and social class."[34] But this adolescent love left a very deep impression on his life and work. Many pages of the trilogy describe the excitement and anguish of the enraptured Kamal.

Decades later, in his semi-autobiographical al-Maraya ("Mirrors," 1972), Mahfuz described the love of the fifteen-year-old narrator (presumably based on his own love) for a twenty-year-old beauty in the neighborhood (with whom he never exchanged a word): "This love was a tyrannical power which devoured me body and soul and cast me into an inferno. . . . It recreated me as a new person yearning for everything that is beautiful and real. Love remained, even after she who had inspired it had disappeared, as an incurable, burning madness that lasted ten years." Because of that infatuation, says Mahfuz, his emotional life suffered from "long and complicated crises as though [he were] under the spell of some black magic."[35]

His religious crisis was also very severe. Mahfuz was brought up in a religious atmosphere both in his home and in his very traditional neighborhood of Jamaliyya. The center of religious activity in this neighborhood was al-Husayn mosque, where, according to popular belief, the head of the Prophet Muhammad's grandson Husayn is buried. People from all over Cairo come to worship in this mosque,

[33] Adham Rajab, "Safahat majhula min hayat Najib Mahfuz," p. 93.
[34] Ghitani, p. 21. See also Fu'ad Dawwara, Najib Mahfuz min al-qawmiyya ila al-'alamiyya (Cairo, 1989), pp. 256–58.
[35] "Safa' al-katib," al-Maraya, pp. 210–14.

the most highly revered shrine in the city. As a child in school, Mahfuz was terribly upset to learn that actually Husayn's head was not buried there, and that the tomb was probably empty and was only a symbol.[36] This was an early serious impairment of his naïve belief.

As a student in high school, Mahfuz read about Darwin's theory of evolution and this shook the very basis of his traditional beliefs. The concept of evolution has become the matrix of his understanding of the history of civilization and of all of his social thought. This intellectual crisis was described by Mahfuz in the trilogy as the experience of the adolescent Kamal.

Thus, for Mahfuz, growing out of childhood meant being driven out of the paradise of religious faith. Mahfuz was to come back to this painful experience in some of his works, shaping it as a story of a young man who is banished from home by his father.[37]

The problem of loss of faith and the desperate effort to regain it is a recurrent theme in Mahfuz's work. It is the subject of the short story "Za'balawi"[38] and of the allegorical novel al-Tariq ("The Way," 1964).[39] It is also the main concern of the novel al-Shahhadh ("The Beggar," 1965), the story of a successful lawyer who loses his interest in family and work and tries desperately to find the ultimate meaning of life.[40] In both novels the anxious search ends tragically, in one case in murder and execution, in the other in madness.

Against his father's will and his older brother's advice, Mahfuz did not choose to study medicine, engineering or law, which were promising from a materialistic point of view, but rather philosophy.[41]

Mahfuz explains: "I began to read essays by Egyptian thinkers. The thinkers were those who were held in respect in that period –

[36] Cf. Qasr al-shawq, p. 79.

[37] See the story of Adham in Awlad haretna (Children of Gebelawi) and cf. the story of Ja'far Ibrahim al-Rawi in Qalb al-layl. In some stories, the condition of man banished from God's presence is depicted as banishment from home by an angry mother; e.g., "al-Sada," in the collection Khammarat al-qitt al-aswad ("The Black Cat Tavern," 1968), pp. 17–30, and "al-Hawi khatafa 'l-tabaq," in Taht al-mizalla (1969), pp. 65–79.

[38] In the collection Dunya Allah, 1963.

[39] Translated by Muhammad Islam as The Search (Cairo, 1987).

[40] Translated by Kristin Walker Henry as The Beggar (Cairo, 1986).

[41] Ghitani, pp. 26–27.

Taha Husayn, al-'Aqqad and others. But literature I considered to be a marginal hobby. . . . Al-'Aqqad raised questions concerning the origin of being and the idea of beauty. That was the origin of my philosophical orientation. The novel did not have prestige, and therefore I did not think about devoting myself to literature and the novel. . . . [42] As I read the philosophical essays of the Egyptian thinkers, al-'Aqqad, Isma'il Mazhar and others, I started to ask myself philosophical questions and I imagined that by studying philosophy I would find the right answers. Doesn't he who studies medicine become a doctor and he who studies engineering an engineer? So, my study of philosophy was bound to answer those questions which tormented me. I imagined that I would know the secret of being and the destiny of man, that is, after I graduated from the university. I would graduate knowing the secret of being. I was amazed how people could ignore the secret of being and instead study medicine or engineering. Naturally, my father was shocked. Do you grasp the simplicity of this thought? [I believed that] just as you studied medicine, you could study the secret of being."[43]

For Mahfuz, the purpose of studying philosophy was to try to find the truth which in the past he had found in religion and which he now wanted to rediscover.

Mahfuz's first published work was an article called "The Dying of Old Beliefs and the Birth of New Beliefs," which appeared in Salama Musa's magazine in 1930, when Mahfuz had just finished high school.[44] In this article Mahfuz argues that religious faith is dying in the modern era and is no longer the guiding moral force that it used to be; it is being replaced by new beliefs, among them communism and socialism. Influenced, apparently, by the French thinker Gustave Le Bon (1841–1931), he writes in this article that socialism is bound

[42] See above, p. 11.

[43] Ghitani, pp. 26–27.

[44] "Ihtidar mu'taqadat wa-tawallud mu'taqadat," al-Majalla al-jadida (Cairo, October 1930), pp. 1468–70. Salama Musa, a Coptic intellectual whose magazine provided an important platform for progressive ideas, was a major influence on Najib Mahfuz. Mahfuz's description of the encounter between Kamal's nephew Ahmad and the Coptic editor of al-Insan al-jadid mirrors his own first meeting with Salama Musa (al-Sukkariyya, pp. 104–11).

to have a great attraction for the masses, but that it is also bound to collapse after its initial success, since it will inevitably fail to fulfill its promise of earthly paradise. In the same article he expresses serious doubts as to the benefits of social revolution. A revolution, he argues (like Le Bon), will end by causing more damage than benefit to society, and the country in which revolution occurs will soon find itself back in the same situation it was in before the revolution. The only way to improve the state of society is through gradual evolutionary progress.[45] (The books of Gustave Le Bon, notably *Les Lois psychologiques de l'evolution des peuples*, *Psychologie du socialisme*, *Psychologie des foules* and *Psychologie de l'education* were translated into Arabic and had considerable influence on Egyptian intellectuals during the first part of the century.)[46] It seems that Le Bon's negative views on revolution, which Mahfuz adopted as a young man, have guided his social thinking to this day. The suspicion with which he viewed Nasser's revolution, years later, seems to have had its roots in these early attitudes.

Mahfuz's pessimistic view of the long-range prospects of socialism did not stem, apparently, from aversion to the aspiration to social and economic equality; indeed, under the influence of Salama Musa, Mahfuz would become an adherent of Fabian socialism.[47] Rather, it reflects his awareness of the limitations of human nature. Mahfuz's views on socialism in this article would seem to disclose his remarkable capacity to distinguish between his personal sympathies and

[45] Mahfuz's ideas in this article can be traced to Le Bon's *Psychologie du socialisme* (Paris, 1898); cf. especially pp. 1–9, 464–65.

[46] See Israel Gershoni and James P. Jankowski, *Egypt, Islam and the Arabs* (New York, 1986), p. 134. *Les Lois psychologiques de l'evolution des peuples* and *Psychologie des foules* were translated into Arabic before World War I by Ahmad Fathi Zaghlul, Sa'd Zaghlul's brother. *Psychologie du socialisme*, translated by Muhammad 'Adil Zu'aytar, appeared in 1925, and *Psychologie de l'education*, translated by Taha Husayn, appeared in the 1930s. Mahfuz pays tribute to Le Bon by having one of his characters write an article on his *Psychologie de l'education*; see *al-Sukkariyya*, p. 111.

[47] Mahfuz's preference for those of his characters who are proponents of socialism, such as 'Ali Taha in *al-Qahira al-jadida* and Ahmad Shawkat in *al-Sukkariyya*, has often been noted; see Mahfuz's response to Raja' al-Naqqash in "*Bayn al-wafdiyya wa'l-marxiyya*," *al-Hilal* (February, 1970), pp. 40–41. In *Bidaya wa-nihaya*, Husayn, the "good" character, comes to believe in socialism. Having read a translation of Ramsay MacDonald's book on socialism, he is reassured that "socialism does not conflict with religion, family or ethics" (*Bidaya wa-nihaya*, pp. 301–302).

what he considers to be an objective assessment of reality – a quality which is so characteristic of his novelistic enterprise.

During his years in the university, Mahfuz became better acquainted with Western thought, both classical (Plato and Aristotle) and modern. He seems to have been influenced especially by Henri Bergson's philosophy of evolution and his concept of *élan vital*. Various concepts typical of Bergson's philosophy – the notion of time as a real being, the belief in the freedom of the spirit, the rejection of materialism and, finally, a distrust of any all-embracing philosophical theory – have shaped Mahfuz's thought and artistic vision. He was also influenced by the American pragmatists – specifically Peirce, James and Dewey. Their influence reinforced his rejection of all isms. In addition to Western philosophy, he studied medieval Islamic philosophy under Mustafa 'Abd al-Raziq, a liberal Muslim thinker who had great personal moral influence on him.

While studying philosophy in the university, he began publishing short articles on various philosophical subjects that interested him. Among the subjects he treats in his articles from this early period are "The Development of Philosophy before Socrates," "The Philosophy of Socrates," "Plato and His Philosophy," "The Concept of Laughter in Bergson's Philosophy," "The Idea of Criticism in Kant's Philosophy," "Bergson's Philosophy," "Pragmatism." At the same time he was also writing and publishing articles on literature: on Chekhov, Ibsen, Moliere, and Shaw (an article on *Back to Methuselah*).[48]

One can gauge the deep personal involvement of Mahfuz in his philosophical studies from the way in which Kamal, his fictional alter ego, describes his attitude to philosophy: "During these hours [of reading and writing philosophy] he would turn into a free traveler, exploring unbounded regions of thought. He reads and reflects and takes notes, which he would later collect in his monthly articles. He is being pushed into this struggle by the desire for knowledge, the love of truth, the spirit of mental adventure, and the yearning to find comfort and alleviate his oppressive mood and his deep-seated feel-

---

[48] A full list of the philosophical and literary articles which Mahfuz published in the years 1930–1945 is provided by Badr at the end of his study of Mahfuz. See Badr, *Najib Mahfuz*, pp. 401–4.

ing of loneliness. He finds refuge from his loneliness in Spinoza's monism, consolation for his personal insignificance by participating along with Schopenhauer in the triumph over desire. He alleviates his sorrow over the misfortune of [his widowed sister] 'A'isha with a dose of Leibniz's philosophy on the meaning of evil, and he quenches his thirst for love with Bergson's poetic philosophy. However, his continuous effort did not save him from the torment of mental confusion. Truth is an object of desire which, no less than a desired person, is evasive and coquettish; it plays with the mind, arouses doubt and jealousy, and induces a violent urge for possession and union."[49]

Even while he was studying philosophy, he continued to be interested in literature although, understandably, he read mostly philosophy. But when he graduated from the university and started work on his Master's dissertation, he found himself in the midst of a deep crisis over the question of whether to devote himself to philosophy or to the writing of fiction.[50] Mahfuz described this crisis in a number of his interviews as an extremely acute and tormenting inner conflict.

"I found myself in a horrible struggle between literature and philosophy, a struggle which cannot be imagined except by one who has experienced it. I had to make a decision or go mad. Then there was in my mind a demonstration staged by the characters of Tawfiq al-Hakim's play, *Ahl al-kahf*, of Yahya Haqqi's story *"al-Bustaji"* and by the little blind fellah who knows nothing of the world beyond the bamboo reeds on the bank of the irrigation canal in [Taha Husayn's] *al-Ayyam*, and by many others from Mahmud Taymur's stories. They all marched in one demonstration. So I decided to leave philosophy and march with them."[51]

Mahfuz's decision in favor of fiction was motivated not only by an attraction to literature, but also by the realization that the systematic study of philosophical theory was not leading him to the ultimate truth as he had hoped. His state of mind at the time is reflected in a conversation between Kamal (Mahfuz's alter ego in the trilogy) and

---

[49] *Al-Sukkariyya*, pp. 17–18.
[50] *'Asir hayati*, p. 131.
[51] Ibid.

his friend Riyad Qaldes.[52] Kamal, the "philosopher," on being introduced to Qaldes, the writer, says: "I am a tourist. I only record
things. I don't know where I stand." He doubts everything, even science: "Some prominent scientists doubt that scientific truth conforms
to actual truth." The editor (who has performed the introduction between the two men) responds: "Religion has taken revenge on you,
you have abandoned it to chase sublime truths, and you have come
back empty handed." Qaldes suggests that literature is the answer:
"Science is the language of the intellect and art is the language of human personality in its totality."[53]

Thus, in 1936, Mahfuz decided that literature would be his field
and abandoned his dissertation in philosophy. From that time on he
stopped writing articles on philosophy, and devoted himself exclusively to the writing of fiction.

In an interview published in 1963, Najib Mahfuz mentioned: "I
once wrote a short story, 'Hikmat al-Hamawi,' which best depicts my
literary life." Given this disclosure, it is worthwhile to examine this
story closely. "Hikmat al-Hamawi" ("The Wisdom of Hamawi," in
al-Majalla al-jadida, 18 March 1936) is the story of a writer who
never publishes because he believes he should write a perfect work
that would somehow reflect the essence of all his life's experiences.
As a young man he writes the story of an early unfulfilled love, but
he keeps it unpublished, so as to be able to review it in later years in
the light of future experience. When as a middle-aged man he re-
reads the work of his youth, he considers what he wrote twenty years
before to be unworthy of publication. He now engages in an extensive and thorough reading of philosophy, ethics and major works of
literature in an attempt to grasp the ultimate truth. He keeps taking
notes and writing comments and reflections on what he reads, but
constantly postpones publication because he expects to correct and
improve his writings in the light of future knowledge and deeper in-
sight. This quest continues for years, but instead of leading him to the
truth, only plunges him into doubt and confusion: "I worshipped
truth and pursued it by all the known paths. Then, when I looked to
see how far I had come, I found myself as far away from it as before,

[52] Riyad Qaldes is believed to be modeled on Mahfuz's friend, the writer 'Adil Kamil.
[53] Al-Sukkariyya, pp. 124–28.

as though I were moving round it in a circle, at a fixed distance." At the end of his life, he loses interest in everything. He finds the experience of life meaningless. He has nothing to be published.

The hero's disillusionment with philosophy parallels Mahfuz's own experience at the time the story was written. On the other hand, Mahfuz's assertion that this story best describes his literary life is somewhat puzzling because Mahfuz, unlike the would-be writer in his story, did publish copiously and did not seem hampered by a desire to correct past work in the light of future experience. Mahfuz's statement about the story "Hikmat al-Hamawi" was made in response to an interviewer's question: "At the age of fifty, have you achieved all that you want for yourself in your personal and literary life?"

Mahfuz answered in the affirmative, and went on to explain that he loves all his works just as a man loves all his children, regardless of their fame or success. He then said, "When I published my first novel, 'Fate's Play' ('Abath al-aqdar), I believed I had accomplished something truly great. Years have passed, and today I see it as 'Children's Play' ('Abath al-atfal) and not as 'Fate's Play'!" He then makes the above-quoted statement about "Hikmat al-Hamawi."[54]

What Najib Mahfuz seems to say here is that at different ages he had different personal experiences and differing views of life, and that his literary works reflect these various phases of his personal development. If he had waited before publishing his earlier, less mature works until he could correct them in the light of future experience, he would never have published anything. Unlike his character Hamawi, he was able to resist the temptation to try to produce "the perfect work of art," and instead wrote and published continuously works which at each stage of his life appeared to him genuinely to express his thoughts and experiences.

The story is, however, very interesting in another respect, in that it tells us something about the writer's impulse to publish, which, as we shall see presently, is motivated by the writer's desire to make a name for himself. "Hikmat al-Hamawi" begins with a brief introduction to the family of the would-be writer: "The family name belonged to a

[54] Dawwara, pp. 234–35.

family of noble origin and high reputation in social status and learning." But nowadays the family name is virtually forgotten: "If the name Hamawi were to be mentioned now, it would have no echo, nor would it stir any memory in the heart" (the opening sentence of the story). The hero of the story (the would-be writer) inherited the good name of the family and had the capacity to make his name survive time by his literary enterprise, despite the family's straitened circumstances. But because he did not publish anything, the formerly famous and respected name sank into oblivion.

Mahfuz's comment on *"Hikmat al-Hamawi"* was made some thirty years after the story was written. But this comment does not just come from the wisdom of hindsight of the fifty-year-old Mahfuz being interviewed. Published in 1936, the story seems to reflect the resolve of the young writer Mahfuz to publish, and not to condemn himself to oblivion, as did the would-be author in his story.

Mahfuz had always been an avid reader, even as a child. His reading ranged widely: the moralistic essays and sentimental stories of Manfaluti (1876–1924), known for his rich sonorous language, the historical novels of Jurji Zaydan (1861–1924), classical Arabic poetry. As a boy he was also very fond of detective stories, translated from English and French, which appeared in cheap popular editions. Mahfuz tells us that, at the time, he even tried to rewrite these detective stories, replacing the characters' names with his own name and those of his friends, and changing some of the settings.

In an interview, reflecting on this stage of his childhood literary attempts, Mahfuz says, "The truth is that the desire to write was there from a very early age, even before its motive became clear. During the period that I was addicted to detective stories, I would copy some of them in a special notebook and write my name on it." The interviewer asks, "Do you mean that you would copy, for instance, a story by Sinclair and write on it 'Copied by Najib Mahfuz'?" Mahfuz answers, "I wish it were 'Copied by...,' because this would have indicated a degree of honesty. But I actually wrote, 'Composed by Najib Mahfuz.'"[55]

---

[55] Dawwara, p. 220.

In another interview Mahfuz recalls his early desire to see his name published. He told Fu'ad Dawwara, "As a young boy, I made a habit of writing letters to various newspaper columnists, either supporting or contradicting their opinions, so that I could see my name in print, even at the cost of its being accompanied by expressions of abuse."[56]

When Mahfuz decided to become a writer, he embarked on an intensive program of reading Western literature. He did this in a typically organized and systematic way, preparing a reading list based on Drinkwater's *Outline of Literature*. Shakespeare, Dickens, Shaw, Ibsen, Tolstoy, Dostoevsky and Proust were all on his list; the non-English authors he read in English translation. Naturally he had his preferences: he tells us that he did not especially like Balzac, Faulkner or Hemingway (except for *The Old Man and the Sea*); he admired Melville, Dostoevsky and Tolstoy. Oddly, he did not like Dickens, to whom he is often compared. Shaw is a particular favorite of his, and he has a special place in his heart for Shakespeare. Galsworthy's *Forsyte Saga*, which Mahfuz read in the mid-forties, made a great impression on him. In a letter to his friend Dr. Adham Rajab, he writes: "*The Forsyte Saga* is a great novel. When you read it you will see that it is the daughter of [Tolstoy's] *War and Peace* and perhaps the sister of [Romain Rolland's] *Jean-Christophe*.[57] It is a very extensive novel, of the kind that you would like me to write, but that is a task I cannot undertake until I leave the government service and become a writer in the true sense of the word. When you read it, give my regards to the heroine Irene (if I remember correctly) whom Galsworthy compares to a picture by Titian. Many a time have I contemplated that picture, with the events of the heroine's story spinning in my head."[58]

His cultural interests were not, however, limited to literature; they included music and fine art. Mahfuz is a passionate lover of Egyptian

---

[56] Ibid., p. 222.

[57] It seems that when Mahfuz wrote this letter (probably in 1947), he had not yet read *Jean-Christophe*, which apparently had been recommended to him by Dr. Rajab. This conclusion is corroborated by Mahfuz's subsequent letter to Dr. Rajab in which he remarks that the latter does not share his enthusiasm for *The Forsyte Saga*; he also mentions that he has not yet found the time to read *Jean-Christophe*, as his friend had urged him to do. Adham Rajab, in *October* (11 December 1988), p. 42.

[58] *October* (11 December 1988), p. 41.

music; his eldest daughter is named after the admired Egyptian singer Umm Kulthum. Even in his youth, Mahfuz was known among his friends for his love and talent for music. While a university student he took courses at the Cairo Institute of Arab Music, studying both theory and practice (he learned to play the *qanun*, an oriental stringed instrument).[59] He also devoted much time to listening to Western music and, with characteristic thoroughness, read books on the composers and their compositions. He told an interviewer, "When I learned, for example, that a composition by Debussy would be broadcast, I would prepare myself to listen to it by reading about him and about the composition."[60] Yet Western music has not taken the place of Arab music in his heart. "You may call it [i.e., the love for Western music] a quiet love," says Mahfuz, "but Arab music remains the foundation."[61]

Since he did not travel abroad, Mahfuz acquainted himself with the masterpieces of world art through books; he read various volumes by Herbert Read on art.[62] "My thirst for art is intense," writes Mahfuz to Dr. Rajab, "I want to lose myself in listening to music and contemplating eternal pictures." In a more prosaic tone, he adds, "I visited a number of bookstores to buy [the art books] that I need but was deterred by the excessively high prices."[63]

Ever since his youth, Mahfuz has been trying to learn as much as he can about the development of modern science and technology, by reading popular summaries of scientific subjects; this reading, he believes, has had a lasting effect on his cultural formation and thought.[64] "I am obsessed with reading about science," says Mahfuz.[65] This interest in science is most suitable for a man convinced, as Mahfuz is, that science is humanity's primary means of progress.

Mahfuz graduated from the university in 1934 and was nominated as a candidate for a government scholarship to continue his studies

[59] Dawwara, pp. 215–16; Ghitani, p. 95.
[60] Dawwara, p. 265.
[61] Ibid., pp. 264–68.
[62] See Ghitani, p. 55.
[63] Letter to Dr. Adham Rajab (30 January 1947), *October* (11 December 1988), p. 41.
[64] Dawwara, p. 216.
[65] Ghitani, p. 45.

in philosophy abroad. But the committee passed him over. Mahfuz believes that the committee discriminated against him, mistaking him for a Copt because of his name.[66] In 1934, with Mustafa 'Abd al-Raziq's recommendation, he obtained a secretarial position in the university administration, where he worked for a number of years. Mahfuz recalls, "There wasn't a great deal of work, the library was right in front of me, and I devoured volumes from it every day. During this period I wrote one hundred short stories and three novels: *'Abath al-aqdar, Radubis, Kifah Tiba.*"[67] Years later, Mahfuz would reveal that he was not really interested in writing short stories: "I did not write short stories for the purpose of writing short stories. I wrote novels. And I went around to publishers, but they refused to publish them. But since I wanted to be published, I wrote short stories. Yes, that was the incentive for writing short stories. Mind you, there is something important that you should understand: I derived the subjects of some of these stories from novels.[68] Some people have said that my short stories were [later] turned into novels; it's the other way around."[69]

In 1939, when Mustafa 'Abd al-Raziq became Minister of Religious Endowments (*awqaf*), he arranged for Mahfuz to be appointed his parliamentary secretary.[70] 'Abd al-Raziq used to excuse him from work in the afternoon, saying, "That's in order for you to have time to write, Najib!"[71] After a few years, when 'Abd al-Raziq left the ministry, Mahfuz was transferred to another, less central position in the same ministry, but not in the main building. His new office was located in Qubbat al-Ghori, a sixteenth century building in the vicinity of al-Azhar and the Jamaliyya quarter. This was a happy turn of events for Mahfuz; it brought him back to his native neighborhood, through whose bazaars and alleys he loved to roam. Another benefit

---

[66] See Adham Rajab, "*Safahat majhula min hayat Najib Mahfuz,*" pp. 96–97; see also Mahfuz's interview with Ghali Shukri, *al-Watan al-'Arabi,* no. 48 (12 February 1988), p. 45.

[67] *'Asir hayati* p. 132.

[68] Mahfuz apparently means to say that he derived the subjects of these short stories from *projected* novels.

[69] Ghitani, p. 38

[70] Raja' al-Naqqash in *al-Musawwar* (October 1988), p. 32.

[71] *'Asir hayati,* p. 132.

for Mahfuz was the public library housed in Qubbat al-Ghori, which made it easy for him to obtain books he wanted but could not afford to buy.[72] He worked in the Ministry of Awqaf until 1955; during his last few years in this ministry he was in charge of welfare loans.

Mahfuz's financial circumstances during these years were straitened: as an average employee he was earning a modest salary with which he also had to support his mother and widowed sister. He seems to have been quite bitter about his low income, and in addition he felt that his job was robbing him of the time he needed for reading and writing. His frustration was aggravated by the fact that he had not yet won the literary recognition to which he aspired.

Mahfuz remembers the 1940s as a period of pessimism and despair. In an interview with Fu'ad Dawwara in 1963, he recalls that he and two other young writers, 'Adil Kamil and Ahmad Zaki Makhluf, were tormented by doubts as to the significance of their literary work: "We suffered a very strange psychological crisis characterized by deep pessimism, by a sense that nothing had value and all was absurd, and by all the other things you read about in modern European literature. We were like the heroes of Camus even before he wrote about them. . . . We were on the point of concluding that any effort spent on literature was totally wasted and worthless. . . . Our psychological crisis was aggravated by the fact that 'Adil [Kamil] and I had entered our novels in the Arabic Language Academy competition, but they were both rejected on grounds of morality. . . .[73] We kept asking ourselves, 'Why do we write?' . . . 'Adil Kamil and Ahmad Zaki Makhluf actually stopped writing because of this crisis." Mahfuz and his friends used to hold their meetings sitting on a round lawn near al-Jala' Bridge. As their mood was gloomy, they called their meeting place and the group itself "the ill-starred circle" (al-da'ira al-mash'uma).[74]

---

[72] Ghitani, pp. 104–5.

[73] Dawwara, p. 233. Mahfuz is referring here to 'Adil Kamil's Millim al-akbar and his own al-Sarab, which were entered for the competition in 1946. 'Adil Kamil's novel was accused of being a "communist" work and al-Sarab was considered too bold in its treatment of sex. On this incident see also Mahfuz's letter to Dr. Rajab, October (December 1988), p. 43.

[74] Dawwara, pp. 233–34.

In 1946 he wrote to his friend Dr. Rajab: "I confess to you that I am tormented by gloomy thoughts for hours; I compare myself to my [journalist] colleagues and I am amazed. Take for example Salah Dhihni, he now lives in an apartment in Duqqi rented for twenty-five pounds, which is more than my whole salary, and he has bought a car for six hundred and fifty pounds and he has a readership of about half a million."[75] In another letter to Dr. Rajab (also in 1946), he says, "I pray to God to save me from my [present] job and arrange an obscure job for me in the basement or on the roof, or else make me win the lottery. In any case, I am using my limited time without wasting any of it. I am satisfied that I read *War and Peace* this year. I shall not rest until I write a novel like it or, at least, one close to it, although I feel that the age of long novels has ended. The writer to-day should adopt a condensed and well wrought style, otherwise – those few who are still faithful to books would cease reading and run away to the cinema."[76]

In a following letter, Mahfuz again mentions his hope of writing a long novel, a *roman-fleuve*, one day: "I want you to know that the idea of a long epic novel keeps tempting me. However, I tell you frankly that I shall not embark upon it until I can devote my whole life to it. It is my intention, many years from now, to ask for retirement as soon as I am entitled to it, then I will devote ten years to this work which will be the quintessence and conclusion of my literary life. But before such time – it is absurd. Think of this: a novel like *Khan al-Khalili* must live in me a whole year [before I write it], and then it takes another year to write; now imagine a novel which is ten or fifteen times as long as *Khan al-Khalili*. So, be patient, dear friend."[77]

Yet, in that same year, 1946, despite his declaration that he would not undertake the writing of a long epic novel until he had fully re-tired, and regardless of his feeling that "the age of the long novel has ended," he began writing the Cairene trilogy – a family saga five

---

[75] *October* (11 December 1988), p. 40.

[76] Ibid., p. 45.

[77] *October* (11 December 1988), pp. 44–45. From this and a few other remarks in the letters, it seems that Dr. Rajab urged Mahfuz to embark upon the writing of a long novel, like Tolstoy's *War and Peace*.

times longer than *Khan al-Khalili*.[78] Mahfuz completed this work in 1952.[79]

Reminiscing in 1980 about his years in the Ministry of Awqaf, Mahfuz admits that he preferred his work as a government employee, for all its drawbacks, to being a journalist, which would have probably increased his income:

> I have always refused to become a journalist, fearing that I would be lost; it is an occupation which is not suitable for me, and I have not prepared myself for it. My work in the government was not boring; I used to deal daily with a multitude of people and meet all sorts of types. My years in the Ministry of Awqaf were very rich [in this respect]. I used to meet those who had claims; they came from very different backgrounds: from a grandson of Sultan 'Abd al-Hamid[80] to a poor fellah who had a share in some *waqf* (endowment).... My period in the Welfare Loans Project was especially interesting. Women would come to give their jewelry as security; all day long I used to talk and argue with those women, who came from the low-class, tradition-bound neighborhoods.[81]

Mahfuz's literary output during his fifteen years in the Ministry of Awqaf was impressive: six novels, including the Cairene trilogy.[82]

The completion of the trilogy was a turning point in Mahfuz's life. After he finished it, in April 1952, Mahfuz stopped writing novels

---

[78] The trilogy, which was originally conceived as one novel called *Bayn al-qasrayn*, contains 1,500 pages.

[79] Beginning and completion dates for the trilogy are derived from Ghali Shukri who gives a list of the dates of composition of Mahfuz's novels, from *'Abath al-aqdar* to the trilogy, based, he affirms, on information given to him by Mahfuz. See Ghali Shukri, *al-Muntami: Dirasa fi adab Najib Mahfuz* (Cairo, 1969), p. 452. It should be noted that 'Abd al-Muhsin Taha Badr argues that we should treat this information with skepticism; he specifically doubts that the trilogy was completed before the 1952 revolution, although he does not offer conclusive proof that this was not the case. See Badr, *Najib Mahfuz*, pp. 237–38. In any event, there is no reason not to accept 1946 as the year in which Mahfuz began to write the trilogy.

[80] The 34th sultan of the Ottoman empire, 'Abd al-Hamid ruled 1876–1909.

[81] Ghitani, pp. 104–5.

[82] *'Asir hayati*, p. 132.

and short stories and confined himself for about five years to the writing of film scripts. This interruption in his literary work aroused all sorts of questions and speculations. Of course, it was only when Mahfuz had become a literary celebrity, following the appearance of the trilogy in 1957, that people began to wonder why this great novelist had not written anything since he had completed the trilogy – reportedly, a few months before the revolution. The fact that the halt in Mahfuz's writing more or less coincided with the Free Officers revolution (23 July 1952) led some people to assume that his literary silence was somehow caused by the revolution. One leading Egyptian critic (who was living outside Egypt at the time) presented it as a "silent protest" against the oppressive nature of the Nasserist regime.[83] The explanation Mahfuz himself gave to interviewers in the early 1960s seemed to confirm the assumption of a causal connection between his literary silence and the 1952 revolution. This is how Mahfuz explained his silence to Fu'ad Dawwara in 1963:

> I had been steeped in the realistic mode until I completed the trilogy in April 1952, and I had plans and ideas for seven other novels in the same direction of realism and [social] criticism. Suddenly, the 1952 revolution occurred, and my desire to write those seven novels died with it. . . . Once the revolution had occurred, many writers began to criticize the society of the pre-revolutionary period. As for me, [after the revolution] I suffered the third interruption in my literary career.[84] When the old social order disappeared, I lost my desire to criticize it. I thought that I was finished as a writer, that I had nothing more to say or write. I said this publicly and I honestly believed it; it was not an exercise in public relations, as some people suspected. I remained in this state from 1952 to 1957; I did not write a single word nor did I have any desire to write. I thought that it [that is,

---

[83] Ghali Shukri, *Thawrat al-fikr* (1965), p. 215. Cf. Sasson Somekh, *The Changing Rhythm: A Study of Najib Mahfuz's Novels* (Leiden, 1973), p. 52.

[84] In the same interview Mahfuz mentions two earlier "halts" (as he calls them) in his literary career: the first when he elected to abandon philosophy and devote himself to literature, the second when, after three historical novels, he decided to write realistic novels on the contemporary scene.

Mahfuz's career as a writer] was finished. Then, I found myself writing *Awlad haretna* and it was published in 1959.[85]

The information given here by Mahfuz is not accurate. *Awlad haretna* is indeed the first literary work he published after the revolution; there is, however, a very strong indication that this was not the first book he wrote after his period of silence. In a passing comment (which would appear to have escaped attention so far) in an interview in December 1957, Mahfuz mentions that he has written "nine long novels [of which] the first is *'Abath al-aqdar*, the middle [one] is the *Bayn al-qasrayn* trilogy and the last is *Tharthara 'ala 'l-nil*."[86] It should be noted that when Mahfuz said this, the last book in the series of nine he mentions had not yet been published, and, indeed, did not appear until 1966. Mahfuz would appear to have delayed publication of this last novel for several years, for fear of official reaction to his characters' uncomplimentary comments on the Nasserist regime.[87]

As for his literary silence, Mahfuz admits, in his 1980 interview with Jamal al-Ghitani, that his earlier explanations were not candid:

> I used to say to those who asked me about that period [of silence] that the revolution had achieved the [desired] goals and there were no [social] problems to provoke me [into writing]. This was an explanation intended to clear me of any suspicion, especially since the question as to my silence had political implications. It seemed to me that my answer provided a reasonable explanation; but was this the true explanation? It was merely an explanation. The truth is that I stopped writing for four or five years. What were the causes I cannot honestly say. . . . Perhaps the trilogy was the cause. It is possible that I fulfilled my

[85] Dawwara, pp. 226–27, from an interview published in 1963. *Awlad haretna* ("Children of Our Neighborhood") was translated into English by Philip Stewart, and published in 1981 under the title *Children of Gebelawi* (London, 1981). Mahfuz omits mention of *Tharthara fawq al-nil* ("Chatter on the Nile"), a novel he may have written in 1957, before writing *Awlad haretna*, but which he kept unpublished for a number of years. See below, p. 85.

[86] *'Asir hayati*, p. 127. It should be noted that the published title of the novel is *Tharthara fawq al-nil*, and not as appears here. The difference is, however, insignificant.

[87] See below, pp. 86, 129.

literary vision in it; but I am not so certain about that, because
I had at the time seven subjects [about which I wanted to
write].... I thought that I was finished [as a writer], because
every writer has an artistic age; Rimbaud stopped writing when
he was twenty-two years old. I told myself, "Let me find something else." I found some comfort in writing film-scripts, and
this involved me with the cinema crowd, but all this did not lure
me away from literature. It was the worst period in my whole
life, it was so bad that I wanted to die.[88]

It is quite clear from the above that Mahfuz's literary silence from
1952 to 1957 had nothing to do with the 1952 revolution.[89] Yet, even
in this conversation, Mahfuz delicately avoids mentioning the
immediate cause of this terrible crisis. In his conversations with
Ghitani in 1980, Mahfuz recalls how his publisher, Sa'īd al-Saḥḥār,
turned down the trilogy on grounds of excessive length, and the
devastating effect this had on him. Although he does not mention
that it was this terrible disappointment which led him to stop
writing, it would appear that this was, indeed, the immediate cause
of his five-year literary silence. This is the story as Mahfuz first made
it public in 1980:

When I finished the trilogy I took it to Sa'id al-Sahhar. It was
one novel called *Bayn al-qasrayn*; its division into three parts is
another story which I will tell you shortly. Sa'id al-Sahhar
looked at it and asked, "What's this?" I said, "It's a new novel
called *Bayn al-qasrayn*." He took it and flipped through its
thousand pages, saying, "How can I print it? It's impossible."
    I returned home heartbroken. In the past I had had as many
as three novels waiting to be published, but this had never depressed me. But that night I broke down. After all those years
of work, after that exhausting effort, could I not publish my
greatest and dearest work?... It was a terrible blow. Indeed, I

---

[88] Ghitani, p. 101.

[89] Somekh, *The Changing Rhythm*, rejected the explanation connecting Mahfuz's literary
silence to the 1952 revolution, and suggested, correctly, that its causes were rather personal
and literary. See Somekh, pp. 52–53. However, Somekh did not possess the information
which Mahfuz disclosed to Ghitani only in 1980.

felt deeply offended when, upon seeing the novel, al-Sahhar told me, "This is not a novel, it's a calamity."[90]

To write the trilogy Mahfuz had had to overcome his fear that readers would be put off by its length, and al-Sahhar's curt rejection shattered all his hopes. That al-Sahhar's refusal to publish the trilogy was indeed the primary cause of Mahfuz's literary silence is corroborated by the fact that in 1957, once the trilogy had been published, Mahfuz resumed his writing.

The trilogy was saved by the writer Yusuf al-Siba'i, a cavalry officer who was a member of the Free Officers group and a close associate of Anwar Sadat.[91] When al-Siba'i heard from Mahfuz that he had written a long novel which he could not publish, he volunteered his help. Al-Siba'i told Mahfuz that he was going to publish a magazine and that he would serialize the novel in it. Mahfuz recalls:

> Yusuf al-Siba'i took the whole novel; it was a handwritten manuscript, and I had no copy of it.... If Yusuf al-Siba'i, God have mercy on his soul, had somehow lost that single copy, the trilogy would have been gone forever.... [Some time later, the literary monthly] al-Risala al-jadida came out, and Bayn al-qasrayn began to appear.[92] It was [my publisher] Sa'id al-Sahhar who noticed that the serialized novel was a success. He said to me, "The novel is a success, but it is impossible to publish it in one volume because it is too big." He suggested dividing it into three parts.... I asked him, "What about the title?" He said, "Give [the three volumes] three names."... That is how Bayn al-qasrayn became a trilogy.[93]

Mahfuz kept the original title (Bayn al-qasrayn) for the first volume and gave the next two volumes other names (Qasr al-shawq and al-

---

[90] Ghitani, pp. 59–60.

[91] Yusuf al-Siba'i was a prolific writer of novels, short stories and plays. He was assassinated in 1978 by Palestinian terrorists, because he had accompanied President Sadat to Jerusalem in November 1977. See Joan Wucher King, Historical Dictionary of Egypt (Cairo, 1984), pp. 571–72.

[92] The literary monthly al-Risala al-jadida, edited by Yusuf al-Siba'i, began to appear in Cairo in 1954. The first volume of the trilogy was serialized in it from April 1954 to 1956.

[93] Ghitani, pp. 59–60.

Sukkariyya).[94] All three titles were names of streets in the old quarter of Jamaliyya where the story takes place, and where Mahfuz spent his early childhood. The first volume appeared in 1956, the other two in 1957.[95]

Between 1952 and 1957 Mahfuz wrote only for the cinema, which he considered to be the competitor of serious literature. He became one of Egypt's best cinematic writers. He had, in fact, started writing film scripts a few years before, but at the time only as a sideline. In 1946 the film director Salah Abu Sayf asked Mahfuz to write the script for a film he was planning to make.[96] Mahfuz accepted the offer, as he explained, for financial reasons.[97] (This happened a few months before he wrote, in the above-quoted letter to Dr. Rajab, that the novelist must beware lest his readers forsake him in favor of the cinema.) In another letter to his friend Dr. Rajab, Mahfuz writes apologetically about his new undertaking: "I heard that the son of a bitch [name omitted by the editor] lied to you about me and accused me of having made a final move to the cinema. Don't believe the bastard! A true artist would not desert his art for any reason. Has the cinema ever satisfied an artist?"[98]

Mahfuz's motives for undertaking to write film scripts, even while complaining of not having enough time for his literary work, were arguably more complex than just his need for additional income. His

[94] *Bayn al-qasrayn* was translated into English by William M. Hutchins and Olive E. Kenny as *Palace Walk* (New York, 1991); *Qasr al-shawq* by William M. Hutchins, Lorne M. Kenny and Olive E. Kenny as *Palace of Desire* (New York, 1991); and *al-Sukkariyya* by William M. Hutchins and Angele Botros Samaan as *Sugar Street* (New York, 1992).

[95] The publisher Sa'id al-Sahhar prefers, understandably, not to recall his initial rejection of the trilogy. Taking credit for the service he rendered to Mahfuz and to Arabic literature he writes, "One day, in 1956 [*sic*], Najib Mahfuz came into my bookstore carrying a large quantity of paper, more than a thousand folio sheets, and he asked me to publish it in one book. Those sheets of paper contained Najib Mahfuz's trilogy. . . . I thought that if the novel were to be published in one book, it would limit sales; I therefore suggested printing it in three parts and Najib agreed." (From the publisher's postscript to a new edition of *Kifah Tiba* issued immediately after Mahfuz was awarded the Nobel Prize.)

[96] Hashim al-Nahhas, *Najib Mahfuz 'ala 'l-shasha* (Cairo, 1975), p. 14. See also Mahmud Fawzi, *Najib Mahfuz – za'im al-harafish* (Beirut, 1989), p. 141.

[97] Letter to Adham Rajab, *October* (11 December 1988), p. 40.

[98] Ibid., p. 41. The letter, which like the rest of Mahfuz's correspondence to Dr. Rajab is not dated, was postmarked Cairo, 30 January 1947.

keen awareness of the cinema's appeal for the masses, apparent in his letters to Dr. Rajab, may well have pushed him to venture into what he obviously considered an enchanting and threatening medium. By the end of the 1950s, when his status as Egypt's foremost novelist had been incontestably established, he had stopped writing film scripts. Mahfuz apparently hesitated to give up this bountiful source of income, but his official appointment as chief censor in 1959 decided the matter: it was inappropriate for him to continue to write for the cinema.[99]

The connection between Mahfuz and the Egyptian cinema turned out, however, to be lasting and fruitful: by 1971, he had written the scripts for eighteen films, and twelve of his novels had been adapted for the cinema.[100] His relationship with Salah Abu Sayf developed into a continuing professional cooperation and a close friendship.[101] Salah Abu Sayf was the first to direct a film based on a published novel by Mahfuz – Bidaya wa-nihaya ("The Beginning and the End"). The film (1960), with Omar Sharif in the leading role, was a great success.

Mahfuz's view of the relative value of the cinema in comparison with literature does not seem to have been affected by his success as a writer of film scripts or by the success his novels have enjoyed in this medium, nor even by the fact that for a number of years he was director of the Foundation for the Support of the Cinema. When an interviewer asked him to comment on Sartre's statement that the cinema had become the most modern medium of artistic expression, Mahfuz answered: "It is certainly true that the cinema is the most modern medium, but we must distinguish between 'most modern' and 'most important.' In my opinion, no other medium of expression surpasses the written word. . . . It is in my writing that I have expressed everything I want to say."[102]

---

[99] Interview with Ahmad Hamrush in al-Jumhuriyya (2 January 1960).

[100] Hashim al-Nahhas, pp. 14 and 28–31.

[101] Abu Sayf directed twelve of the thirty films for which Mahfuz wrote the script, or which were based on his novels.

[102] Interview with 'A'ida al-Sharif, al-Ādāb (Beirut, March 1967), p. 28.

Mahfuz's despair of literature, following the completion of the trilogy, occasioned a permanent change in his life: he got married. Some twenty-five years later, for the first and only time, he spoke about this at some length in an interview: "I got married in 1954; this happened when I had stopped writing novels during my period of literary despair. I was writing film scripts at the time. Perhaps the emptiness from which I was suffering played an important role in inducing me to get married. What was it that frightened me off marriage? It was literature. This was an erroneous concept. The details are all in the diaries which I used to write daily. Afterwards, I stopped writing them. When I read them now, I am amazed to see how wrong I was [about marriage]. I debated with myself in my diaries whether I should get married or not; I thought that marriage would destroy my literary life and so I concluded that I should reject marriage.[103] Later, after I had started to write again, I believe that my being married, in fact, helped me [in my literary work]."[104]

Mahfuz relates, "My mother urged me to get married and arranged many quite reasonable matches for me; frankly, they were not bad at all, but I refused. . . . One day, a friend of mine introduced me to his wife and his sister-in-law, and I found myself marrying the sister of his wife. . . . Only a few members of my family knew about it. I was afraid to break the news to my mother, because at the time she was preparing another match for me. Even my brother and sister, who knew about my marriage, advised me to keep it a secret [from mother]. I revealed it to her gradually, so as not to shock her."[105]

To many of Mahfuz's friends, his marriage remained a secret for years. He does not seem to have had any qualms about misleading an inquisitive interviewer into believing that he was a bachelor when, in fact, he had already been married for three years.[106] Interviewing Mahfuz early in 1963, the critic Ghali Shukri said to him, "Your private life is like a locked box, and it is impossible for any researcher or critic to evaluate your works in the light of information about

---

[103] Mahfuz's doubts about marriage are echoed in the thoughts and conversations of Kamal in the trilogy. See, e.g., *al-Sukkariyya*, pp. 226, 283, and 323–28.

[104] Ghitani, pp. 113–14.

[105] Ibid., p. 113.

[106] See above, p. 23.

Najib Mahfuz as a person and not just as an artist. What is the reason for this iron curtain behind which you hide your life among us?
Why is it that you revealed to the public only two months ago that
you are a married man [some nine years after the marriage took
place]?" Mahfuz answered: "There is nothing hidden in my private
life and I have made it public and keep making it public to the point
of boredom. My marriage was not a secret; my family and personal
friends – friends not colleagues! – knew about it from the first day. I
concealed it from my colleagues because I did not want it to become
a topic of foolish speculation in the papers and on the radio."[107]

The following story (which I heard from a well-known Egyptian
writer) illustrates Mahfuz's secretiveness about his marriage: "Najib
Mahfuz, Yusuf al-Siba'i, myself and a few others used to meet in a
café where we held long discussions until late at night. Yusuf al-
Siba'i, God have mercy on his soul, was at the time the only one
among us who had a private car, and, generous man that he was, he
would drive us back to our homes. Mahfuz used to get out of the car
near his mother's house, but then, as we found out much later, he
would walk a couple of miles to his home. He took all this trouble to
prevent us from discovering that he was no longer a bachelor living
with his mother."[108]

Mahfuz was afraid that marriage would entrap him in "a mesh of
social relationships forcing [him] to waste [his] time on visits and
courtesy calls," but this, he notes with relief, did not happen.
Mahfuz's wife had no close relatives in Cairo, and his brothers were
apparently considerate of his need to devote his free time to his literary work. "When my brothers would come to visit me, I would not
sit with them most of the time. They would greet me and then go
with their wives to sit with the family. My brothers got used to this;
they knew me. I remember that when my brother Muhammad visited
us, after lunch I would sit with him for a short while, but then he
would say, 'Get back to your work, I know you. I came to sit with the
children.'... After my marriage, there was naturally a change in my
routine: I devoted Friday mornings completely to the family, and we

---

[107] Interview with Ghali Shukri, *Hiwar* 3 (March–April 1963), p. 63.
[108] The writer who told me this story asked me not to mention her name.

used to go out to parks; in the summer vacation we were together most of the time. . . . My wife got to know my temperament and my routine, and she has always been understanding and supportive. Another wife might have become tired of me, but this did not happen."[109]

In 1955, thanks to Yahya Haqqi's recommendation, Mahfuz was transferred to the Ministry of Culture, where he worked until his retirement in 1971 at the age of sixty.[110] At this ministry he worked first as director of the minister's bureau.[111] In 1959, Tharwat 'Ukasha, the new Minister of Culture, appointed Mahfuz chief censor. This signified a promotion in the hierarchy but was a rather strange role for Mahfuz, who is known as an ardent advocate of freedom of expression.[112] It seems that Tharwat 'Ukasha, a career officer but a highly cultured man, wanted Mahfuz in this post precisely to serve as a buffer and an intermediary between writers and artists and the regime.[113] In addition to his work as chief censor, Mahfuz was chairman of the Foundation for the Support of the Cinema.[114] He was apparently a very conscientious worker: he told an interviewer, "When I have a job I carry it out properly, my official work is not a form of escapism but a responsibility."[115] At the end of 1966, when Tharwat 'Ukasha became

[109] Ghitani, pp. 114–15.

[110] When Mahfuz began to work in this ministry, it was called the Ministry of National Guidance (*wizarat al-irshad al-qawmi*); it was later divided into two: the Ministry of Information and the Ministry of Culture, for which Mahfuz worked.

[111] The minister who appointed Mahfuz on Yahya Haqqi's recommendation was Fathi Ridwan. See *al-Musawwar* (21 October 1988), p. 19.

[112] Commenting on the proposed constitution in 1971, Mahfuz said, "I expect a lot from the constitution; however, first in order of priority is freedom of expression. . . . The intellectual should be guaranteed the right to play his role clearly and directly, without need to resort to indirect forms of expression." See *al-Akhbar* (2 June 1971), p. 3.

[113] Tharwat 'Ukasha was a member of the inner circle of the Free Officers. An author and translator (his translations into Arabic include Ovid's *Metamorphoses* and *Ars amatoria*), he served twice as Minister of Culture: October 1958 to September 1962 and September 1966 to November 1970. See Tharwat 'Ukasha, *Mudhakkirati fi 'l-siyasa wa'l-thaqafa* (Cairo, 1987–1988).

[114] This body was reorganized in 1962 as the Foundation of Cinema, Radio and Television; in 1966, it was re-formed as the Public Foundation for the Cinema. See 'Ukasha, vol. 2, p. 328.

[115] *Al-Jumhuriyya* (2 January 1960).

Minister of Culture for the second time, he reorganized the ministry and once again appointed Mahfuz director of the Foundation for the Support of the Cinema. Tharwat 'Ukasha credits Mahfuz with having rescued the foundation and the cinema industry from organizational and financial chaos.[116] Finally, in 1970, Mahfuz was appointed special consultant to the minister, a position he held until his retirement in 1971.[117]

Mahfuz's work in the Ministry of Culture taxed his time considerably more than did his less prominent job in the Ministry of Awqaf, and now that he had become a sought-after interviewee, his complaints about this were made public: "My official work takes most of the day, and then, at night, I take my pencil and I write for two hours at the most. After that – I have no more strength. People call what I write 'literature,' but I call it 'government employees' literature'."[118] On another occasion, when the interviewer referred to him as a "full-time writer," Mahfuz protested, "Not at all! I am a government employee."[119]

Once he determined to be a writer, he set himself a strict program of work which enabled him to become a prolific writer despite the fact that, until 1971, he was employed full-time as a government official. He followed a fixed and regular routine: specific hours for writing, for reading, for meeting with friends. His punctuality in keeping to his routine became the butt of jokes; it was said that his neighbors could set their watches by the time he started his morning walk.[120] It is perhaps thanks to this quality that he was able to write as much as he did. Every afternoon, for thirty-seven years, he would sit and write after returning from the office. So far he has written fifty-two volumes of novels, short stories and short plays, eight collections of essays and many screenplays.

---

[116] 'Ukasha, vol. 2, pp. 328–29 and 343.

[117] *Al-Musawwar* (October 1988), p. 19. The dates of Mahfuz's years of service in his various posts in the Ministry of Culture are not easy to ascertain; some of the dates given in Mahfuz's interview in *al-Musawwar* are clearly mistaken. The dates given here, while based on the interview in *al-Musawwar*, have been corrected and supplemented from other sources.

[118] *'Asir hayati*, p. 128.

[119] *Al-Jumhuriyya* (2 January 1960).

[120] See Muhammad 'Afifi's humorous article, "*Najib Mahfuz rajul al-sa'a*," *al-Hilal* (February 1970), pp. 136–41.

Najib Mahfuz has always been preoccupied by politics.[121] He said once in an interview: "In everything I write you will find politics. You may find [among my works] a story without love or some other theme, but not without politics, because it is the pivot of our thinking."[122]

Yet Mahfuz, like other Egyptian intellectuals of his time, was severely restricted in his ability to express his political and religious views openly. He lived in a society where open criticism of the regime or any supposed slight against Islam could lead to ostracization or punishment. This was true of Egypt both under the monarchy and under Nasser. In addition Mahfuz tends naturally to avoid confrontation, even when he faces no danger beyond social discomfort and inconvenience. This is exemplified by his unwillingness openly to declare his rejection of Marxism at a time when it was in vogue in Arab intellectual circles. When, in 1976, Amina al-Naqqash invited him to reveal the Marxist sympathies she claimed to have detected in his books, Mahfuz wrote in reply: "The truth is that I have a high opinion of Marxism insofar as it implements social justice, and because of its universalistic vision and its reliance on science; but I reject its dictatorial system and its materialistic philosophy."[123] Here Mahfuz, faithful to the Fabian socialism he had espoused many years before, rejects the essence of Marxism while creating the impression of accepting it in part.[124]

Mahfuz's natural tendency to avoid confrontation was exacerbated by the real dangers of excessive candor in such a climate. In particular, he feared banishment from Egypt; he viewed political exile as the worst of punishments. In a letter written in 1946, Mahfuz warned his friend Dr. Adham Rajab, who was studying in England at the time, not to make public his criticisms of the Egyptian government. He wrote: "But as for your [suggestion] to speak up about the situation in one of the associations, I strongly advise you to be subtle

---

[121] Mahfuz's intensive interest in politics has always been recognized by the Egyptian critics. See Ibrahim 'Amir, "*Najib Mahfuz siyasiyyan*," *al-Hilal* (Cairo, February 1970), pp. 26–37.

[122] Ghitani, p. 78.

[123] Amina Al-Naqqash, "*Hiwar ma'a Najib Mahfuz*," *Afaq 'arabiyya* (February 1976).

[124] Mahfuz made a similar response to Raja' al-Naqqash some six years earlier; see "*Bayn al-wafdiyya wa'l-marxiyya*," *al-Hilal* (February 1970), pp. 40–41.

and clever, for it is quite possible that the Egyptian ambassador will somehow learn of your views; [you should take heed] unless you want to live in exile like the former khedive."[125] Mahfuz himself, throughout his career, tried to act with the caution he recommended to Dr. Rajab and constantly resorted to allegory to express his views on politically and religiously sensitive matters.[126]

A supporter of the Wafd from his youth, Mahfuz regarded the 1952 revolution and the officers' regime with ambivalence. He welcomed the demise of the hated monarchy, but deeply resented Nasser's curtailment of freedom of speech and the limitations placed upon civil liberties. He likewise resented Nasser's involving Egypt in what he regarded as senseless and unnecessary wars.[127] As early as 1972 Mahfuz began to speak in closed circles of the need to make peace with Israel, and when President Sadat flew to Jerusalem in November 1977 and initiated the peace process, Mahfuz gave him his full support. He has continued to support relations with Israel, despite the fact that most Arab writers and intellectuals, including some of his close friends, remain hostile to Israel.[128] For over twenty years now Mahfuz has been voicing his views on matters of general interest in a weekly column in *al-Ahram*,[129] and the liberal attitudes he has often expressed have angered fundamentalist Islamic circles in Egypt. His public stand against the death sentence passed on Salman Rushdie incurred the wrath of Shaykh 'Umar 'Abd al-Rahman, who declared both Salman Rushdie and Najib Mahfuz apostates, and argued that had a *fatwa* been issued against Najib Mahfuz after the publication of *Awlad haretna* thirty years earlier, this would have served as a warning to Rushdie, who might then have taken heed.[130] On the afternoon of the 14th of October 1994, an attempt was made

[125] Adham Rajab, *October* (11 December 1988), p. 40.

[126] See Samia Mehrez, "Respected Sir," in M. Beard and A. Haydar (eds.), *Naguib Mahfouz: From Regional Fame to Global Recognition* (Syracuse, 1993), pp. 61–81. For a discussion of Mahfuz's use of allegory, see below, pp. 131–33, 268–69.

[127] See below, pp. 147, 150.

[128] On Mahfuz's attitude to the Arab-Israeli conflict, see Reuven Snir, "The Arab-Israeli Conflict as Reflected in the Writings of Najib Mahfuz," *Abr-Nahrain*, 27 (1989), pp. 120–25.

[129] These articles have been published in three volumes, edited by Fathi al-'Ashri and published in Cairo by al-Dar al-Misriyya al-Lubnaniyya.

[130] See Samia Mehrez, "Respected Sir," pp. 66–68.

on Mahfuz's life. A Muslim fanatic stabbed him in the neck, seriously wounding him. The attack was interpreted by some as having been timed to coincide with the anniversary of the anouncement of Mahfuz's selection as a Nobel Prizewinner. Shaykh 'Umar 'Abd al-Rahman, who is accused of involvement in the New York Twin Towers bombing, is suspected of having instigated the attack on Mahfuz.[131] This attack did not deter Mahfuz from continuing to express his views in support of religious tolerance and in defense of the rights of the Coptic minority.

Mahfuz is known for his faithful attachment to his friends, whom he meets regularly in cafés, or in the home of one of the group – though never at Mahfuz's house. His old high-school friends from the 'Abbasiyya neighborhood constituted one group which he met regularly, at a certain café at exactly the same time each week. His close literary friends were another circle (which included the writer 'Adil Kamil and the humorist Muhammad 'Afifi), who called themselves al-ḥarāfīsh ("the riff-raff"). This group had its origins in al-da'ira al-mash'uma ("the ill-starred circle"), the small group of young writers who had started to meet in the late 1930s.[132] Gregarious by character, this hard-working, disciplined and highly organized man has meetings with friends as a regular part of his weekly schedule. Mahfuz is also known to have a good sense of humor and an extremely quick wit; once he reportedly beat twenty men in a café in a contest of witty repartee, responding by himself to the whole lot of them.[133]

[131] See Mary Anne Weaver, "The Novelist and the Sheikh," *The New Yorker* (30 January 1995), pp. 52–54.

[132] On the *harafish* see *al-Musawwar* (October 1988), pp. 52–53 (a piece by Muhammad Shadhili); Muhammad 'Afifi, "*Najib Mahfuz rajul al-sa'a*," *al-Hilal* (February 1970), pp. 136–41 (this article is reprinted in *al-Musawwar*, October 1988). The name *al-harafish* was adopted by the group after they encountered it in Tahtawi's *Takhlis al-ibriz fi talkhis bariz* as a term describing the noisy riff-raff to be found in the bistros of Paris. See Muhammad Shadhili, as above, p. 52. The rare middle-Arabic term *harafish* and the existence of a literary group of the same name became a talking point in Arabic literary circles after the publication of Mahfuz's novel *Malhamat al-harafish* ("The Epic of the Riff-Raff," 1977), which has no connection whatsoever with the literary group. On this novel, see below, p. 90.

[133] Adham Rajab, "*Safahat majhula min hayat Najib Mahfuz*," pp. 94–95.

Mahfuz is also a family man; he has a wife and two daughters. He keeps his family life completely separate from his literary life. Since his marriage in 1954, he and his family have always lived on the banks of the Nile, the river which he dearly loves.

CHAPTER 3

The Works of Najib Mahfuz

What one cannot theorize about, one must narrate.

Umberto Eco

I do not believe that a literary work can be an answer
to anything. A literary work is essentially a question.

Najib Mahfuz

It is perhaps inevitable that the works of a writer whose literary
output extends over a period of more than sixty years should invite
attempts at classification by style or content.[1] I have chosen to forgo
any attempt at a rigid categorization of Mahfuz's works, preferring
to present a more or less chronological survey.[2] This chapter sketches
Mahfuz's development as a writer and presents the major themes and
ideas which preoccupy him. Particular attention will be paid to the

---

[1] E.g., Nabil Raghib, *Qadiyyat al-shakl al-fanni 'ind Najib Mahfuz* (Cairo, 1975),
categorizes Mahfuz's entire literary output as follows: "The romantic historical stage,"
"The realistic social stage," "The disconnected psychological stage" and "The stage of
dramatic shaping." 'Abd al-Muhsin Taha Badr, *Najib Mahfuz: al-ru'ya wa'l-adah* (Cairo,
1984), sees Mahfuz's work up to the completion of the trilogy as a progression toward
"critical realism," and the chapters of his study are accordingly named as follows: "The
roots of the vision and the artistic beginnings," "The fantastic vision," "[First] contact with
reality," "Towards realism" and "Critical realism."

[2] The literary scholar Jabir 'Asfur has already called attention to the arbitrary nature of
such classifications. See Jabir 'Asfur, "*Nuqqad Najib Mahfuz*," in Ghali Shukri (ed.), *Najib
Mahfuz: Ibda' nisf qarn* (Cairo, 1989), pp. 245–50.

early stories of the thirties and forties, which, although not remarkable for their narrative art, are nevertheless of great interest, as they help us understand the author's psychological make-up, his moral concerns and his urge to write and publish. They also anticipate themes which will reappear throughout his later work.

While Mahfuz's literary output is very impressive in quantity and variation of narrative style, not all of his works maintain the same high literary standard. Years of steady development and improvement of his art culminated in the trilogy (1956–57) and, a few years later, in the very different but equally brilliant short novel *al-Liss wa'l-kilab* ("The Thief and the Dogs," 1961).[3] Since then, however, although he has not produced a work of the same literary stature, Mahfuz has retained the interest of his readers and his position as Egypt's most popular writer. This unique phenomenon may be explained by his unabated creative energy and his continued involvement in Egyptian social and political life: in both his literary works and in his weekly column in *al-Ahram* Mahfuz continues fearlessly to comment on Egyptian affairs, and thereby serves, in effect, as the literary conscience of his country.

Mahfuz began his literary career as a short story writer, publishing some forty stories before his first novel appeared in 1939. Between 1932 and 1946, he published nearly eighty stories in various Egyptian magazines. The early stories (written before 1936) appeared first in Salama Musa's *al-Majalla al-jadida*, and later in other magazines, notably al-Zayyat's *al-Riwaya* and *al-Risala*.[4] His first short story, however, did not appear in any of the above-mentioned publications, but in Muhammad Husayn Haykal's *al-Siyasa al-usbuʻiyya*; this was the only story he ever published in this magazine.[5] In retrospect, it is symbolic that Mahfuz's first work of fiction appeared in 1932 in this particular issue of Haykal's magazine, on exactly the same page as an advertisement announcing the appearance of the third edition of Haykal's novel *Zaynab*, widely regarded as the first Egyptian realistic novel.

---

[3] Translated by Trevor le Gassick and Mustafa Badawi and revised by John Rodenbeck as *The Thief and the Dogs* (New York, 1989).

[4] Ahmad Hasan al-Zayyat served as editor for both these journals.

[5] This story, "*Fatra min al-shabab*," appeared on 22 July 1932; it is discussed below.

Critics and literary historians have noted that these stories are not very successful examples of the genre; many of them have rather elaborate plots that stretch over a long period of time, and include a large number of characters – hardly the stuff of the short story. They represent a considerably lower literary standard than was achieved by other Egyptian writers of short stories in the 1920s, notably Mahmud Taymur, Tahir Lashin, and the 'Ubayd brothers, Shehata and 'Isa. Furthermore, these stories reflect a level of narrative art markedly lower than that achieved by Mahfuz in his early novels published between 1939 and 1946.

While the short stories of this early period are generally mediocre, his novels of the 1940s progressively improve. This puzzling phenomenon can be better understood in the light of Mahfuz's explanation that these works were not conceived as short stories, but were in fact derived from projected novels.[6] There are possibly some exceptions; there are short stories which appear to have been written as such, rather than as novel outlines, such as "Yaqzat al-mumya'" ("The Mummy's Awakening," 1939), "Marad tabib" ("A Doctor's Illness," 1941) and "Badlat al-asir" ("The POW's Suit," 1942).

Mahfuz's very first story, "Fatra min al-shabab" ("A Period of Youth," 1932), is quite obviously based on autobiographical materials.[7] "Fatra min al-shabab," covering in about 1200 words a period of some eight years in the life of the hero, may very probably have been condensed or extracted from Mahfuz's unpublished autobiography al-A'wam ("The Years") which he had modeled on Taha Husayn's al-Ayyam ("The Days").[8] It is written in the third person, possibly a reflection of the influence of Taha Husayn's al-Ayyam which is also a third person autobiographical story.

The story begins when a twelve-year-old boy and his family leave their native old-fashioned, traditional part of the city and move to a new neighborhood. The boy is painfully conscious of being poorer than most of the other boys in the new neighborhood, but neverthe-

---

[6] Jamal al-Ghitani, Najib Mahfuz yatadhakkar (Beirut, 1980), pp. 38–39, and see below, pp. 62–63, 65–66.

[7] The title of the story would appear to paraphrase the subtitle of Muwaylihi's Hadith 'Isa ibn Hisham – Fatra min al-zaman ("A Period of Time"). See above, p. 6.

[8] See above, p. 10.

less succeeds in being accepted. He falls in love (presumably some time later) with one of the girls there, a coquettish beauty with whom many of the local boys are fascinated. The girl is well aware of her charms, and enjoys the fact that many are attracted to her. The hero cannot understand her behavior, whereas she knows of his love for her, and has full control over him. "Only one thing she could not know: the sincerity of his love for her."

He tries to distract himself from this hopeless love by devoting himself to reading and the acquisition of knowledge, but eventually comes to view his absorption in books as futile and decides to commit suicide by drowning himself in the Nile. When he rows out to inspect the site of his watery grave on the night preceding the appointed suicide date, he is awakened to the beauty of nature and decides that he does not want to die. Now he decides to live for the sake of life, not for a woman or for learning, but for life itself. He now wonders, "How could he have placed Woman so high in his heart? She is nothing but a plaything for the pleasure of the body, and a picture to please the soul, and she does not deserve to be worshipped. The life which he was about to abandon by suicide became a purpose in itself . . . and knowledge, which he once thought to be a goal, now became a means for enjoying life by perceiving its affairs and discovering its hidden beauty." The young author's conclusion – that life is an end in itself – has remained an essential component of Mahfuz's thought ever since.

The hero of the story asserts that, having been awakened to the beauty of the world, he has overcome the painful infatuation that nearly destroyed him. It seems, however, that at the time of writing, Mahfuz, unlike his alter ego in this story, had not quite overcome his own painful adolescent love experience in real life: the story mentions that when the hero accidentally meets the girl who was once the object of his admiration, "his heart flutters and his soul is filled with desire."

This story was probably composed a few years after Mahfuz's traumatic emotional experience. As has been noted before, Mahfuz said many years later that the "incurable burning madness" of love lasted for ten years. It may therefore be conjectured that when "Fatra min al-shabab" ("A Period of Youth") was written, his emotional wounds were not quite healed.

It is important to note that it is the idea of beauty which gives new meaning to the life of the hero in this story. Forty years later, in *al-Maraya* ("Mirrors," 1972), Mahfuz again describes a traumatic adolescent love experience (based on the same personal experience) which "created of [him] a new person yearning for everything that is beautiful and real." Some two years after "A Period of Youth" was published, Mahfuz chose "The Concept of Beauty in Islamic Thought" as the subject of his master's dissertation.

His second story, "*Thaman al-duʿf*" ("The Price of Weakness," *al-Majalla al-jadida*, 3 August 1934), appears to be an outline of a novel. This is the story of a man who displays various character flaws, primarily an acute lack of self-confidence. He is the youngest son of aging parents. His father, in the past known for his strength and authority, is now weak with age and illness. "He did not display any emotion towards his child, and all that the child saw in him was a stern, ill-tempered man who was easily angered." His mother gave her youngest son all the love and attention, "which she had previously divided among her six [older] children." In this particular detail (being the youngest of seven children, with some years between himself and the one who preceded him), the hero of the story is obviously similar to Mahfuz.

The author suggests that the psychological problems of the hero are the result of his having been brought up by a very stern, but nearly absent father and by a very indulgent mother. (In various novels, *Khan al-Khalili*, *al-Qahira al-jadida*, *al-Sarab* and the trilogy, Mahfuz depicts male characters whose unfortunate psychological make-up results, according to the author, from having an indulgent mother and a very stern father, who otherwise takes little interest in raising his children.) When the hero is old enough to play with other boys, he finds himself weaker than the rest and consequently the victim of their mischievous harassment. Seeking protection, he attaches himself to the strongest boy, who, in return for the weak boy's daily allowance, becomes his friend and protector. (It should be recalled that Mahfuz once revealed that he had been the weakest of his classmates in the Qur'an school and that they used to snatch his food from him.)[9]

9 'Abd al-Tawwab 'Abd al-Hayy, *'Asir hayati* (Cairo, 1966), p. 128, and see above, p. 25.

The hero in "The Price of Weakness" loves one of his neighbors' daughters, but because of his excessive shyness he dare not ask for her hand in marriage. His mother speaks with the girl's mother on his behalf, and arranges for them to be considered a couple. A very poor student, he lags behind his peers in school, and is still finishing high school when one of his peers – his childhood friend and "protector" – graduates from the police academy as an officer. The self-confident police officer takes a fancy to the hero's sweetheart, and elopes with her. The marriage is not successful and the young woman returns home, divorced, within two months.

In the meantime the hero, who has become a minor government official, is scheduled to be transferred to work in a provincial town. His mother, concerned about who would take care of him, suggests that he should now marry his former sweetheart, the divorcee. The hero, however, does not agree, even though he still loves this woman, because he is afraid he would not fare well in the comparison that the young woman would be bound to make between him and her former husband, the police officer. The price of weakness is a life of loneliness.

Another story which contains autobiographical elements from a later period is "*Hikmat al-Hamawi*," which reflects Mahfuz's disillusionment with philosophy and his subsequent decision to become a writer.[10]

Two of Mahfuz's other early stories deal with corruption in government circles in Egypt, and the hardships encountered by young educated Egyptians who are not lucky enough to be well-connected.

"*Mahr al-wazifa*" ("The Price of Office," *al-Risala*, 9 August 1937) is a story about four friends who graduate from the Cairo University law school. Two, who are from influential families, get high-ranking jobs in the government, the third, with his family's financial assistance, is able to start a career as a lawyer, while the fourth, whose family is neither well-connected nor rich, must resort to a broker who arranges government positions for a fee. Since this young man cannot afford a high price, he can buy his way only into a very low-ranking secretarial job.

[10] See above, pp. 33–34.

In "*al-Qay'*" ("Vomit," *al-Risala*, 7 July 1941), we read about a low-ranking official, Sa'id Kamil, who advances quickly to become director general of a ministry, thanks to his beautiful wife's becoming the mistress of the minister. The story unfolds in the memory of the main character, Sa'id, who reflects on his career while bedridden in illness after his retirement. He recalls that many years before, when he was a minor official, he learned that the ministry had decided to transfer him to a provincial town in Upper Egypt. To avert that administrative decision (for Cairenes, a transfer to Upper Egypt has always been tantamount to a punishment), his very beautiful wife, Amīna (whose name means "faithful"), goes to plead with the director, one Sulayman Pasha Sulayman.

Sulayman Pasha Sulayman, a rich, pleasure-seeking bachelor, is willing to accede to Amina's request to keep her husband in Cairo on condition that she become his mistress. After some hesitation, both the husband and his wife accept the condition. Sa'id not only stays in Cairo, but gets rapid promotion. When Sulayman Pasha Sulayman becomes a minister, Sa'id succeeds him as director and earns the title of pasha, thus becoming Sa'id Pasha Kamil.

Years pass. One day, Sa'id Pasha returns home unexpectedly early, and finds his wife in the bedroom with some other stranger. She does not let him in until the man sneaks away. In his fury, he waves his cane and by mistake hits her leg. Staring at him with a cold, hard eye, his wife says, "How dare you hit the leg that elevated you?" Continuing to reflect on his past, Sa'id remembers a later scene when one day, as he was returning in his car from a high-school graduation ceremony, where he had delivered a speech and presented prizes to the students, some young man, possibly a student, shouted at him, "How dare you hit the leg that elevated you?"

The memory of that moment is now tormenting the sick man. His wife Amina enters his room, asking him tenderly, "How are you?" He looks at her, amazed that she has mysteriously kept her youth and beauty even though she is only eight years younger than him. He thinks, "It is as though every year as I grow older, she grows a year younger. When will she wither and cringe away from her own image in the mirror?"

In both "*Mahr al-wazifa*" and "*al-Qay'*," Mahfuz exposes one of the major ills of Egyptian society at the time: the fact that young people could neither find employment nor advance in government service unless they could make use of family connections or somehow bribe those in power. Mahfuz, who spent thirty-seven years as a government employee, had a first-hand knowledge of the experience of young educated Egyptians seeking office in the government service. He also knew and despised the dubious ways by which people sought promotion. Mahfuz's second contemporary novel, *al-Qahira al-jadida* ("The New Cairo," 1946), embraces the central themes of both these stories in its main plot line.

Mahfuz saw the Turko-Egyptian aristocracy as the source of social and political corruption in Egypt. In the story "*al-Qay'*," he specifically mentions that Amina, the beautiful but shameless wife, is of Turkish origin.[11] (With regard to the high-ranking official, Sulayman Pasha Sulayman, he need not even mention this; at the time, most high-ranking officials were of Turkish or Circassian origin.)

In "*Yaqzat al-mumya'*" ("The Mummy's Awakening," *al-Riwaya*, 1 April 1939),[12] Mahfuz uses allegory to challenge the existing political order. His story expresses the hope of seeing the downfall of the alien monarchic dynasty of Muhammad 'Ali.[13]

Some of Mahfuz's early stories are philosophical or moral parables. "*Al-Sharr al-ma'bud*" ("Evil Worshipped," *al-Majalla al-jadida*, 27 May 1936) describes the settlement of a nomadic tribe and the emergence of urban life with the necessary functions of judge, police chief, and doctor. The community seems to be progressing well, when a religious teacher appears preaching high moral ideals. He calls on people to return to the pure, pristine form of their religion, which has been corrupted by superstition and innovation. The people respond, and the need for the services of the judge, the police chief, and even the doctor consequently decline. These three therefore decide that they must get rid of the person whose preaching has made their functions redundant. They stir up violent opposition to the

---

[11] Ihsan, the heroine of *al-Qahira al-jadida*, whose intimate relations with a high-ranking official secure the promotion of her husband, is also of Turkish origin. On the significance of Ihsan's Turkish origin, see below, p. 190.

[12] Also included in *Hams al-junun*, pp. 81–98.

[13] This allegorical story is discussed in detail in Part Four, see below, pp. 168–70.

preacher, and succeed in banishing him from the city. The established order is again secure.

In a revised and somewhat longer version of this story published three years later, Mahfuz describes the religious teacher as engaging the people in debate on questions of good and evil.[14] The doctrine he preaches is simple: if everyone adheres to ideals of beauty and moderation, both rich and poor will be happy and content. In this version of the story the judge, the police chief and the doctor arrange the teacher's disappearance, only to discover that the community continues to follow his teachings even after he has gone. The three conspirators resort to a further stratagem: they invite a beautiful and seductive dancer into the district, in the certain knowledge that she will cause competition and conflict. The peace of the community is, indeed, soon shattered, and the judge, the police chief and the doctor regain their power and status. The revised version's addition of a beautiful dancer as a means of causing strife is significant: her influence reveals the power of eros, which is hopelessly irrational, and which Mahfuz employs to typify the irrationality of the instinctual element in human behavior.[15]

"Evil Worshipped" is patently a parable on the feasibility of establishing a perfect, harmonious society. At the beginning of the story it seems that Utopia might be achieved; but by the end, human nature has reasserted itself, and the ideal society has receded. This story would seem to reflect the conflict in Mahfuz's mind between the Fabians' optimistic view of human nature and the pessimistic view maintained by Gustave Le Bon.[16]

The story *"Afw al-malik Userkaf"* ("King Userkaf's Forgiveness," *al-Riwaya*, 1 December 1938) explores the question of loyalty. The Pharaoh Userkaf is advised by the gods to test the loyalty of his subjects. In order to do so, he departs from his kingdom, appointing

---

[14] This version appeared in *al-Riwaya* (15 October 1939), and was later included in the collection *Hams al-junun*.

[15] Cf. *Qalb al-layl*, pp. 114–15, and see below, p. 101.

[16] Here, as in his first published article, "The Dying of Old Beliefs and the Birth of New Beliefs," Mahfuz expresses his yearning for Utopia, but concludes reluctantly that it cannot be attained. See above, p. 30.

his son interim ruler. When he returns, he finds that his son has betrayed his confidence and will not vacate the throne for him; he has also married the king's young wife. Others are no better: the chief minister, the commander of the army and the high priest have all switched their loyalties while the king was absent. Banished from his own kingdom, Userkaf allies himself with a malcontent governor with whose help he stages a rebellion against his son, the ruling Pharaoh. Userkaf wins the war and regains power. Rather than face her former husband, the treacherous queen commits suicide. Userkaf, however, forgives all those who betrayed him: the heir apparent, the chief minister, the commander, etc. He explains his decision to the bewildered and amazed governor who helped him win the war: "Who would give me another heir apparent, a more pious priest, a more capable chief minister?... Furthermore, I wish the queen had not committed suicide; I would have asked her to sit on the throne again by my side. And as for sincerity, my dear Governor, I am suspicious of everyone. I do not trust you any more than I trust those others."

The story ends with a statement that King Userkaf lived the rest of his life in a state of emotional isolation and with no friend other than his dog. The story's moral message is therefore ambiguous. Does it preach constant suspicion, or is it, in fact, a warning against excessive suspicion and against testing people's loyalty? The argument in favor of the second interpretation would appear to be corroborated by a quotation from another story by Mahfuz, written some fifty years later. "Beware of being suspicious of all people, lest you become lonely and abandoned by all," one of the characters warns the narrator in *"al-Fajr al-kadhib"* ("False Dawn," 1989).[17]

Hayat li'l-ghayr ("Life for the Sake of Others," *al-Riwaya*, 1 July 1939) which tells the story of an unmarried man of thirty-six who is in love with his neighbors' sixteen-year-old daughter, appears to be a sketch of a novel. To some extent, the story line of the main charac-

---

[17] *"Al-Fajr al-kadhib,"* p. 23. It would seem, therefore, that 'Abd al-Muhsin Taha Badr misconstrues the story *"'Afw al-malik Userkaf"* when he concludes, "the moral of this story is that a wise man should have a pessimistic view of the world and be suspicious of everyone, even of those closest to him." See 'Abd al-Muhsin Taha Badr, *al-Ru'ya wa'l-ada: Najib Mahfuz* (Cairo, 1984), p. 80.

ter and his selfless devotion to his younger brother foreshadow the main character of Mahfuz's first realistic novel, *Khan al-Khalili*.[18]

The problem of madness is the subject of the short story *"Hams al-junun"* ("The Whisper of Madness," *al-Risala*, 19 February 1945).[19] While reflecting Mahfuz's interest in psychology and in the nature of madness, this story is arguably an attempt to deal with a general cultural problem rather than a plausible description of an individual case. The various incidents described by Mahfuz in this story are too disparate to be considered symptoms of any one particular mental illness: they seem to have been concocted to fit an allegorical scheme. Madness here is the name for a rebellion against the social and cultural shackles which limit human freedom.

Although the short stories published in the 1930s and 1940s lack artistic brilliance and would not seem to herald the appearance of a great writer, they nonetheless display some of Mahfuz's unique qualities as a narrator. Almost without exception, the stories are told in a way that keeps the reader interested and absorbed. Another quality displayed even in these poorly-constructed stories is the author's capacity to depict human emotions and interpersonal relations effectively in just a few words. The range of characters covered in these stories is wide: Turko-Egyptian aristocrats, lower-middle class Egyptians, students, prostitutes, poor children. Many of the stories attack the Turko-Egyptian upper class; Mahfuz ridicules their superficial aping of French culture, their vanity and their dissolute moral behavior. Some deal with problems of poverty and social injustice. Most stories are set in contemporary Egypt, but some, of a markedly philosophical nature, are set in ancient times.

The history of the publication of Mahfuz's short stories is worth noting. Twenty-eight of his early stories were collected and republished in a volume called *Hams al-junun* ("The Whisper of Madness").[20] For years, this collection's date of publication caused

[18] See below, pp. 174–75.

[19] For further analysis of *"Hams al-junun,"* which is also the title-story of Mahfuz's first collection of short stories, see below, pp. 108–9.

[20] Twenty-four of the stories included in *Hams al-junun* appeared in various Egyptian magazines; four others have not been found in magazines and may have been published for the first time in this volume. See the bibliographic list in Badr, *Najib Mahfuz*, pp. 405–9.

confusion among scholars. The list of Mahfuz's works which appears at the end of most of his books (and which indicates the year of the first edition and the year and number of the current edition for each work) cites 1938 as the original publication year for this collection. This date has puzzled the researchers because some of the stories could not have been written before 1941. This is especially obvious in the story "The POW's Suit," which assumes the presence of Italian prisoners of war on Egyptian soil.

Some of the stories included in the collection *Hams al-junun* appeared in various Egyptian magazines in the years 1939 to 1945. Scholars have also noted with some surprise that there seems to be no reference whatsoever to the appearance of the book *Hams al-junun* in literary magazines prior to 1949.[21] In an attempt to understand this strange phenomenon, one critic hypothesized that there had been an original 1938 edition, but that this had been superseded by a later edition which included more recent stories.[22] However, the truth behind this discrepancy emerged when Mahfuz revealed that *Hams al-junun* was really published some ten years after the claimed date of 1938. He revealed this some time in the late 1970s, to the literary historian Dr. 'Abd al-Muhsin Taha Badr, who was preparing a study on Mahfuz.[23]

He furnishes some more information on this subject in a later interview. "The person who made the collection *Hams al-junun* is the late 'Abd al-Hamid Jawda al-Sahhar. I didn't want to publish this collection; at that time, I had already published the three historical novels, *al-Qahira al-jadida* and *Zuqaq al-midaqq* [published in 1947].[24] He came and said to me, 'Why don't you publish a collection of short stories?' I said, 'What collection? Now? The time for that has long since passed.'. . . Al-Sahhar [the publisher] insisted on publishing a collection of short stories, so I gave him a huge number of magazines whose names I don't even remember. When he saw that I

---

[21] Sasson Somekh, *The Changing Rhythm: A Study of Najib Mahfuz's Novels* (Leiden, 1973), p. 46.

[22] See Ahmad Haykal, *al-Adab al-qasasi wa'l-masrahi fi misr*, 3rd ed. (Cairo, 1979 [1951]), p. 92, n. 2.

[23] Badr, *Najib Mahfuz*, pp. 72–73. (Badr's book originally appeared in 1978.)

[24] Mahfuz neglects to mention here his *Khan al-Khalili*, which was published before *al-Qahira al-jadida* and *Zuqaq al-midaqq*.

was very uncomfortable [with the idea], he said, 'So then, let's give the real date of writing of these stories; when did [the editor and publisher] al-Zayyat suggest you publish a collection of your stories?' I said, 'In 1938.' Al-Sahhar said, 'Then you should consider that [proposed] collection your first book and date it 1938.' Consequently, the reader doesn't know that *Hams al-junun* was published for the first time after the appearance of *Zuqaq al-midaqq* [in 1947] and not in 1938, as appears in the list of my works which you find in every book."[25]

Mahfuz's first three books were historical novels with subjects derived from Egypt's age of the Pharaohs. Even before he began to publish his own fiction, he published a translation of a small English book by one Reverend James Baikie that gave a popular description of everyday life in Pharaonic Egypt.[26] Years later, Mahfuz explained that he had done the translation to practice his English; clearly, however, the choice of this particular work reflected his special interest in Egypt's Pharaonic past, as did his choice of subjects for these first three novels.[27] This interest stemmed from his concept of Egyptian national identity, in which he followed the lead of Egyptian intellectuals such as Ahmad Lutfi al-Sayyid, Muhammad Husayn Haykal, Taha Husayn, Tawfiq al-Hakim, and Salama Musa.

These men maintained that the Egyptian national identity is essentially neither Arab nor Islamic, but is inherently and distinctly Egyptian, having its roots in the land and in the great civilization that emerged from it. According to this view, modern Egyptians should see themselves as heirs to a glorious Pharaonic past. The corollary to this view was an animosity towards the Arabs and towards what these intellectuals termed the "Arab mentality" – characterized, in their view, by "barbarism, violence, lack of imagination, addiction to momentary pleasures and an incapacity to create a stable civilization."[28]

---

[25] Ghitani, p. 38.

[26] James Baikie, *Ancient Egypt* (London: Adam Charles Black, 1912). This small, eighty-eight-page book, with color illustrations, was obviously intended for young readers.

[27] Ghitani, p. 39.

[28] See Israel Gershoni and James P. Jankowski, *Egypt, Islam and the Arabs* (New York, 1986), pp. 96–111.

Consistent with their view of Egypt's national identity and with their liberal world view was their strong advocacy of full equality for the Copts, Egypt's indigenous Christians.[29] These intellectuals recognized, of course, that since the conquest of Egypt by the Arab Muslim armies in 639 CE and the subsequent Islamization of its people, Arabic has become the language of all Egyptians. But they insisted that the Arabic language (which the Egyptians share with all Arabs) and the religion of Islam (which they share with all Muslims, Arab and non-Arab alike) are not the determining components of the national identity. Islam should not be allowed to play a role in politics; religion, they maintained, should be a private matter only.[30] Najib Mahfuz, it appears, has accepted these views and continues to maintain them to this day.

Just as the Pharaonic setting of Mahfuz's first three novels was motivated by the modern quest for a distinctive Egyptian identity, so did their content reflect Mahfuz's other essentially modern concerns and attitudes. Mahfuz fictionalized Pharaonic history and made it a vehicle for his views on contemporary issues.

The first novel, 'Abath al-aqdar ("Fate's Play," 1939), is set in the court of Khufu (Cheops), the Pharaoh who ordered the building of the great pyramid of Giza. The story, sustained by a plot of political intrigue and gallant love, enables Mahfuz to express his views on government, education, and moral behavior. The plot for the story was inspired by an Egyptian legend recounted by Baikie in *Ancient Egypt* which Mahfuz had translated several years earlier. In Mahfuz's story, the Pharaoh attempts to thwart a magician's prophecy that the succession to the throne will pass from his family to that of the high priest of the god Re. It is only at the end of the book – and of his life –

---

[29] On "Pharaonicism" and its chief proponents see ibid., pp. 164–90; see also Nadav Safran, *Egypt in Search of Political Community* (Cambridge, 1961), pp. 95, 144–47.

[30] In 1925, 'Ali 'Abd al-Raziq (brother of Mustafa 'Abd al-Raziq, Mahfuz's professor) expounded the arguments for the separation of Islam and government in his book *al-Islam wa-usul al-hukm* ("Islam and the Bases of Political Authority"). The book met with violent opposition in conservative circles, and its author was ousted from the corps of the *'ulama'* ("religious scholars"). However, his views were apparently widely accepted among Egyptian liberal intellectuals. See: Gershoni and Jankowski, pp. 60–74; Albert Hourani, *Arabic Thought in the Liberal Age* (London, 1962), pp. 183–92; Safran, pp. 139–43.

that he realizes his ruthless attempt to change the course of Fate has proved futile.

The story of the Pharaoh's unsuccessful attempt to defy Fate serves as a frame for the main story, which is an account of the upbringing and exploits of the hero, the high priest's son, Dadaf. By virtue of his education, talent, perseverance, loyalty and other fine qualities, Dadaf distinguishes himself as a commander in the Pharaoh's army. When the crown prince rebels against his father and attempts to kill him, Dadaf saves the Pharaoh's life. The Pharaoh rewards him by giving him his daughter in marriage and appointing him successor to the throne. The story strongly suggests that a ruler should be morally restrained in exercising power and that he should avoid shedding innocent blood. At the end of his life, the Pharaoh records in his Book of Wisdom the lessons experience has taught him; this is his legacy to his people.

The title of Mahfuz's book, "Fate's Play," suits the frame story, but the greater part of the book recounts the achievements of Dadaf, who advances by virtue of talent and effort. This reflects an outlook very different from the underlying assumption of the frame story. Hence, the book appears to convey two conflicting messages: the frame story demonstrates the invincibility of Fate, while the main story celebrates man's capacity to shape his destiny by his own efforts. However, the contradiction between the message of the main story and that of its surrounding frame has not, so far, attracted attention. Most critics have seen the book simply as an expression of Mahfuz's belief in the overpowering dominance of Fate.[31]

The title of the novel would appear to be the source of this misconstruction. But "Fate's Play" ('Abath al-aqdar) was not the book's original title; Mahfuz named it "The Wisdom of Cheops" (Hikmat Khufu). However, Salama Musa, the publisher, changed the title to "Fate's Play," thereby influencing the way the book was understood and distracting attention from the other aspect of its message.[32]

---

[31] Badr maintains that "the purpose of the author in this kind of novel [i.e., "Fate's Play"] was to show us the vanity and uselessness of human action." Badr, Najib Mahfuz, p. 142. See also Somekh, p. 61.

[32] See interview with Ghali Shukri, al-Watan al-'arabi, 48 (12 February 1988), p. 45. In a conversation in February 1989, Mahfuz told me that he believed that Salama Musa was

Throughout his work, Mahfuz has repeatedly emphasized the importance of individual action and responsibility. He is clearly no fatalist. In an interview in 1988 he succinctly states his position: "I believe in work [*'amal*] and in the result of work, but there is also an element of luck [*wa-lakin al-huzuz mawjuda*]. However, predestination [*al-qadar*] in the sense of abolishing man's freedom [of action] – no, because man is subject to punishment and reward, and so he has to be free."[33]

The book shows how hard work and perseverance can shape destiny; it concludes with the downfall of those who have shed innocent blood, and celebrates the final triumph of loyalty and love.

Mahfuz's identification with the Pharaonicist school of Egyptian nationalism is revealed here not only in his choice of subject and setting but also by various details throughout the book. The hero falls in love with Pharaoh's daughter – whom he will eventually marry – when she is disguised as a *fallaha* (an Egyptian peasant girl) and he has no idea of her true identity. In the form of nationalist ideology described above, the fellah was viewed as the embodiment of the Egyptian spirit: "Ancient Egypt or the Egypt of the Pharaohs is still alive among our fellahin," wrote Salama Musa in 1926.[34] The love between the hero – who is not of royal lineage – and Pharaoh's daughter qua *fallaha* symbolizes the triumph of the eternal Egyptian spirit. This image of Egypt as a peasant girl prefigures Mahfuz's use, twenty-eight years later, of a young *fallaha*, Zahra, in the novel *Miramar*, to represent Egypt.

'Abath al-aqdar depicts the Bedouin of Sinai, whose raids threaten Egypt's peace and security, as barbaric and uncouth. This negative view of the (Arab) Bedouin, too, conforms to the above-mentioned form of Egyptian nationalist ideology.

An idea which Mahfuz expresses directly and emphatically is that the pyramids attest to the greatness of the Egyptian people more than

---

unhappy with the title *Hikmat Khufu* because Khufu was the name of his son.

[33] *Al-Musawwar* (October 1988), p. 73.

[34] Salama Musa, *Mukhtarat Salama Musa* (Cairo, 1926), p. 195; see also Gershoni and Jankowski, pp. 205–7. The monument erected in 1928 to celebrate the rebirth of modern Egypt took the form of a statue of a peasant woman resting her hand upon the head of a sphinx. See Gershoni and Jankowski, p. 186.

to that of the Pharaoh. He describes the workers who constructed the pyramids as being moved by faith and determination, "imposing human will upon eternal Time."[35] This echoes Tawfiq al-Hakim's view that the ancient Egyptians were obsessed with an ambition to master time and place, and subordinate them to the national will.[36]

The second novel, *Radubis* (1943), recounts the story of a young Pharaoh's infatuation with a beautiful courtesan (Radubis) and his fateful struggle with the powerful clergy. Both themes reflect the author's modern concerns. He employs the love story to express his views on the potential destructiveness of love, and the story of the struggle between the Pharaoh and the clergy is an object lesson on the danger inherent in a religious establishment that wields economic and political power.[37]

Some Egyptian critics interpreted this novel as a warning to the young King Farouk not to let his inclination to debauchery interfere with the exercise of his royal duties, lest he be overthrown by popular rebellion. This, however, is an anachronistic reading of the novel, as King Farouk was at this time still in the early years of his reign and had not yet earned a reputation for dissolute behavior.[38]

In the third of his historical novels, *Kifah Tiba* ("The Struggle of Thebes," 1944), Mahfuz tells the story of the war of liberation waged by the Egyptians, under the leadership of Prince Ahmas, against the Hyksos, invaders from the north who occupied Egypt for over a century (1700–1580 BCE). The final victory of the indigenous Egyptians over the foreign occupiers and their expulsion from Egypt was intended by Mahfuz and understood by his readers to herald the end of the British occupation of Egypt. It is significant that the young Pharaoh Ahmas, the hero of the war of liberation, is torn between his sense of duty to his people and his loyalty to his Egyptian sister-wife,

---

[35] *'Abath al-aqdar*, p. 9.

[36] See Tawfiq al-Hakim, *Taht shams al-fikr* (Cairo, 1938), pp. 106–7. Cf also Gershoni and Jankowski, pp. 145–46.

[37] In some significant points *Radubis* appears to have been influenced by Anatole France's *Thais*. Mahfuz has mentioned that he read and admired Anatole France; see Fu'ad Dawwara, *Najib Mahfuz min al-qawmiyya ila al-'alamiyya* (Cairo, 1989), p. 217.

[38] 'Abd al-Muhsin Taha Badr points this out in his study of Mahfuz. See Badr, *Najib Mahfuz*, p. 155.

on the one hand, and his love for the fair-haired, blue-eyed daughter of the King of the Hyksos, on the other.

This was probably intended to represent through allegory the conflict between Mahfuz's aversion to the British as foreign occupiers and his attraction to Western culture, and to English literature in particular. Some years later, Mahfuz described this conflict in the trilogy, expressing it through the thoughts of Kamal, his alter ego.

Kifah Tiba was highly praised, especially by a young literary critic by the name of Sayyid Qutb, who saw it as the most important of the historical novels written in Egypt. The critic ended his review with the statement that if he had the power, he would distribute the book free to every young Egyptian man and woman and would call a gathering to honor the author whom, he affirmed, he did not personally know.[39] In the spirit of Egyptian nationalism of the time, Qutb expressed in his article the same degree of resentment toward all those nations which had invaded and occupied Egypt throughout the ages: Hyksos, Romans, Turks, Arabs and Europeans.[40] It is interesting to note that Qutb, who within a few years would become one of the leaders of the Muslim Brotherhood, did not distinguish between Muslim (Arab and Turkish) and non-Muslim foreign rulers. It is especially striking that he included in his list of "foreign oppressors" the Arabs, whose occupation of Egypt introduced Islam into that country.

In 1966 Sayyid Qutb was put to death by Nasser for having led a Muslim Brothers' plot against him. Mahfuz, who has always been opposed to religious extremism and has often decried the fanaticism of the Muslim Brotherhood, has nevertheless always faithfully remembered the name of Sayyid Qutb, the first critic to note his special talent as a novelist. In fact, one of the chapters of his *al-Maraya* portrays a fictitious character modeled closely on the enigmatic personality of Sayyid Qutb.[41]

After writing these three historical novels, Mahfuz abandoned his

---

[39] *Al-Risala 586* (Cairo, 18 September 1944); quoted in Fadil al-Aswad (ed.), *al-Rajul wa'l-qimma* (Cairo, 1989), pp. 49–55.

[40] Ibid., p. 54.

[41] "'Abd al-Wahhab Isma'il," *al-Maraya*, pp. 261–67.

plan to write a series of novels tracing the history of Egypt from Pharaonic to modern times and turned to the contemporary scene.[42]

Khan al-Khalili (1945) is set in the early years of World War II (from September 1941 to August 1942).[43] It is interesting to note that the family in this novel moves from their home in the more modern Sakakini quarter to the old Khan al-Khalili, for fear of air raids; this incident is based on Mahfuz's own experiences in 1941: because of his fear of the air raids, Mahfuz persuaded his mother (with whom he was living at the time as a bachelor in the 'Abbasiyya quarter) to move to the old Azhar quarter, which borders on Khan al-Khalili.[44]

As a result of this correspondence between Mahfuz's life and the story of the family's move for fear of air raids, some people, apparently, believed that Ahmad 'Akif, the main character in *Khan al-Khalili*, was modeled on Mahfuz himself. Mahfuz denies this identification:

> Some people ask me, "Doesn't the personality of Ahmad have something of you in it?" This is completely untrue. Ahmad is a real person. He was a minor official in the university administration [where Mahfuz himself worked from 1936 to 1938]. He actually read the novel after it came out but did not recognize himself in it. He didn't realize at all that he was the inspiration for the main character. This, incidentally, proves a very curious thing: a person's view of himself and other people's view of him – they are indeed very different from each other! The "Ahmad 'Akif" I knew was merely a minor official in the

---

[42] Ghitani, pp. 43–44.

[43] Mahfuz, in the list supplied at the end of each of his books, gives the publication dates of *Khan al-Khalili* and *al-Qahira al-jadida* as 1946 and 1945 respectively. Sasson Somekh has shown, however, that reviews of *Khan al-Khalili* appeared in 1945, whereas reviews of *al-Qahira al-jadida* did not appear until 1946. See Somekh, pp. 198–99. This suggests that the true order of publication is: *Khan al-Khalili*, 1945, and *al-Qahira al-jadida*, 1946. On this matter see also Rasheed El-Enany, *Naguib Mahfouz: The Pursuit of Meaning* (London and New York, 1993), pp. 220–21. An additional proof that *al-Qahira al-jadida* was not published until 1946 is Mahfuz's letter to his friend Dr. Adham Rajab, dated 6 July 1946, in which he promises to send him a copy of *al-Qahira al-jadida* by next post. See Adham Rajab, "*Khitabat bi-khatt Najib Mahfuz*," *October* (11 December 1988), p. 40.

[44] Muhammad 'Afifi, *al-Hilal* (February 1970), pp. 95–96.

university administration, but he thought that he knew everything in Egypt. He had only a high school diploma, but he
believed that he had mastered all the knowledge in the world.
He was superficial and fickle. The risk I took was that had he
known I was inspired by him in *Khan al-Khalili*, my life might
have been in danger; he might have attacked me, because he
was truly a deranged character.[45]

Mahfuz succeeds in giving a vivid picture of life in Khan al-Khalili,
one of the streets of Cairo's medieval Jamaliyya quarter (where he
himself was born). In this book, too, Mahfuz devotes much attention
to the big ideological and cultural debates of the time. Ahmad 'Akif,
a hapless low-ranking official, is a protagonist of cultural con-
servatism, his rival a communist. Mahfuz has them both sound too
extreme and one-sided in arguing their respective positions, but it is
the conservative in particular whose arguments are pathetically
ridiculous, for they reveal his ignorance as well as his intellectual
pretentiousness.

Once again it was the critic Sayyid Qutb who highly praised this
novel, ranking it higher than Tawfiq al-Hakim's *'Awdat al-ruh*: "The
genuine Egyptian features in *Khan al-Khalili* are clearer and stronger,
whereas in *'Awdat al-ruh* there are various French shadings. . . . *Khan
al-Khalili* is free of the lengthy repetitions that weigh on *'Awdat al-
ruh*. . . ."[46] This was a great compliment (and a daring one for the
critic) because Mahfuz was a relatively unknown young novelist,
whereas Tawfiq al-Hakim was already a literary celebrity.

The next novel, *al-Qahira al-jadida* ("The New Cairo," 1946), is set
in 1934, and has for its main characters a group of Egyptian students.
Through these characters, the author presents the major ideological
orientations dividing the Egyptian intelligentsia at the time: one of the
students is an Islamic fundamentalist; another a secularist and a socialist; a third supports the Wafd, the popular national party (which Mahfuz
himself had loyally supported ever since high school), and the fourth (the

---

[45] Jamal al-Ghitani, *Najib Mahfuz yatadhakkar* (Beirut, 1980), pp. 64–65.

[46] Sayyid Qutb's review of *Khan al-Khalili* (*al-Risala*, 17 December 1945) is included in
Ghali Shukri (ed.), *Najib Mahfuz: Ibda' nisf qarn* (Cairo, 1989), pp. 35–39. Citation here is
from the latter, p. 39.

main character) is a cynical careerist who does not care for any ideal.[47] In his review of *al-Qahira al-jadida*, Qutb wrote that he regarded Mahfuz's works as "the real beginning of the creation of genuine Arabic novels. For the first time, indigenous Egyptian flavor and aroma appear in a literary work with a [universal] human quality. . . ."[48]

A comparison of *Khan al-Khalili* and *al-Qahira al-jadida* shows that the former displays a more mature style, narrative structure and use of language than the latter. It may well be that although, as research has shown, *al-Qahira al-jadida* appeared a year later than *Khan al-Khalili*, it was actually written earlier; this may be the reason why Mahfuz listed it as the earlier work.

In *Zuqaq al-midaqq* ("Midaqq Alley," 1947), Najib Mahfuz describes the changing social reality of a traditional Cairene neighborhood under the impact of World War II. There is no one main character in the story, which portrays a gallery of characters, most of them of the lower and lower-middle classes.

The following year Mahfuz published *al-Sarab* ("Mirage"), the story of a young man beset by a host of neuroses caused by his having been brought up by an over-indulgent mother. For years he is unable to have normal relations with women, but eventually finds satisfaction in a relationship he establishes with a buxom widow in her forties. In *al-Sarab* Mahfuz attempts to demonstrate the devastating psychological and social effects of the hypocritical and repressive attitudes to sex current at the time. Though not one of Mahfuz's best novels, it continues to be one of his most widely read.[49]

In 1949 he published *Bidaya wa-nihaya* ("The Beginning and the End"), the story of a Cairene family of the lower-middle class whose father dies, leaving four children, three sons and a daughter.[50] The youngest of the three sons, an ambitious and vain character, enters the military academy after finishing high school. The year is 1936, when the military academy opened its doors for the first time to young Egyptians who were not sons of the aristocracy. (This was the

---

[47] See below, pp. 182–85.

[48] Sayyid Qutb, review of *al-Qahira al-jadida*, reprinted in *al-Rajul wa'l-qimma*, p. 58.

[49] *Al-Sarab* was in its thirteenth printing by 1987, outstripping even such novels as *Khan al-Khalili*, *Zuqaq al-midaqq* and *al-Liss wa'l-kilab*.

[50] Translated by Ramses Awad as *The Beginning and the End* (New York, 1989).

class that included Nasser, 'Abd al-Hakim 'Amir, Sadat, and some other members of the inner circle of the Free Officers who led the 1952 revolution.)

The novel ends with the suicide of the vain and selfish officer. The negative judgment passed by the author on this character anticipates, in a way, Mahfuz's negative view of the military men who led the revolution of 1952. The analogy between the fictitious figure of the officer Hasanayn and the leaders of the Free Officers revolution was not, apparently, lost on perceptive Egyptian readers. In the film made from the novel *Bidaya wa-nihaya* in 1960, Hasanayn is portrayed as a selfish opportunist. The journalist 'A'ida Sharif recounts a discussion which took place in the Casino al-Opera café shortly after the film's release. Some of those present criticized the director, Salah Abu Sayf, for his unsympathetic portrayal of Hasanayn, but Mahfuz supported him. 'A'ida Sharif, who was among those present, challenged Mahfuz: "Some time ago, the critic Ahmad 'Abbas Salih wrote that Hasanayn was not an opportunist but a person of high ambition, whose striving represents the revolution; and you agreed with him at the time." Mahfuz smiled and said, "Every interpretation has two edges."[51]

This answer is characteristic of Mahfuz's tendency to avoid confrontation and of his adroit use of the slyly enigmatic response. In this case, the critic's interpretation of Hasanayn as a symbol of the revolution was clearly intended as a positive judgment. But Mahfuz's cryptic response offers an opposite interpretation: what could be a more damning verdict on the revolution than its personification in the character of the vain, self-destructive Hasanayn?

In an interview in 1986, when asked about the apparently prophetic nature of some of his works, Mahfuz recalled a meeting with Anwar al-Sadat in the early 1960s, at which Sadat told him that he had read *Bidaya wa-nihaya*. Sadat asked: "How could you have made the officer Hasanayn commit suicide? He's us, that officer [*da ihna, al-dabit da!*]."[52] The suicide of the young officer at the end of the story is indeed prophetic: it will be recalled that 'Abd al-Hakim

[51] 'A'ida Sharif, "*Dhikrayat wa-hadith ma'a Najib Mahfuz*," *al-Ādāb* (March 1967), p. 26.

[52] 'Abd al-Rahman Abu 'Awf, *al-Ru'a al-mutaghayyira fi riwayat Najib Mahfuz* (Cairo, 1991), p. 165.

'Amir, Nasser's deputy and Commander-in-Chief of the Egyptian army, committed suicide on 14 September 1967, in the wake of Egypt's military defeat in June of that year.

Mahfuz seems to prefer the humble and patient Husayn, the second of the three sons in *Bidaya wa-nihaya*. Significantly, like Kamal in the trilogy, he would like to become a teacher; but, since he must work to help his family and so cannot go to teachers college, he takes a job as a secretary in a school. This son is considerate of others and proves loyal to family and friends; it is he who will continue the family line. The strongest character of the novel is, however, the mother who, in her patience and wisdom, is able to survive all the troubles and hardships that life brings her.

Mahfuz's next novel was the Cairene trilogy, on which he worked for a number of years, and which he completed in the spring of 1952, a few months before the Free Officers revolution.[53] The novel's main character is Kamal, the author's alter ego, who grows up in the shadow of his autocratic father, Sayyid Ahmad. A ten-year-old child at the beginning of the story in 1917, Kamal is a thirty-seven-year-old bachelor when the story ends in 1944.

The story traces three generations of a Cairene family between 1917 and 1944. With the story of Sayyid Ahmad's family as the main plot line, the novel gives a detailed picture of middle-class life in Cairo and a dynamic account of Egypt's major political and social developments throughout that period. Against a background of many alternating milieus (family home, bazaar, café, office, brothel, university lecture hall, etc.), Mahfuz treats a multitude of subjects: Egyptian nationalism, family relations, love, the place of the writer in society, secular positivism versus religious faith, socialism versus Islamic fundamentalism and many other social and cultural issues.

The death of Sayyid Ahmad's second son, Kamal's older brother, in anti-British demonstrations in 1919, casts a long shadow over Sayyid Ahmad's family. Although Mahfuz views the 1919 rebellion with admiration, as a heroic action and a genuine expression of the feelings of the whole nation, he frankly describes the not-so-heroic

[53] See above, p. 40. For a full analysis of the trilogy, see below, pp. 198–225.

stance that other members of Sayyid Ahmad's family took at the time. (This is very characteristic of Mahfuz: he does not give up his critical vision or his irony even when describing things dear to him; intellectual honesty has precedence over personal bias.)

Both the father and the mother strongly oppose their son's participation in the nationalist movement. The father, like the rest of his friends, is an enthusiastic supporter of the nationalist call for independence. He regards his signature of the petition in support of Sa'd Zaghlul – signed by many thousands of Egyptians in November, 1918 – as a bold nationalist action. But he will not have his son risk himself by participating in the student demonstrations, and goes so far as to try to make him swear on the Qur'an that he will desist from any anti-British activity. Later, after his son's death, he takes great pride in being "the father of a martyr." The mother is not interested in politics at all; she cares only for the well-being of her family. She, too, refuses to let her son risk his life, but, unlike the father, she does not quite understand her son's nationalist attitude nor his hatred for the British: "Why do you hate them? Aren't they people like us, with children and mothers?" When the son declares, "A nation cannot live if it is ruled by foreigners," the mother responds, "We are alive even though they have been ruling us for a very long time. I gave birth to all of you children under their rule. They don't kill people; they don't desecrate the mosques, and Muhammad's nation is fine and well."[54] Finally, she sums up her position: "These matters are none of our business. If our ministers believe that the English should get out of Egypt, let them push them out by themselves."[55]

Sayyid Ahmad's eldest son does not take part in the national upheaval; years later, however, he will boast of having been one of the leaders of the 1919 demonstrations, along with his martyred brother.

Kamal, a mere child in 1919, naturally shares the nationalist enthusiasm and anti-British sentiment of the grown-up members of his

[54] *Bayn al-qasrayn*, p. 399.

[55] Ibid., p. 400. The attitude of the mother here is similar to that of the mother in *Bidaya wa-nihaya*, who tells her sons, when they rejoice at the conclusion of the Anglo-Egyptian treaty of 1936: "There is no compensation whatsoever for the loss of young life.... Occupation, independence, I don't see the difference between them. We would do better to pray to God to alleviate our [own] distress and to replace our hardships with ease" (*Bidaya wa-nihaya*, pp. 175–76).

family. When Kamal sees British soldiers for the first time, when they encamp near his home, he says in amazement, "How beautiful they are!" His brother asks him sarcastically, "Do you really like them?" The child answers naïvely, "Very much indeed. I imagined that they would look like demons."[56] Within a few days, Kamal comes to befriend these soldiers and visits them in their encampment daily upon his return from school. As Kamal grows, he is torn by an inner strife that has been typical of generations of modern educated Arabs: the conflict between the pull of the indigenous traditional culture on the one hand, and the attraction to the imported modern culture on the other. Kamal, who becomes a teacher, significantly chooses English as his subject. In an interview in 1988, Mahfuz mentioned that he, like so many of his generation, suffered from the crisis of "cultural duality."[57]

With the publication of the Cairene trilogy, Mahfuz was recognized as the master of the modern Arabic novel, and it was expected that in his next novel he would somehow celebrate the new reality created after 1952 by the Free Officers revolution. This, as we know, did not happen, and Mahfuz did not emerge from his literary silence until 1959, when he published *Awlad haretna* ("Children of Our Neighborhood") in serial form in *al-Ahram*, Egypt's leading newspaper.[58]

In *Awlad haretna* Mahfuz deals allegorically with the problems of civilization, as it has evolved under the aegis of the three monotheistic religions until the modern age. He explores the nature of religion, secular authority and knowledge, and the relationship between these three. In the section of the allegory relating to the modern era, Mahfuz focuses on the problem of science and the scientific approach, as opposed to religion and the traditional worldview. Religious circles in Egypt were outraged by the book, which pious Muslims regarded as a blasphemy. The book's division into five

---

[56] *Bayn al-qasrayn*, p. 427.

[57] *Al-Musawwar* (21 October 1988), p. 15

[58] *Al-Ahram* (21 September–25 December 1959). The book was translated into English by Philip Stewart, and published in 1981 as *Children of Gebelawi* (London, 1981); the title of this translation will be used here throughout.

parts and 114 chapters may be considered as a mischievous allusion respectively to the five books of Moses and the 114 suras of the Qur'an.

The book deals with another very sensitive subject: the nature of power. It criticizes the oppressive rule of the officers – represented allegorically in the story as club-wielding thugs who brutally oppress the people. For both of these reasons *Awlad haretna* has never been published in book form in Egypt; it was, however, published in Lebanon in 1967.[59]

The neighborhood (*hāra*) of the book's title represents the whole of humanity, although it should be noted that the human history encompassed here by Mahfuz is essentially that of the three great monotheistic religions. The term *hara* signifies a quarter in Old Cairo, whose division into ten to fifteen *hara*s dates back to Fatimid times. "Physically, a *hara* is a subsection of a city. Having only limited access, usually through a street terminating in an open square, it is equipped with walls and gates which can be closed at night and, in addition, barricaded completely during times of crisis. Socially, the *hara* is a group of persons usually unified by ethnic and/or occupational characteristics.... Politically, it is often a unit of administration and control."[60] The people of Mahfuz's *hara* inhabit a physical setting which belongs to no particular historical period and which supplies no specific place names relating it to any actual locale. We are, however, given enough hints to indicate that the description of the neighborhood is based on a quarter in Old Cairo in pre-modern times. This neighborhood borders on the desert (*khala'*, literally "empty space") and life there is described in a way which suggests a pre-modern era: there are no references to cars, telephones or any other form of modern technology. It should be noted that this *hara*, although presumably located in Cairo, and although many of its features are drawn from Mahfuz's memories of his early child-

---

[59] Beirut, Dar al-Ādāb, 1967. On the religious opposition to the book and attempts to prevent its publication, see Samia Mehrez, "Respected Sir," in M. Beard and A. Haydar (eds.), *Naguib Mahfouz: From Regional Fame to Global Recognition* (Syracuse, 1993), pp. 65–69. For an analysis of some philosophical aspects of *Awlad haretna* see below, pp. 101–3; for its political significance, see pp. 133–35.

[60] Janet L. Abu-Lughod, *Cairo: 1001 Years of the City Victorious* (Princeton, 1971), p. 24.

hood in Jamaliyya, is a fictional locale where realistic elements are used to create a mythological environment which represents the whole world. Having created this environment, Mahfuz was to return to it again and again in a number of his later novels and short stories.

In 1961 Mahfuz published an eagerly awaited new novel, *al-Liss wa'l-kilab* ("The Thief and the Dogs"), whose appearance was a milestone in the development both of Mahfuz's art and of modern Arabic fiction.[61] It introduced Arab readers to themes of existentialist literature – alienation, despair, loss of meaning – and to modern narrative techniques, such as stream of consciousness. The political content of the book was also of great significance: it was a powerful expression of disenchantment with the 1952 revolution, by Egypt's foremost novelist.

The story begins when the hero, Sa'id Mahran (the thief of the book's title), is released from jail on the anniversary of the revolution, in honor of which his prison term has been shortened. He finds that the world has not changed for the better since pre-revolutionary days. He wants to avenge himself on those who have wronged him – primarily his one-time henchman, 'Ileish Sidra, who deceived him with his wife Nabawiyya and took Sa'id's place as Nabawiyya's husband and head of the gang. His other adversary is Ra'uf 'Alwan, a journalist closely associated with the regime. In the years before the 1952 revolution, when the hero was just a boy, this journalist (at that time, still a student) had been the hero's spiritual mentor, and had encouraged him to believe that there was nothing wrong in stealing from the rich, since they had no right to their money and property. Now, however, this journalist shows no sympathy for the thief; he gives him some money and tells him not to approach him again. Now the editor of a government-owned magazine, the journalist lives in luxury in a villa resembling those of the wealthy and powerful whom he had once condemned.

When Sa'id realizes that his former mentor Ra'uf 'Alwan is not ready to help him, he feels betrayed by him, too. Convinced that it is his mission to destroy "the traitors," he tries to kill both his former

---

[61] For further discussion of the book see below, pp. 115–16, 136, 226–35.

henchman and Ra'uf, but fails. In a café frequented by underworld characters, Sa'id meets Nur, a prostitute he has known for many years. Nur, who has always loved Sa'id, now gives him refuge in her apartment, in an isolated building bordering on a cemetery. Nur would like Sa'id to abandon his vengeful schemes and escape with her to Upper Egypt, her place of origin, where they could live quietly together. Sa'id, however, does not give up his raging desire for revenge. After a few nights, Nur does not return home; she disappears, and Sa'id can no longer hide in her apartment. A fugitive from the police, he tries to hide in the cemetery. In the final scene, surrounded by policemen and tracker dogs, Sa'id is shot dead.

The literary-aesthetic qualities of the book drew such enthusiastic acclaim that the book's potentially embarrassing political implications were somehow dimmed. The critics observed, of course, that the novel contained elements of social criticism, but interpreted these as directed against opportunists who distorted the true nature of the revolution. They chose not to see the book as a negative comment on the regime itself. The more profound implication of this novel, that the revolution had failed to bring about any real change for the better, could not be mentioned in Egypt. The Egyptian expatriate Anwar Abdel-Malek, however, wrote in Paris: "The work of fiction [al-Liss wa'l-kilab] slashed through the euphoria of the newspapers and the daily proclamations of victory. It portrayed the condition of a man who is still downtrodden. The most successful novel by Egypt's best contemporary novelist concludes in crisis and drama, not with a happy ending."[62]

Al-Liss wa'l-kilab was followed by a series of other short novels similar to it in style, more sparing in descriptive detail and with a larger proportion of dialogue and interior monologue than Mahfuz's earlier realistic novels. Social reality is described only when necessary as a background to the problems of the individual which, in the main, are not social (poverty, oppression, etc.), but rather existential: anxiety, loneliness, loss of purpose.[63] This change in form and style

[62] Anwar Abdel-Malek, *Egypt: Military Society* (New York, 1968), p. 319. Abdel-Malek's book was originally published in French (Paris, 1962).

[63] See Menahem Milson, "Naǧīb Maḥfūẓ and the Quest for Meaning," *Arabica*, 17 (1970), pp. 178–86.

corresponds to the shift in Mahfuz's thematic focus; with attention directed essentially to the inner world of the individual, the use of interior monologue becomes more prominent. The amount of dialogue increases, while the language becomes more terse and loaded with hints and symbols. In all these short novels, the main characters are alienated, lonesome and forlorn.[64]

It should be emphasized that, despite the obvious differences between Mahfuz's novels of the 1960s and those he wrote in the 1940s and 1950s, there was no sudden revolution in his writing. The third volume of the trilogy (al-Sukkariyya) points both thematically (the problem of alienation) and stylistically (an increase in the proportion of dialogue) in the direction which Mahfuz was to take in the 1960s.

In 1962 Mahfuz published al-Summan wa'l-kharif ("The Quail and Autumn"),[65] whose hero, 'Isa al-Dabbagh, is a high-ranking government official dismissed in the wake of Nasser's revolution. Embittered and forlorn, he leaves his home in Cairo and moves to self-imposed exile in Alexandria. Despite his friends' entreaties, he cannot bring himself to adjust to the new order. One of his friends, also formerly a high-ranking official in the old regime, tells him that he has found spiritual comfort in Sufism, but for 'Isa this is not a solution.

Typically, this alienated hero is reluctant to make any permanent commitment; he refuses to look for another job, and has no desire to establish a family. When he does eventually marry for economic reasons, he cannot bring himself to love his wife. Painfully aware of the emptiness of his existence, he tries to reestablish his connection with Riri, a former prostitute with whom he used to live and who has borne him a child. But it is too late. He has no chance of regaining his daughter, Ni'mat; he has lost the right to fatherhood by his callous behavior towards her mother.

The hero's name, 'Isa al-Dabbagh, is significant. 'Isa, Arabic for Jesus, represents the high ideals to which the hero pretends; it also ironically represents the hero's belief that he has served as a scape-

---

[64] The novels I am referring to are the following: al-Liss wa'l-kilab (1961), al-Summan wa'l-kharif (1962), al-Tariq (1964), al-Shahhadh (1965), Tharthara fawq al-nil (1966).

[65] Translated into English by Roger Allen as Autumn Quail (Cairo, 1985).

goat for the wrongdoings of others. He tells his friends, "I sometimes find consolation in seeing myself as Christ, bearing the sins of a nation of sinners."[66] The *dabbagh* ("tanner") practices what is considered the most repugnant of professions, because of the foul stench associated with the work. This is an allusion to the corruption which soiled the reputation of both 'Isa and the Wafd party. The daughter he has lost is called Ni'mat, which means "God's favors."

Al-Tariq ("The Way," 1964, appeared in English as *The Search*) is the story of a young man named Sabir (meaning "the patient one," an obviously ironic name), who, following the death of his mother, sets out on a desperate search for his father, from whom his mother had separated before he was born. Sabir becomes involved with a married woman, murders her rich, elderly husband, is caught and, at the end of the story, is awaiting execution.

The book is, in fact, a parable on man's search for a heavenly Father and his uncontrollable desire for transcendental meaning and guidance.[67] The name of the father, Sayyid Sayyid al-Rahimi (which in approximate translation can be rendered as "Lord Lord Merciful"), would seem to make this interpretation inevitable.[68]

Tharthara fawq al-nil ("Chatter on the Nile," 1966)[69] depicts a group of Cairo intellectuals – government officials and people from the media and the entertainment world – who meet nightly on a houseboat on the Nile where they engage in drinking, drugs, sex and idle talk. They are morally dissolute and intellectually confused. The story portrays a dismal picture of the mood and manners of Cairo's intelligentsia under the Free Officers' regime. It contains some very caustic remarks made by the characters about the regime, which they regard as a reign of fear.

Although it was not published until 1966, and is usually regarded as one of Mahfuz's short novels of the 1960s, *Tharthara fawq al-nil*

[66] *Al-Summan wa'l-kharif*, p. 70.
[67] See my article, "Naǧīb Maḥfūẓ and the Quest for Meaning."
[68] While the book has been more or less generally recognized as a parable on a religious quest, the critic Fu'ad Dawwara has offered a different interpretation, regarding *al-Tariq* as an allegory of Egypt's modern political history. See Dawwara, *"al-Tariq: auwaluhu 'ahr wa-akhiruhu jarima,"* in *al-Majalla*, 91 (July 1964). Reference from Dawwara, *Najib Mahfuz*, pp. 105–30.
[69] Translated by Frances Liardet as *Adrift on the Nile* (Cairo, 1993).

would appear, in fact, to have been written in 1957.[70] Mahfuz, probably for fear of official reaction, delayed publication. His fears were indeed justified: when the book appeared, 'Abd al-Hakim 'Amir, Nasser's deputy, was angered by the uncomplimentary allusions to the regime; he complained about the matter to Nasser, and demanded that Mahfuz be punished. He was saved by the intervention of the minister of culture, Tharwat 'Ukasha.[71]

In describing the houseboat setting, Mahfuz may well have drawn on a personal experience he describes in a letter to Dr. Rajab (probably from 1947): "I have met a young writer this summer, a talented and pleasant young man, who owns a houseboat. Here we stay until midnight, dividing our time between hashish and women; and your brother has quite changed his nature – though only for the duration of the summer vacation, of course. Furthermore, he has taught me to play poker, may God forgive him, and I have become a gambler, and I am only a step away from [needing] a specialist in venereal diseases. Look what a bad end this writer has come to!"[72]

In the 1960s Mahfuz began to publish short stories once more: the collection *Dunya 'llah* ("God's World") appeared in 1963. Says Mahfuz, "The stories in the collection *Dunya 'llah* are the first I have ever written out of a genuine desire to write a short story."[73] It should be recalled that Mahfuz has explained on various occasions that in the 1930s he really wanted to write novels, but since he was unable to find anyone willing to publish them, he wrote instead short stories "derived" from his projected novels.[74]

The themes of Mahfuz's short stories of the 1960s are similar to those found in his novels of this period: the existential problems of

---

[70] See above, p. 43. The novel first appeared serialized in *al-Ahram* in 1965, and was published in book form the following year.

[71] Mahfuz to Ghali Shukri, *al-Watan al-'arabi* (29 January 1988), p. 45.

[72] Letter to Dr. Adham Rajab, "*Khitabat bi-khatt Najib Mahfuz*," October (11 December 1988), p. 42.

[73] Ghitani, p. 101

[74] See above, pp. 38, 63, 65–66. The collection *God's World*, trans. Akef Abadir and Roger Allen (Minneapolis: Bibliotheca Islamica, 1973) is not a translation of *Dunya 'llah* but an assembly of twenty stories from a number of Mahfuz's collections, from *Hams al-junun* (1948?) to *Shahr al-'asal* (1971).

the individual and the larger problems at the very foundations of civilization. Many of these stories are symbolical or allegorical. Their
ideational content is usually more pronounced than in the novels of
this period, because of the nature of the genre. In the short stories, as
in the novels, universal problems are perceived in a particularly
Egyptian setting.

Short stories have now become a regular part of Mahfuz's literary
repertoire. Since *Dunya 'llah* he has published fourteen collections of
short stories, many of which appeared in the literary section of *al-
Ahram*. A number of these stories have a more or less veiled political
theme; some of them are surrealistic. The appearance of the more
enigmatic of these often allegorical stories invariably provoked argument among intellectuals as to their meaning and Mahfuz's intent.[75]
Mahfuz himself refused to provide any explanation. He told an interviewer that, some days after the appearance of the story *"Luna bark"*
("Amusement Park," one of his more enigmatic surrealistic short
stories, published in the collection *Bayt sayyi' al-sum'a*, 1965), one
of his friends told him, "I know the hidden meaning of the story."
Mahfuz recounted that he answered his friend, "If so, please help
me by telling me what it is, so that I, in turn, can tell those who ask
me."[76]

A surrealistic atmosphere, verging on the absurd, is especially
characteristic of the collections *Taht al-mizalla* ("In the Bus Shelter,"
1969), *Shahr al-'asal* ("Honeymoon," 1971) and *al-Jarima* ("The
Crime," 1973). Mahfuz explained on several occasions that the situation and general mood in Egypt following the military debacle of
1967 could not be expressed other than surrealistically.

The novel *Miramar* (1967) revolves around seven characters – five
men, representing different generations, political persuasions and
social backgrounds, who lodge in pension "Miramar" in Alexandria,
and two women: the aging Greek proprietress of the pension and the

---

[75] E.g., see below, p. 141 n. 23. Mahfuz's reluctance to provide explanations for his
works has already been noted in connection with the character of Hasanayn in the film
version of *Bidaya wa-nihaya*; see above, p. 77.

[76] Interview with 'A'ida Sharif in *al-Ādāb* (March 1967), p. 29.

young maid Zahra, a beautiful *fallaha* who has come to the big city from her native village seeking independence and education.[77]

Miramar resembles Mahfuz's previous novels of the 1960s in that most of its characters are lonesome and alienated. It differs, however, from these earlier novels in two respects. First, this is Mahfuz's only contemporary novel which, as a whole, takes place outside Cairo. Second, it has a different narrative form: it is a quartet; the story is told by four of the protagonists, each from his own viewpoint.

The Alexandria locale is of great symbolic significance: from Mahfuz's Cairo-centric point of view Alexandria represents exile and alienation. In fact, all the characters, except for the Greek proprietress, are away from home. The symbolic meaning of Alexandria is already anticipated in the earlier short novel *al-Summan wa'l-kharif* (1962), where the hero, a high-ranking government official dismissed from office by the new revolutionary regime, attempts "to get away from it all" by going to Alexandria.

Mahfuz was not the first Egyptian novelist to write a novel narrated from four different points of view. He was preceded, six years earlier, by a younger novelist, Fathi Ghanim, who wrote a similarly constructed novel called *The Man Who Lost his Shadow*.[78] But it was through *Miramar* that the quartet form became "naturalized." Some critics have drawn the inevitable analogy between Mahfuz's "Alexandria quartet" and Lawrence Durrell's *Alexandria Quartet*. However, Mahfuz's approach in *Miramar* seems to owe more to Akira Kurosawa's film *Rashomon* (1950) than to Durrell's novel. In fact, since the beginning of the 1960s, Mahfuz's narrative art has been greatly influenced by cinematic narrative techniques. He has always been fascinated by the elusiveness of truth and reality, and cinema (which he has always liked and which he came to know at close hand through script writing and through his work as director of the Foundation for the Support of the Cinema) seems to have suggested to him new ways of portraying the many facets of reality. Mahfuz used the

---

[77] The novel was translated into English as *Miramar* by Fatma Moussa-Mahmoud (London, 1978).

[78] Fathi Ghanim (b. 1924), *al-Rajul alladhi faqada zillahu* (Cairo, 1962). English translation by Desmond Stewart (London, 1966).

quartet form again in the short novel *al-Karnak* (1974)[79] and in *Afrah al-qubba* ("The Festivities of the Dome," 1981).[80]

Al-Karnak, which paints a depressing picture of life under Nasser, aroused controversy and, in some cases, animosity towards Mahfuz.[81]

In 1972, with the publication of *al-Maraya*, a collection of fifty-five self-contained fictional profiles which he himself called "a novel," Mahfuz began to move away from the classical model of the novel. This tendency to episodic composition reappears in many of his later works, such as *Malhamat al-harafish* (1977), *Layali alf layla* (1982), *Rihlat Ibn Fattuma* (1983) and *Hadith al-sabah wa'l-masa'* (1987). This new departure may have been prompted by two factors: on the one hand a feeling on Mahfuz's part that he could neither surpass nor repeat his supreme achievements – the trilogy and *al-Liss wa'l-kilab*; and on the other, a desire to experiment with a narrative style akin in some measure to the Arab indigenous tradition of storytelling, which was episodic in both its popular and its classical manifestations.[82] It is interesting to note that Mahfuz's adoption of the episodic style was preceded, in the early sixties, by his return to the short story form, which he had abandoned some twenty years before.

Malhamat al-harafish ("The Epic of the Riff-Raff," 1977)[83] tells the story of sixteen generations of the al-Naji family. In this story Mahfuz returns to the semi-mythological setting he used for the first time in *Awlad haretna* – a *hara* (neighborhood) in Old Cairo in an undefined pre-modern era. The eponymous father of the family is 'Ashur, who begins life as a foundling abandoned outside the walls of the local Sufi monastery and grows up to be an honest, hard-working and good-natured man. When the neighborhood is stricken by plague he, his wife and their three sons flee to the desert. On their return home six months later, they discover that they are the only

---

[79] A translation appears in *Three Contemporary Egyptian Novels* by Saad Al-Gabalawy (New Brunswick, 1984).

[80] Translated by Olive Kenny and revised by Mursi Saad El Din and John Rodenbeck as *Wedding Song* (New York, 1989).

[81] See below, pp. 130–31.

[82] I have borrowed the term "episodic" from Rasheed El-Enany, *Naguib Mahfouz: The Pursuit of Meaning* (London and New York, 1993).

[83] Translated by Catherine Cobham as *The Harafish* (New York, 1994).

survivors; hence the family name: *al-naji* means "survivor." 'Ashur becomes the leader of the resettled *hara*, embodying an ideal of upright leadership as he confronts and overcomes a wicked rival. After 'Ashur's mysterious disappearance, one of his sons succeeds him as the neighborhood *futuwwa* ("ringleader," "strong-man") and continues his tradition of just rule until he dies, and violence and corruption take over.

The *harafish*, the poor people of the neighborhood, whom 'Ashur and his son protected, now once more fall victim to the oppressive rule of the local hoods (*futuwwas*) and to exploitation by the rich. After generations of strife and jealousy, one of 'Ashur's descendants – another poor but honest and kind man who, like the ancestor whose name he bears, possesses unusual physical strength – leads the *harafish* in rebellion against their oppressors and establishes himself as the local *futuwwa*, securing for the neighborhood a new, just regime.

Malhamat al-harafish is an attempt on the part of Mahfuz to understand and explain the interaction between human nature and the social and political order. This book in some ways resembles *Awlad haretna* which was published eighteen years earlier. Both novels are situated in the *hara*, and in both Mahfuz exposes the corrupting effects of wealth and power. However, unlike *Awlad haretna*, which deals allegorically with particular stages of history, *Malhamat al-harafish* does not attempt to illustrate any particular era, and focuses primarily on personal desires and fears: sex, greed, the various forms of love, the inevitability of death and the yearning for the infinite.

The title of the book aroused comment because it resurrected the word *harāfish*, a medieval term which had long fallen into disuse. *Harafish* – the plural form of the little used *harfūsh* – means "riffraff" or "ruffians," but Mahfuz redeems this derogatory term and applies it to the poor and underprivileged classes in general.[84] In choosing this term for the title of his book, Mahfuz was indulging in a private joke: several years previously, he and his literary friends had begun to refer to themselves as the *harafish*.

Afrah al-qubba (1981) is a short novel about a young playwright

---

[84] On the historical meaning of *harafish* see EI[2], s.v. "*harfūsh*."

and his first successfully performed play. From birth, the life of the hero has been closely connected with the theater: his father is a prompter and his mother a box-office cashier. The theater manager and the actors are frequent guests in the family home, where guests and hosts alike nightly indulge in drinking, sex and drugs.

The plot of the successful play, which serves as a pivot for the novel, is taken from the life of the young playwright's own family, and the novel's four narrators – the playwright himself, his parents and an actor – appear as characters in the play. The parents and the actor are horrified by the play – which represents the playwright as having informed the police of his parents' activities as drug dealers and as having killed his wife and young son – because they mistakenly believe it to be an unaltered representation of reality. They do not realize that although the play is founded on actual people and events (the playwright's parents were indeed imprisoned, his wife and son did indeed die), these are represented not as they really were, but as the author's imagination has reshaped them.

Mahfuz uses this story to explore the tense and often tragic relationship between the writer and society and also, possibly, to reflect his own experiences following the publication of *al-Karnak*, when he was accused of disloyalty and ingratitude towards his country. In addition to making use of the quartet form to show how personal perceptions of reality inevitably differ, *Afrah al-qubba* also stresses the gap between truth and its fictionalized representations.

Al-Baqi min al-zaman sa'a ("You Have One Hour Left," 1982) is the story of an Egyptian family from the mid-1930s until after the signing of the Camp David peace agreement between Egypt and Israel in 1978. The various ideological and political affiliations dividing Egyptian society are all represented in the novel by members of the family.

Layali alf layla ("The Nights of a Thousand Nights," 1982) evokes the *Arabian Nights* (known in Arabic as the *Thousand and One Nights*) not only in its title and by borrowing several of its main characters, but also in its frame-story structure. Thirteen loosely related tales are enclosed within a story about King Shahriyar, the murderous king of the *Arabian Nights*. Mahfuz's "Nights of a Thousand Nights" begins at the point where the *Arabian Nights* ends:

Shahriyar has already decided to spare Sheherazade's life and marry her. A series of stories ensues, recounting events in the kingdom and enabling Mahfuz once more to explore the power of love, the temptations of lust and greed and the uses of political power for good and evil. King Shahriyar, who has become a searcher after truth, invites Sinbad to tell him about his marvelous voyages and hears from him the moral lessons he has derived from his experiences. The first of these is: man often mistakes illusion for the truth. When asked how it is possible to distinguish between the two, Sinbad replies: we must use the senses and reason God has given us (pp. 247–48). He further says that the preservation of outworn traditions is foolish and destructive, that freedom is essential to the life of the spirit and that without it even Paradise is worthless (pp. 250–51). By the end of the book, Shahriyar has given up his kingdom and become an ascetic. He has learned that joy and pleasure are short-lived, and that absolute truth is unattainable.

This is not the first time that Mahfuz has clothed his philosophical and social views in variations on the *Arabian Nights*. Several years earlier, in his one-act play *al-Shaytan ya'iz* ("Satan Preaches"), he retold the *Arabian Nights* story, "The City of Brass."[85]

Rihlat Ibn Fattuma ("The Travels of Ibn Fattuma," 1983)[86] purports to be the travel journal of one Qindil Ibn Fattuma who, dissatisfied with life in his homeland, the Land of Islam (*Dar al-Islam*), undertakes a journey in search of a social Utopia.

The description of the countries he visits allows Mahfuz to present his views on different societies and stages of human development. The first two countries Ibn Fattuma encounters are the Land of Sunrise (*Dar al-mashriq*) and the Land of Confusion (*Dar al-hayra*). The former is a pagan society with a primitive social order, the latter a quasi-feudal regime. For different reasons, Ibn Fattuma finds life in both unbearable, and he makes his way to the Land of the Arena (*Dar al-halba*). This is a liberal capitalist society in which "God is reason and freedom is its prophet" (p. 107). Ibn Fattuma, however,

---

[85] This play appeared at the end of a collection of short stories of the same name, published in 1979. The story of the City of Brass occupies the 602nd to the 623rd of the *Arabian Nights*.

[86] Translated by Denys Johnson-Davies as *The Journey of Ibn Fattouma* (London, 1992).

is shocked at this society's indifference towards the weak and the poor and he leaves for the Land of Safety (*Dar al-aman*), a society theoretically guided by total justice which is in fact a brutal Soviet-style dictatorship. His journey toward Utopia leads him next to the Land of Sunset (*Dar al-ghurub*), a serene and beautiful land where people have assembled from all over the world to prepare for the journey to the Land of the Mountain (*Dar al-jabal*), which is believed to be the land of the heart's desire. The Land of Sunset, is, however, overrun by the conquering army of the Land of Safety, and its inhabitants are given the choice of living in a socialist dictatorship or leaving for the Land of the Mountain with their preparations incomplete. They choose to leave, and although they succeed in crossing the border into the Land of the Mountain, Ibn Fattuma's record comes to an end before the mountain itself is reached. Mahfuz's book leaves the reader uncertain as to whether or not Ibn Fattuma's diary can ever have a sequel. The name of the hero, Ibn Fattuma, was clearly chosen to evoke the name of the famous fourteenth century traveller Ibn Battuta, the Marco Polo of the Muslim world, whose *Rihlat Ibn Battuta* is a classic of Arabic literature.[87]

Mahfuz returns to the multi-vocal narrative technique (though not in a quartet form) in the short novel *Yawm qutila 'l-za'im* ("The Day the Leader was Killed," 1985),[88] and in *al-'A'ish fi 'l-haqiqa* ("He Who Lives in the Truth," 1985). In the former, the story is told by three of the characters, each one alternating with the others in several turns. The latter is told by fourteen persons.

"He Who Lives in the Truth" is the story of Akhnaton (c. 1360–1344 BCE), the Pharaoh who established a new religious system. In the story a young Egyptian, a decade or so after the death of Akhnaton, becomes interested in the intriguing figure of this Pharaoh and sets out to discover the truth about him. The search consists of a series of encounters with various people, fourteen in number, who personally knew Akhnaton, and who tell his story from fourteen different perspectives. The name of the novel, "He Who Lives in the

---

[87] See *EI*², s.v. "Ibn Baṭṭūṭa."

[88] Translated by Malak Hashim as *The Day the Leader Was Killed* (Cairo, 1989). For a discussion of this story and its political intent, see below, p. 143.

Truth," is deliberately ambiguous, in more than one way. The Arabic word signifying "truth" also means "reality" and the preposition signifying "in" means also "for the sake of." Thus, the title can also read "He Who Lives for the Sake of the Truth." The identity of the subject, "He Who...," is also ambiguous; it refers to Akhnaton, the King who believed he had found the true religion, as much as to the young narrator who launches a search for the truth about the dead king. What drives the young narrator of this story is indeed the most important impulse of Mahfuz's entire literary enterprise: the desire to grasp the elusive truth. Since Mahfuz is convinced that no one individual can perceive a full, objective picture of reality, he produces fourteen witnesses, each of whom presents his own version of the story.

It is worthwhile noting that in this novel, as well as in an earlier book published in 1983 entitled *Amam al-'arsh* ("Before the Throne") Mahfuz returned to the Pharaonic setting, which he had not used for decades, as though to remind Egyptian readers of the uniqueness of Egyptian identity – a national identity which precedes Arabism and Islam.[89]

Al-Fajr al-kadhib ("False Dawn," 1989) is a collection of thirty short stories set in modern Cairo. The themes and characters are familiar. Perhaps the most distinctive feature of this collection is that in many of the stories the main character, like the author himself, has reached a point at which he takes moral stock of his life. The pervading spirit is one of equanimity.

Qushtumor (1988), Mahfuz's latest novel, tells the story of a group of five friends in Cairo over a period of seventy years. All five were born in 1910 (one year before Mahfuz's birth), and grew up in al-'Abbasiyya (the neighborhood in which Mahfuz lived from the age of twelve until his marriage in 1954). The narrator, who is one of the group, recounts the individual fortunes of each of his four friends against the backdrop of the political vicissitudes of Egypt throughout their lifetime. The story is recounted in the form of the reminiscences of an old man, who views the world and the life he has lived with serenity:

---

[89] On the content of *Amam al-'arsh*, see below, pp. 144–55.

The 'Abbasiyya we knew – is anything left? Where are the fields and the orchards? . . . Where are the houses and their gardens? Where are the villas and the mansions, where are the respectable matrons? All we see now is a jungle of cement and iron, and hordes of mad cars. All we hear is clamor and uproar. Heaps of waste surround us.

Since the present denies us any cause for happiness, we are driven to the [gardens of] the past to gather some of its vanished harvest. We do this even though we know we are deceiving ourselves. Although we remember the evils and suffering with which the past was filled, we cannot help but enjoy this source of magic and fantasy.[90]

The book ends as the narrator is aroused from his reflections by the voice of one of his friends reciting the ninety-third chapter of the Qur'an (*Surat al-Duha*):

By the light of day, and by the fall of night, your Lord has not forsaken you, nor does He abhor you.
The life to come holds a richer prize for you than this present life. You shall be gratified with what your Lord will give you.
Did He not find you an orphan and give you shelter?
Did He not find you in error and guide you?
Did He not find you poor and enrich you?
Therefore do not wrong the orphan, nor chide away the beggar.
But proclaim the goodness of your Lord.[91]

Is it possible that Mahfuz, ever fond of creating enigmas and riddles, sees in the last sentence quoted here – which is also the last line of his final novel – an allusion to his own literary enterprise?

[90] *Qushtumor*, p. 146.
[91] Ibid., p. 147. The translation of the Qura'nic verses is that of N. J. Dawood, *The Koran*, Penguin Books.

PART TWO

RECURRENT IMAGES, PERSISTENT IDEAS

CHAPTER 4

Rational Man, Rebellious Devil

In this and the following two chapters, I propose to explain some important aspects of Mahfuz's conceptual world by analyzing several interrelated themes which occupy a central place in his works. These are embodied in certain literary images which recur with remarkable persistence.[1]

Let us begin our examination of Mahfuz's vocabulary of images by way of one of his short stories: "The Other Face" ("*al-Wajh al-akhar*"), published in the collection *Taht al-mizalla* (1969). The narrator is a famous educator telling the story of his long friendship with two brothers, one a police officer and the other a criminal, both of whom he has known since childhood. His sympathies, quite understandably, lie with the policeman. The struggle between the brothers reaches its climax when the police officer is appointed chief of police in the city where his criminal brother operates. The narrator tries in vain to arrange a reconciliation between the two. Eventually the police kill the criminal. When the narrator hears of his death he is deeply distressed, and sinks into a state of moral and emotional confusion. His value system has been turned upside-down and he realizes that, whereas in the past he has regarded the police officer as the ideal hero, he has now come to view the slain criminal as his

---

[1] Jabir 'Asfur has called attention to the fact that, while critics often use expressions such as "Mahfuz's world" or "Mahfuz's vision," these terms have so far been insufficiently analyzed and have been given no precise meaning. Jabir 'Asfur, "*Nuqqad Najib Mahfuz*," in Ghali Shukri (ed.), *Najib Mahfuz: Ibda' nisf qarn*, (Cairo, 1989), pp. 238–43.

ideal. He announces his decision to abandon education for art. The subject of his first painting is to be a nude woman. He says that reason has failed him, and that he now prefers to act destructively and madly.[2]

Let us consider more closely the characters and motifs in this story, which is really an essay in the fictional mode on the conflict between human passions on the one hand and social order on the other. In the fictional structure of the story the narrator, *qua* educator, is presented as having attempted to mediate between the two brothers. Mahfuz hints a number of times that the conflict between the two is actually a struggle between two aspects of the human personality which pull in opposing directions.[3] The very name of the story, "The Other Face," suggests this notion of inner ambivalence. Speaking of the criminal brother, the narrator says to the policeman, "He is not a creature of another species. He is a captive of those passions which we have undertaken to repress." The policeman answers, "That is the difference between civilization and barbarity." The conflict between the brothers represents a problem of universal dimensions; it is concerned with the very foundations of civilization. The policeman describes his brother in the following terms: "a mad storm, an uncontrollable eruption, a raging bull." On the other hand, the policeman is referred to as characterized by rationality (*'aql*). When pronounced by the criminal brother, however, "rationality" sounds like a vice rather than a virtue.

To clarify this point further, we may quote here a brief conversation in which the narrator informs the criminal that his brother, the police officer, would like to see him.

> [The criminal:] Damn it! He is, as they say, the very model of reason, and with time he's probably become even more obnoxious.
>
> [The narrator:] His wish [to meet you] undoubtedly stems from good motives.

---

[2] "I have wasted my life in the company of rational people" (*laqad ada'tu ayyami fi suhbati 'l-'uqala'*), *Taht al-mizalla*, p. 64.

[3] The narrator says: "A curious reality dawned on me: they have been fighting each other all their lives even from the cradle . . . Each of them is soon going to find out that he has been fighting his own flesh and blood, in other words, a part of himself"; ibid., p. 59.

[The criminal:] Ever since the cradle he has wanted to do away
with me.

[The narrator:] He wanted you to follow the same path in life as he
did.

[The criminal:] Reason ... equilibrium ... order ... diligence ...
morality. In my eyes he's the very symbol of death.

Unbridled passions are often referred to as "madness." This attribute
is ascribed a number of times to the criminal brother. Once the
narrator has shifted his preference to the criminal, he declares that he
has chosen to abandon the company of rational people and become a
madman. He says, "I shall turn away from those who are rational
and respectable, and let the whirlpool sweep me away. Let them be
happy and useful, and let me be mad and destructive and may Satan
accept me."

In Mahfuz's works the sexual instinct ranks foremost among those
elements which defy rationality.[4] Some of the offences ascribed to the
criminal are connected with sex (pimping, sexual assault, etc.). In the
final scene, which dramatically demonstrates the narrator's conversion, we see him stepping towards his model, the nude woman.

On the day the criminal is killed, the narrator suffers a sudden in-
flammation in one of his legs, which leaves him with a limp. This
infirmity seems to suggest that with the criminal's death the narrator's very person has been injured. Hinting that the struggle between
the two brothers may actually have taken place in the mind of the
narrator, Mahfuz has him say: "We were three and we were one." In
this dramatic story of ideas we are faced with a system of concepts
and symbols aligned in two contrasting sets: order, rationality and
the police on one side; primeval instincts and passions, crime, madness and nudity on the other. Satan, too, appears as an enemy of
order; in the final scene of the story the narrator exclaims: "Let Satan accept me!"[5] This, as we shall presently see, is a point of great
significance in the symbolical language of Mahfuz.

Let us now pursue our investigation by examining the central mo-

---

[4] Cf. the role of the dancer in Mahfuz's early story *"al-Sharr al-maʿbud"* ("Evil
Worshipped"), see above, pp. 63–64.

[5] *Taht al-mizalla*, p. 64

tifs and symbols of the story as they occur in other, both earlier and
later, works by Mahfuz. First we shall consider the great allegorical
romance *Awlad haretna*. This work, which depicts the history of
mankind from Adam's time to the modern age, is divided into five
parts, each dealing with a different stage of history. The first part,
which tells the story of the patriarchal lord Jabalawi and his sons
Adham and Idris, is an allegory on the beginning of civilization. The
name Adham is a close approximation to Adam, while the name Idris
is phonetically and morphologically similar to Iblis, the Qur'anic
name for Satan. When choosing a superintendent for his estate, the
father passes over Idris, his eldest son, and picks Adham for the job.[6]
Idris, arrogant and violent by nature, reacts to his father's decision
with fury, and, in retribution, is banished from his father's house.
Adham and his wife, too, are soon to be banished by the father.
Adham's offence is that, at his brother's request, he has attempted to
discover what is written in the patriarch's will. The meek Adham did
not want to do this but was unable to resist the temptation, because
his wife coaxed him into it. This and numerous other details remind
us repeatedly of the Biblical story of the Fall.

Idris's violent conduct is described in some instances as "madness."[7] Adham, for his part, asks his brother to "return to reason or
rationality."[8] When his wife tempts him to look at his father's will,
Adham prays, "O God, give her back her reason."[9] In contrast to the
violent Idris, Adham is described as humble, patient, obedient and
restrained. When Adham is asked by his father what caused him to
act as he did against his better judgment, he answers, "The Devil."[10]

---

[6] The parallelism between the first part of *Awlad haretna* (pp. 11–112) and the Qur'anic
stories of Satan's banishment and Adam's fall is manifested in the very structure of the story
as well as in a variety of details. One specific motif is perhaps worth noting as an example:
God taught Adam the names of all things, and thus demonstrated to the angels that Adam
was best qualified to serve as His deputy on earth (Qur'an, 2: 31–34). Similarly, Adham is
praised by his father for knowing the names of the tenants of the estate (*Awlad haretna*,
p. 14).

[7] E.g., *al-ghadab jannanani* ("anger maddened me"), *siyah jununi* ("mad screams"),
Awlad haretna, pp. 36 and 57 respectively.

[8] Ibid., p. 29.

[9] Ibid., p. 43, and cf. p. 45 where Adham says to his wife: "I hoped to hear from you the
voice of rationality" (*sawt al-'aql*).

[10] Ibid., p. 48.

Idris is also described as a drunkard, or as one who becomes "drunk and boisterous," and he says of himself, "wine has ruined my reputation."[11] It should be recalled that in the story "*al-Wajh al-akhar*" the criminal brother is accused, among other things, of *'arbada* ("boisterousness"), a term used mainly to characterize drunks. We may better understand the significance of these images of Satan and drunkenness if we bear in mind their Islamic connotations. According to Islamic tradition (based on the Qur'an) Iblis (Satan) was banished by God as punishment for his arrogance and disobedience, for he alone of the angels refused God's order to prostrate himself before Adam.[12] Arrogance and disobedience are precisely the qualities for which Idris is condemned in *Awlad haretna*.

Wine and all alcoholic drinks are strictly forbidden in Islam. Many Muslims disregard this prohibition, but the awareness that wine is forbidden is always present. Hence, for Muslims, drunkenness suggests not only the expected implication of impropriety, but also that of disobedience towards God. (In Islamic mysticism [Sufism], however, wine and drunkenness have a different significance: they symbolize the yearning for God and mystical trance or ecstasy. Mahfuz, we know, is well acquainted with the concepts of Sufism, and, indeed, we find in his works that wine and drunkenness may suggest both rebelliousness and ecstatic joy.)[13]

Criminality becomes a permanent aspect of the lives of Idris and Adham: Idris makes his living as a thief and highwayman;[14] one of Adham's sons kills the other; Idris's daughter has a clandestine affair with Adham's son and is henceforward considered little better than a prostitute. Summing up the situation, Idris says with bitter irony: "The illustrious Jabalawi now has a whore for a granddaughter and a murderer for a grandson."[15] All the descendants of the great patriarch are revealed to be the issue of a murderer and a woman perceived to be a whore. This is Mahfuz's way of reminding his readers that sexuality and aggression are innate human qualities.

[11] Ibid., pp. 81, 101 and 36 respectively.

[12] Qur'an 15:28–43; 7:10–12; 38:73–77; and see *EI*², New edition, s.v. "Iblīs."

[13] In many of Mahfuz's stories we encounter Sufi characters, Sufi terminology and, occasionally, a discourse on the mystical approach to life.

[14] *Awlad haretna*, p. 57.

[15] Ibid., p. 109.

The novel *Bidaya wa-nihaya* ("The Beginning and the End,"
1949), the story of a lower middle-class Cairene family, is Mahfuz's
most extensive novel in his realistic phase prior to the trilogy. The
novel opens when the head of the family, a minor government official, dies, leaving a wife and four children – three sons and a
daughter. The eldest son is a handsome youth of exceptional physical strength; a drop-out from school, he drifts into underworld life to
become a bouncer in a café in the brothel district, a drug dealer and
the lover and protector of a prostitute. We last encounter him when,
wounded by rival gangsters and on the run from the police, he seeks
temporary asylum at his mother's house, which he leaves as soon as
he can stand on his feet again, since he does not want to compromise
his family.

The sister, who has had no education, has to work as a seamstress
in private homes to support her mother and two younger brothers,
who are still in high school. A rather plain-looking girl with no
dowry, she has few bright prospects for a suitable match. She is seduced by a young grocer who secretly promises her marriage, but
does not keep his word. Driven by poverty, loneliness, despair and
the need to assert her femininity, she begins to prostitute herself. This
is of course unknown to her family; she finds the opportunity for her
brief escapades when she goes out to work as a seamstress.

When Husayn, the middle brother, finishes high school, he faces a
difficult choice: to fulfill his long-standing wish to study to be a
teacher, or to go out to work and earn money. If Husayn goes to
teachers college, his younger brother, who still has another year in
high school, will not be able to go to college himself when the time
comes, because the family cannot sustain two sons in college.
Husayn, considerate of others and possessed of a deep sense of family responsibility, decides to go out to work in order to help his
family; he accepts an appointment as a secretary in a school outside
Cairo. The youngest brother is selfish, ambitious and vain. He is obsessed with the social conventions of the upper class which he would
like to join. He is, therefore, all the more agonized by the poverty of
his family. He takes care to conceal his family's humble circumstances from his classmates. When he finishes high school, he refuses
to continue his studies in a teachers college, which is free, and

chooses instead to enter the military academy, which requires tuition fees but is socially more prestigious. He is able to follow and eventually complete his studies in the military school at the cost of considerable hardship to his family, and not without some financial help from his criminal brother.

One day the sister is arrested while she is with one of her clients. The police notify her brother, the military officer, discreetly, in order to spare his reputation. For his sake she is released without charges. After her release, her brother pressures her into committing suicide for the sake of "family honor." Having watched his sister drown herself, he is gripped by remorse, and realizes for the first time how ruinous his vanity has been. At the very end of the book we leave him as he too is about to commit suicide.

In this summary I have tried to underline those aspects of the personality of the brothers and sister which offer parallels to the characters of the two brothers in "al-Wajh al-akhar" and of the descendants of the great patriarch Jabalawi in Awlad haretna. To recapitulate these points in Bidaya wa-nihaya: the eldest brother is a criminal, the youngest an officer – admittedly not a police officer, but still one of the "uniform-wearing" apparatus. The young man actually would have preferred to study at the police academy were it not for the higher fees required there. The middle brother wants to become a teacher; the sister becomes a prostitute.

I believe that the story of these two brothers in Bidaya wa-nihaya offered Mahfuz a realistic illustration of the ideational clash allegorized in "al-Wajh al-akhar." In Bidaya wa-nihaya the possibility of conflict seems to be envisaged by the criminal brother when his young brother (who is still unaware of his criminal pursuits) comes to seek his financial help in joining the military academy.

> [The older brother:] The military academy? Excellent! Thank God you haven't chosen the police academy!
> [The younger brother:] It's too expensive.
> [The older brother:] I don't mean that, but I don't like police officers.[16]

---

[16] Bidaya wa-nihaya, p. 241.

The sister is guilty of an offence to which she has been condemned by her sex and situation; she is driven to prostitution not only by poverty but also by sexual deprivation.

I shall quote here part of the conversation between the sister and brother, after the sister's release from police custody. The brother asks her about her scandalous conduct:

> "How could you do this? You? Who could imagine such a thing?"
> She sighed and said in submission and despair,
> "It was God's decree."
> Angrily he shouted,
> "No, the Devil's decree."
> She answered in the same rueful voice,
> "Yes."[17]

When again he asks her how she has fallen into sin, she answers once more, "It was the Devil's decree." To this the brother retorts, "You are the Devil, you have ruined us all."

Just as the allegorical representation of various human inclinations in *Awlad haretna* and "*al-Wajh al-akhar*" can be seen as derived from the realistic example of the brothers and sister in *Bidaya wa-nihaya*, so, too, we find in Mahfuz's earlier works what could be termed the realistic model of the patriarchal lord, Jabalawi. I have in mind here Sayyid Ahmad 'Abd al-Jawad, the head of the family in the trilogy.[18]

The parallelism between the picture of the father in the trilogy and the great patriarch Jabalawi in *Awlad haretna* is admittedly only partial. Although the majestic Jabalawi is no ascetic (he has numerous wives and children), he, unlike Sayyid Ahmad, has no frivolous aspect to his personality. Still, just as Yasin, the debauched son of Sayyid Ahmad in the trilogy, claims to have taken after his father in his lechery, so does Idris in *Awlad haretna* claim to have acquired his ruthlessness from his father Jabalawi.[19] When Adham rebukes his brother Idris for treating people rudely, the latter retorts: "It is your

---

[17] *Bidaya wa-nihaya*, p. 371.
[18] See below, p. 198.
[19] *Qasr al-shawq*, p. 400. Cf. M. Peled, "Yasin the Gate-Crasher," *Middle Eastern Studies*, 9 (1973), pp. 341–46.

father who taught me to treat people rudely and mercilessly."[20] Yasin and Idris both consider their perverse conduct to be derived by heredity or imitation from their fathers, whom they attempt to hold in some way responsible for their transgressions. The excesses of these two recalcitrant sons (sexual indulgence in the one case and violent aggressiveness in the other) would seem, indeed, to result from inherited inclinations; hence their imputations are not completely groundless. The parallelism between the case of Yasin and his father and that of Idris and his may illustrate the analogy between the realistic and the mythical in the mind of Mahfuz. The figure of the elusive father in the novel *al-Tariq (The Search)* – whose attributes are power, wealth, generosity and an insatiable appetite for women – is also reminiscent of Sayyid Ahmad.[21]

The figure of the law-breaker as a rebel against the established order is already to be found in some of Mahfuz's earliest works. In the story "*Yaqzat al-mumya'*" ("The Mummy's Awakening," 1939) we are told of a hungry fellah who attempts to steal some of the meat that a rich pasha has given to his dog. The poor fellah, who is caught by the pasha's servants and taken to the village police, is called a thief by his oppressors.[22] The juxtaposition of "thief" and "dog" in the story "*Yaqzat al-mumya'*" is worth noting, as it recurs in the novel "The Thief and the Dogs."

The thief in *al-Liss wa'l-kilab* ("The Thief and the Dogs," 1961) rebels against social injustice.[23] The "dogs" in the title literally refers to the police tracker dogs which surround the thief at the end of the story. It is also the term used by the thief for the police themselves, and for all those who have betrayed him. In a conversation between the thief and his lover, the prostitute, he says, "The majority of our people are not afraid of thieves, nor do they hate them; but they instinctively hate dogs."[24] At the end of the story the thief is shot dead by the police; his fate is similar to that of the criminal in "The Other Face."

[20] *Awlad haretna*, p. 65.
[21] See above, p. 85.
[22] On "*Yaqzat al-mumya'*" see below, pp. 168–70.
[23] See above, pp. 82–83 and below, pp. 226–35.
[24] *al-Liss wa'l-kilab*, p. 126

The thematic connection between the Devil and various forms of law-breaking (theft, prostitution and sexual offenses), madness or ir-rationality is suggested time and again by the language used. We have seen examples of this in the story "*al-Wajh al-akhar*" and in *Awlad haretna*; such usages occur, however, in most of Mahfuz's works. By way of example, I shall note here some of the expressions occurring in *al-Liss wa'l-kilab*. The hero (the thief) says to himself: "You are driven by your nervous impulses without reason [*bi-la 'aql*]"; to threaten his adversaries he shouts: "I'm the Devil himself." The newspaper article about the thief mentions, among other things, "his hidden madness."

In the story "*al-Wajh al-akhar*" the outcome of the struggle be-tween order (the policeman) and rebellion (the criminal) is the destruction of the rebellious hero. The conflict, however, is not re-solved, for, as we have seen, the sedate educator (the narrator) now declares himself to be a destructive madman; formerly one of the props of the established morality, he now denounces the values he once upheld. The story's conclusion may be seen as a kind of poetic justice: the narrator, who first seemed to side with the police-men, now assumes the role of the vanquished criminal.[25] To be sure, the way in which the narrator challenges the established order dif-fers from that of the criminal. His challenge is manifested in madness, not in crime, but, as has already been observed, madness and law-breaking are intertwined in many of Mahfuz's works.

The cultural meaning of madness is explored in one of Mahfuz's early stories, "*Hams al-junun*" ("The Whisper of Madness," 1945).[26] The hero of this story one day begins to question all social conven-tions and habits and, what is worse, to defy them. One morning he asks himself: "Why don't we strip off these clothes and throw them to the ground? Why don't we appear as God created us?" Without acting on his thought he sets out for a walk. Passing near a sidewalk restaurant, he is grieved by the sight of people eating there while hun-

---

[25] On the particular significance of poetic justice in allegorical works, see Angus Fletcher, *Allegory* (Ithaca and London, 1964), p. 307.

[26] *Al-Risala*, 19 February 1945. For an English translation see Nagib Mahfuz, *God's World: An Anthology of Short Stories*, trans. with an introduction by Akef Abadir and Roger Allen (Minneapolis, 1973), pp. 47–54. See above, p. 66.

gry children in rags are sitting nearby. He snatches a chicken from one of the tables and throws it to the ground near the hungry children.[27] Following this incident, he attacks a distinguished looking gentleman in his favorite café, and hits him in the back of the neck. This he does for no good reason, except that he feels like it. Outraged, the victim of the attack retaliates with slaps and kicks, and the hero barely escapes and leaves the café. On his way he notices an attractive young woman walking with a male escort, and he feels an urge to touch her breast. He cannot see why he should not give in to this urge and does just that, which of course brings upon him the angry reaction of the people around, in the form of curses, insults and beating. This does not exhaust his desire for more adventures, and he remembers his thoughts from the morning about the absurdity of wearing clothes. He removes his clothes and "appears naked as God created him." We should now return to the question with which the author opens his story: "What is madness?" In the attack on the man in the café, madness takes the form of unprovoked aggression. In the incident with the young woman, it is a defiance of the norms controlling the relations between the sexes. Nudity, in which the attack of madness described in the story reaches its climax, is seen by the hero as the natural free state of man "as God created him." The scene in which the "madman" feeds the hungry children is an expression of protest against the social order.[28]

The problem of madness versus rationality is a central theme in the short story "*Qaws quzah*" ("Rainbow," 1965).[29] Tahir ("the pure one"), a high-school student, is in love with a girl of his own age. Since her family is about to leave Egypt for a number of years, he wishes to become formally engaged to her before they go. His parents are modern, educated people; the father is an educator and the mother an inspector in the Ministry of Social Affairs. The household runs to a well-organized routine. His father's favorite expression of approval is: "This is the very essence of reason." The parents regard

---

[27] It is interesting that the children in rags are referred to here as *al-'araya*, i.e., "the naked ones." Ibid., p. 8.

[28] The protest against social injustice voiced here is similar to the above-mentioned theme of the poor fellah in "The Mummy's Awakening," who stole to satisfy his hunger.

[29] In the collection *Bayt sayyi' al-sum'a* ("A House of Ill Repute").

Tahir's desire to become engaged as an immature whim, which must be given up. Tahir is resentful of the supposedly rational routine of the family, and expresses this in various ways. Looking up at the sky one evening, he says, "How I envy its freedom." Appalled, his father asks him, "Don't you like order, Tahir?" Tahir's rebellion against the fixed routine of his family comes to a head when he sets fire to his room. He is pronounced mentally ill, and is taken to hospital. The director of the hospital tells the parents that this is the best place for Tahir. To this the father responds, "Indeed, sir, this is the very essence of reason."

The analysis of "*Hams al-junun*" and "*Qaws quzah*" seems to suggest that in elaborating the theme of "madness," Mahfuz's interest is not primarily psychological, but rather cultural and moral. The pathological state of the individual is seen by him as an extreme form of a universal human predicament: the conflict between social order and freedom, between the civilization of *homo sapiens* and the instincts of man, the animal.

In *Qalb al-layl* ("The Heart of the Night," 1975), Mahfuz spells out this intrinsic contradiction which bedevils both man as an individual and humanity as a whole. *Qalb al-layl* – ostensibly the confession of an aging man reviewing his childhood, education, loves and political views – is, in fact, a philosophical essay in fictional garb. The protagonist recalls his quarrel with his grandfather, who brought him up in his house. This overpowering patriarch, who resembles Jabalawi in *Awlad haretna*, would like his grandson to marry the girl he has chosen for him, whereas the hero wants to follow his own passions. The grandfather considers this disobedient behavior (he says to the young man, "You are recalcitrant"), whereas the young man declares that this is freedom. The old man retorts, "This is madness, and the madman will have to leave my old house." To which his grandson answers, "In madness lies true paradise."[30]

The hero of *Qalb al-layl* further explains his views on this inner conflict between rationality and irrationality:

---

[30] *Qalb al-layl*, p. 66. It should be noted that the old (or ancient) house (*al-bayt al-'atiq*) is one of the terms signifying the sanctuary of the Ka'ba, (see Qur'an, 22:29, 33). Its use here is yet another allusion to the religious significance of the grandfather and his house in *Qalb al-layl*.

I would first like to present to you my views on a universal tragedy, namely, the tragedy of *homo sapiens* (*al-insan al-'aqil*).
Before reason was created, man was in harmony with himself and
with his life. It was a harsh life of struggle which he was unable
to control; he was like any other animal. But when he was given
reason, he undertook the burden of a new trust, a responsibility
which he could not possibly escape and, at the same time, was
not suited to bear. . . .[31] What is taught by reason is opposed by
the natural instincts. To this day the instincts have had the upper
hand, at least in public life. It is only in science that reason has
achieved absolute dominance. In everything else it yields to the
instincts; the products of science itself are consumed by the instincts. While reason retains its own language in the sphere of
scientific research, the language to which the millions respond is
still the language of emotion and instinct: songs of nationalism
and patriotism and racism, stupid dreams and delusions. This is
a universal tragedy. Its red clouds will not disperse until the voice
of reason rises high, and instincts subside, wither and die.[32]

According to this view, which Mahfuz shares, the irrational impulses
affect man not only individually, but collectively as well. In fact, it is
emphasized here that the dominance of the irrational impulses over
the collective behavior of social groups is almost absolute. The
remark about the products of science being consumed by the instincts
seems to refer to the fact that those in power manage to enlist the
scientists in their service; consequently, politics, which is dominated
by irrational factors, may be said to have subordinated science,
which is the accomplishment of reason.[33]

Kamal, the pensive hero of the third part of the trilogy, *al-
Sukkariyya* (who represents the author's intellectual perplexity),[34] is

[31] The terms used here (*hamala* "to carry" or "to bear," *amana* "trust") are Qur'anic, cf.
Qur'an 33:72. This is an interesting example of Mahfuz's habitually unorthodox use of the
vocabulary of the Qur'an.

[32] *Qalb al-layl*, pp. 114–15.

[33] Mahfuz expressed this idea in the story of 'Arafa, the magician in *Awlad haretna*. 'Arafa,
who in the allegory stands for the man of science (the name 'Arafa is derived from the verb "to
know"), falls under the control of the superintendent of the estate (who represents political
power) and is forced to surrender to him the magical exploding bottle he has invented.

[34] See above, p. 21.

fascinated by the sight of the enthusiastic masses at a nationalist rally.[35] In the midst of the crowd he feels that "reason has been sealed up in a bottle for a while and the repressed forces of the soul break loose . . . and the instincts spring forth." Tired of his thoughts and doubts, he feels like joining those masses "to revive his bloodstream and acquire warmth and youth." The masses appear to him to be acting without reason [bi-la 'uqul], yet he perceives in their assembly "the dignity of conscious instincts."

The recognition that collective behavior is dominated by irrational impulses is not, then, new to Mahfuz; his attitude towards this phenomenon, however, appears to have changed. In al-Sukkariyya (which was completed before the 1952 revolution) Mahfuz speaks with admiration and envy of the masses who act without being held back by reason. Twenty-three years later, in the passage from Qalb al-layl quoted above, horror and revulsion have replaced admiration and envy: Mahfuz now speaks of "stupid dreams and delusions" cherished by the masses, and he mentions in this context the ominous "red clouds" of revolution.

This later attitude is already reflected in Mahfuz's short story "al-Majnuna" ("The Mad One," 1968).[36] The "mad one" in this story is a senseless war between two neighboring quarters. It would seem that Mahfuz has become keenly aware of the dangers inherent in the irrationality dominating relations between national or religious groups. In this connection we should mention the story "Ruh tabib al-qulub" ("The Spirit of the Healer of Hearts"), in which the rebellious crowd is several times referred to as mad.[37] The policeman says, "When people go mad they lose their awe of the police." In the confrontation between the "mad" crowd and the law-enforcement apparatus of the state, Mahfuz's sympathies lie with the crowd. He realizes nonetheless that the irrational crowd can be viciously manipulated. Mahfuz's attitude to the phenomena he categorizes as "madness" is ambivalent. He

---

[35] Al-Sukkariyya, pp. 41–44.

[36] In the collection Khammarat al-qitt al-aswad ("The Black Cat Tavern," 1968), pp. 141–52.

[37] In the collection Shahr al-'asal ("The Honeymoon"), published in 1971. See my article "Religion and Revolution in an Allegory by Najib Mahfuz: A Study of Ruh tabib al-qulub," in Miriam Rosen-Ayalon (ed.), Studies in Memory of Gaston Wiet (Jerusalem, 1977).

recognizes the dangers of anarchy, but cannot help sympathizing with those who "go mad" under pychological and social pressures they can no longer withstand.

We have so far encountered nudity in two stories by Mahfuz, written some thirty years apart: *"Hams al-junun"* and *"al-Wajh al-akhar."* In the more recent of the two, *"al-Wajh al-akhar,"* nudity occurs as the *only* attribute of the female model of the so-called mad artist. In the earlier story, nudity is described as the most complete form of rebellion against accepted social and cultural norms. Nudity recurs in many of Mahfuz's works. The following are some examples.

In *Hikayat haretna* ("Stories of our Neighborhood," 1975), a volume of short stories presented as autobiographical reminiscences, Mahfuz recalls a childhood memory of seeing a naked woman for the first time. "I saw Sitt Umm Zaki [the family's neighbor, and his mother's friend] completely naked, sitting on a couch in the sun and combing her hair, completely naked. A strange and dazzling view. She was as big as a cow." The woman invites the little boy to massage her back, which he does diligently and to her great satisfaction. Jokingly she tells him, "You are a demon from paradise."[38] She warns him not to tell his mother, and he promises to be discreet. The promise given, she repeats, "Indeed you are a devil."[39] The link between latent eroticism, paradisaic happiness and secret sin is all too clear in this scene. The use of the ambiguously loaded terms "demon" and "devil" is, of course, significant. Mahfuz is not naïve in his views of eros; he perceives its darker aspects. In another volume of semi-autobiographical sketches, *al-Maraya*, published in 1972, he recalls how, at the age of nine or ten, he was taken to a brothel by a teenage relative, under the pretext of going to the movies. He does not understand where he is; all he knows is that while his teenage relative enters one of the rooms with a woman, he is assigned to another woman who is supposed to take care of him. She takes him into

---

[38] Her phrase "a demon from paradise" (*'ifrit min al-janna*) may reflect the notion found in Islamic tradition that demons (*jinn*) serve as attendants in paradise. The expression *'ifrit min al-janna* appears to be modeled verbally on the Qur'anic expression *'ifrit min al jinn* (Qur'an, 27:39).

[39] *Hikayat haretna*, pp. 6–7.

a room where, after taking a shilling from him, she proceeds to undress herself. The sight frightens and fascinates him simultaneously.[40] Nudity also occurs as a central image in "*Mawqif wada'*" ("The Moment of Separation," 1971),[41] where the nudity of the two protagonists (two men stranded in the desert) represents the loss of all past norms and habits. This image recurs in the story "*al-'Ury wa'l-ghadab*" ("Nudity and Anger," 1973).[42]

In these stories, nudity, both male and female, is connected with the pre-civilized, natural state of mankind, and is intended to invoke it. However, a certain difference may be discerned between the symbolic function of male and female nudity. For Mahfuz, female nudity represents sensuality and sexuality; male nudity primarily signifies renunciation of the accepted social norms and relinquishment or loss of all possessions. In Mahfuz's view, men are preoccupied to the point of obsession by metaphysical inquiries, political ambitions or social ideologies, whereas women – engrossed as they are in the biological processes of existence – regard these as relatively unimportant concerns. Hence, for Mahfuz, female nudity symbolizes the persistence and vitality of the natural instincts, while male nudity is a manifestation of rebellion.

---

[40] *Al-Maraya*, pp. 19–22.
[41] In the collection *Shahr al-'asal*.
[42] In the collection *al-Jarima* ("The Crime"), published in 1973.

CHAPTER 5

Home and Homelessness

In each of the six novels Mahfuz published in the 1960s, the hero has left home, either by choice or by force of circumstance. In each case "home" is a metaphor.

In the first of these novels, *al-Liss wa'l-kilab* ("The Thief and the Dogs"), the homeless hero, Sa'id Mahran, takes refuge with a Sufi sheykh who was his father's spiritual mentor, and who rekindles childhood memories.[1] Sa'id's arrival at the sheykh's house is described as follows: "He stood for a moment on the threshold, looking and remembering when he'd crossed it last. What a simple house, just like those of Adam's day."[2] But the religious guidance offered by the sheykh is incomprehensible and unsatisfactory. When Sa'id approaches his own former mentor, now a successful and popular journalist, he is callously rejected and driven out of the journalist's luxurious villa. Seeking revenge, Sa'id can find no rest; he loses Nur, the prostitute who has long been in love with him and who has taken him into her home, and ends his life lonely and homeless.

For our purposes it is important to note that the two men with whom Sa'id hopes to find refuge and who he hopes will help him are in some way father figures. To be sure, each represents a very different system of beliefs and behavior, but, unfortunately for Sa'id, neither of these competing options is viable for him. Although the sheykh does not reject Sa'id cruelly, as the journalist does, staying in

---

[1] See above, pp. 82–83.
[2] *Al-Liss wa'l-kilab*, p. 21.

the Sufi's house is implicitly conditional upon terms which Sa'id cannot accept. The precepts of Islam no longer have any validity for him,
and he finds the language of faith irrelevant and incomprehensible.

Sa'id is the first in a series of homeless characters typical of
Mahfuz's novels of the 1960s. In 1962 he published *al-Summan wa'l-
kharif* ("The Quail and Autumn"), whose hero, 'Isa, a high-ranking
government official dismissed in the wake of Nasser's revolution,
leaves his luxury apartment in Cairo and moves to furnished rooms
in Alexandria.[3] When his mother dies 'Isa sells the family home, to
which he refers as "the old house." (In Arabic one word, *bayt*,
denotes both "house" and "home.") 'Isa's move to Alexandria underlines his alienation from his own people. It should be remembered
that Alexandria in the early 1950s – the period in which the novel is
set – had a markedly Greek character.[4] 'Isa rents a furnished apartment from a Greek family and reflects, as he looks out of the window, "Everywhere you look, you see Greek faces – on the balconies,
in the windows, in the street. I am an alien in a city of aliens ... in
the café you constantly hear their foreign language, so you imagine
you have actually emigrated ... and these foreigners whom you have
long viewed with suspicion – now you love them more than your
own compatriots, and you seek consolation among them because you
are all foreigners in a foreign country."[5]

Mahfuz's four subsequent novels – *al-Tariq* ("The Way," 1964), *al-
Shahhadh* ("The Beggar," 1965), *Tharthara fawq al-nil* ("Chatter on
the Nile," 1966) and *Miramar* (1967) all depict characters who find
themselves homeless, socially alienated and intellectually perplexed.

The obviously allegorical qualities of *al-Tariq* set it apart from
Mahfuz's other short novels of the 1960s.[6] Its hero, however, shares
one important characteristic with the heroes of the other novels of
this period: he does not live in the family home. After his mother's
death, he sells her house and from then on lives in hotels and pen-
sions.

---

[3] See above, p. 84.

[4] Until 1956 Alexandria had a very large non-Egyptian population in which Greeks
predominated. In the wake of the 1956 war most of these foreigners were forced to leave.

[5] *Al-Summan wa'l-kharif*, p. 83.

[6] See above, p. 85.

'Umar, the hero of *al-Shahhadh* ("The Beggar"), is not a beggar at all, but a rich lawyer in Cairo.[7] In his mid-forties he loses all interest in his family and his work and embarks on a desperate search for meaning in life. He leaves home and goes to live as a hermit in a hut on the edge of the desert. The name of the novel echoes the term "dervish" (Persian for "poor man") which is the standard term for a Sufi who begs for his living.

The hero of *Tharthara fawq al-nil* ("Chatter on the Nile") is a minor government official who has lost his wife and daughter. Depressed and grieved beyond all possibility of consolation, he daydreams at his desk at work and spends the rest of his time on a houseboat on the Nile where a group of dissolute Cairo intellectuals regularly meet.[8] Here, again, the alienation of the hero is underlined by his lack of a home or family. The instability and insularity of life on a houseboat reflect both the hero's unstable and alienated world and the general fragility of human existence.

The characters in *Miramar* have all lost their homes for one reason or another, and have taken up residence in Hotel Miramar in Alexandria.[9] The symbolic significance of Alexandria as an alien city has already been noted. Indeed, all the guests of the pension are, to a certain extent, exiles.

These novels of the 1960s, with their homeless heroes, are very different from the Cairene trilogy, whose center is the family home, with its established order and hierarchy. Each of the stories of the 1960s describes a different set of circumstances, but in each homelessness is a metaphor for a state of social alienation and intellectual confusion.

The key to the metaphor is to be found in Mahfuz's novel *Awlad haretna* ("Children of Our Neighborhood," 1959).[10] In this novel the father, Jabalawi, banishes his son, Adham, from the family home, in what is clearly a modern version of the Biblical story of Adam's fall from God's grace. From this point in the story, the father's home (invariably referred to as "the Big House") becomes forbidden territory to his many descendents, while Jabalawi himself retreats into com-

---

[7] See below, pp. 236–37.
[8] See above, pp. 85–86.
[9] See above, pp. 87–89.
[10] See above, pp. 80–82, 101–3.

plete seclusion. In the final chapter of the story, one of the patriarch's descendents, several generations down the line, ventures secretly into the Big House – seeking help in his campaign against the injustice and persecution which have pervaded the entire neighborhood – and discovers that the father, whom the family has revered for so long, is a senile cripple. This secret invasion of the Big House causes Jabalawi's death. In Mahfuz's rendering of the story, the banished hero is Man, who must make his way in a world from which God has absented himself.

The theme of expulsion from the family home recurs in *Qalb al-layl* (1975) whose hero rebels against the authority of his grandfather when he comes of age. To assert his freedom the young man gives up the safety and ease of the patriarchal home.[11] In *Afrah al-qubba* (1981) the young playwright, who is the novel's main character, is bitterly disillusioned by his father and comes to detest him. He also realizes that the family home, to which he refers as "the old house" (*al-bayt al-qadim*), has become a house of ill repute.[12] He leaves home in order to achieve independence and to fulfill his mission as a writer.

Home, in Mahfuz's vocabulary of the 1960s, has two inter-related metaphoric meanings: it signifies both God's grace and protection and the sheltered world of childhood. Life in the family home represents the lost childhood of humanity and of every individual. A final comment on the word *bayt* ("house" or "home") may further highlight the religious connotations inherent in it: as noted above, Islam's holiest sanctuary in Mecca is referred to in the Qur'an as *al-bayt al-'atiq*, meaning "the ancient house." It should be recalled that the terms "the big house" (*al-bayt al-kabir*) and "the old house" (*al-bayt al-qadim*) were used to describe the family home in *Awlad haretna*, *al-Summan wa'l-kharif* and *Afrah al-qubba*. The similarity between these terms and the Qur'anic expression is obvious.

---

[11] See above, p. 110.
[12] *Afrah al-qubba*, p. 160.

CHAPTER 6

Absent Father, Persevering Mother

In a number of Mahfuz's stories the father is dead or otherwise unable to fulfill his duties. This theme deserves our special attention for two reasons: Mahfuz is writing of a patriarchal society in which the absence of the father assumes particular significance; the recurrence of this theme in many variations in his works reveals the author's preoccupation with the subject.

This absence is most glaring in *Bidaya wa-nihaya*, in which the father dies as the story opens. The family's sense of loss is further aggravated by the sons' discovery that their father was not the powerful, influential man they had believed him to be.

After the father's death, the family is held together and sustained by the strong-willed mother: "The mother alone was the mainstay of the family. . . . She was not defeated by [the loss of her husband and the resulting economic hardship], nor did she complain; she did not lose her essential qualities of perseverance, determination and strength."[1] She is greatly admired by her son Husayn, who at one point compares her to the land of Egypt itself. Riding the train from Cairo to Tanta to take up his position as a secretary at the school there, Husayn looks out at the countryside to escape his dreary thoughts. "He looked again at the flat land stretching all the way to the horizon. Silent, patient, and good. Without thinking about it, he remembered his mother, who was just like the green earth in her pa-

---

[1] *Bidaya wa-nihaya*, p. 174

tience and generosity, while the plow of Time was leaving its marks on her."[2] The description of the queen mother – the embodiment of the Egyptian spirit in *Kifah Tiba* – anticipates the description of the mother in *Bidaya wa-nihaya*: she, too, is referred to as the "patient mother," and the effects of Time on her face are described in much the same way.[3]

In *al-Qahira al-jadida* we encounter another example of what may be called "the father who failed." Because of his illness, the father is unable to support his son at university. In *Khan al-Khalili* the father is a retired, low ranking government official who has become a recluse. It is the mother who manages the household, while the elder son is the breadwinner. The hero of *al-Sarab* grows up without a father, as his parents were divorced before he was born. In the allegorical novel *al-Tariq*, published sixteen years later, the father similarly disappears before the son's birth. In *al-Shahhadh* the father abandons his family in his search for mystical experience, leaving his pregnant wife alone to take care of their two daughters and give birth to their son. Saniyya al-Mahdi, the mother of the family in *al-Baqi min al-zaman sa'a* (1982), maintains the house and keeps the family united after the father leaves to live with his new second wife. It is generally recognized that this novel is an allegory on the history of Egypt since the 1930s; the mother, Saniyya, represents Egypt.[4]

In all these novels the fathers are portrayed as irresponsible, selfish and misguided. Acting in accordance with the conventions of society, they unintentionally cause terrible damage to their families. Thus, for example, the grandfather in *al-Sarab* marries his daughter to a worthless fly-by-night, merely because the young man is of "good family," and condemns her to a life of unhappiness and misfortune. In *Bidaya wa-nihaya* we learn that it was the deceased father who had objected to his daughter's studies beyond elementary school – a decision which arguably contributed to her becoming a prostitute.

The juxtaposition of mother and father is most conspicuous in Mahfuz's Cairene trilogy, where the contrast between them is drawn

---

[2] Ibid., p. 199.   [3] *Kifah Tiba*, pp. 141, 163.

[4] See Mahmud Ghanayim, "Microcosm and Macrocosm in Najib Mahfuz's *al-Baqi min al-Zaman Sa'ah*," in *Writer, Culture, Text*, ed. Ami Elad (Fredericton, Canada, 1993), pp. 47–55.

in very sharp lines. The image of Sayyid Ahmad appears at first sight to contradict Mahfuz's view of the father as described above: a vigorous and energetic man and a highly respected merchant, he is absolute master of his household. However, as the story proceeds, the image of Sayyid Ahmad is diminished in various ways. While imposing an extremely strict code of behavior on his family, he himself regularly spends the night drinking and merrymaking with his friends in the company of women of pleasure. A pious Muslim during the day, he is a debauchee by night. With time, the despotic father becomes less of an imposing all-powerful figure: his sons come to know about the other, secret part of his life and to realize that he is far less influential in society than they had believed.

Amina, the mother, gradually becomes somewhat more independent: she can go out to visit her married daughter and worship in al-Husayn mosque. Toward the end of the story, an interesting reversal of roles between father and mother occurs. Whereas at the beginning the mother stays awake every night, waiting for her husband to return from his frolicking, years later it is the father, sick and half-paralyzed, who anxiously awaits his wife's return from her daily family visits and prayer in the mosque. It is the mother, meek and submissive, who wins the love of her children, the respect of the neighbors and the sympathy of the reader. Mahfuz has disclosed in various interviews that the image of the mother in the trilogy is largely derived from that of his own mother, although, he insists, his mother was not held prisoner in the house as the mother in the trilogy was.

Although Sayyid Ahmad's role in the trilogy is far more substantial than that of the deceased father in *Bidaya wa-nihaya* (who lives on only in his family's memory), the two have several significant traits in common. In both cases the children gradually become aware that they have exaggerated their fathers' power and influence; and in both cases the fathers oppose their daughters' education.

The figure of a powerful, autocratic patriarch underlies the conceptual structure of *Awlad haretna*, where the father, Jabalawi, is an allegoric representation of God. Jabalawi, too, fails his family: secluded in his "Big House," he is apparently unaware of the persecution inflicted on his descendants by the neighborhood thugs.

Mahfuz seems to view women, especially mothers, with much greater sympathy than he views men. In many of his stories, men are rather negative in character: selfish, arrogant, vain, debauched, or utterly confused and lacking a sense of purpose in life. By contrast, he often presents women as models of selfless devotion and perseverance; this last quality is especially esteemed by Mahfuz as "the quality which makes it possible to endure life." These contrasting attitudes to father and mother are probably rooted in Mahfuz's own childhood experience.[5]

It is Mahfuz's female characters who personify Egypt and the Egyptian people, while men represent political authority, of which, as we know, he is highly critical. The allegorical roles Mahfuz assigns to women, as opposed to those he allocates to men, clearly reflect his personal sympathies and his rejection of the values and conventions of patriarchal society.

[5] See above, p. 22.

CHAPTER 7

One Vision, Three Narrative Modes

In the above analysis I have attempted to delineate the essential features of Mahfuz's conceptual world, intentionally disregarding the question of chronological development. Although the year of publication of each work cited is given, so that it can be fitted into a chronological framework, the images and ideas are treated, so to speak, synchronically. I shall now come to a question I have so far suspended: how the development of Mahfuz's artistic vision has affected the significance of the images discussed above.

In the following discussion I shall be distinguishing between three modes of fiction: allegory, mimesis and myth. Each of these modes stands in a particular relation to one of three levels of reference. Allegory is used to illustrate abstract ideas. Mimesis is the endeavor to depict concrete phenomenal reality. Myth is meant to represent the archetypal, which, as its name indicates, is believed to be more fundamental and more constant than the phenomenal.[1] To be sure, one hardly finds any one of these three modes in a pure form.[2] Neverthe-

[1] The following quotation from Claude Levi-Strauss may underline this point: "On the one hand, a myth always refers to events alleged to have taken place in time: before the world was created, or during its first stages – anyway, long ago. But what gives the myth its operative value is that the specific pattern described is everlasting; it explains the present and the past as well as the future." Claude Levi-Strauss, "The Structural Study of Myth," in William A. Lessa and Evon Z. Vogt (eds.), *Reader in Comparative Religion: An Anthropological Approach*, 3rd ed. (New York, 1972), p. 292.

[2] Cf. Angus Fletcher, *Allegory* (Ithaca and London, 1964), pp. 7–10. The allegorical, in order effectively to convey ideas, must contain elements of the mimetic. Mimetic works of

less, this tripartite distinction is important as an analytical tool. It may help us in determining which mode is predominant in a given work, or, as is more frequently the case, in understanding the various forms of convergence and mixture of different modes.

When we read Mahfuz's early stories, we cannot help but feel that these works do not so much provide a direct reflection of reality as illustrate the author's ideas on human nature in general and Egyptian society in particular. This is not to say that Mahfuz was not interested in accurately portraying the contemporary social scene; his intention, however, is didactic. We should recall here some facts concerning Mahfuz's intellectual formation, which may help us to understand his literary approach when he wrote his early stories. During this period he was profoundly influenced by Salama Musa, in whose journal, *al-Majalla al-jadida*, he published his articles in the early thirties.[3] Mahfuz subscribed to the socialistic beliefs of Salama Musa (Fabian socialism), and absorbed some of his views on the proper role of literature. Salama Musa, a sworn rationalist, believed that science (understood to include both the natural and social sciences) would be humanity's salvation. Literature, he believed, can be beneficial only if it is put at the service of society. This the conscientious writer should do by deriving his ideas from science and making his literary works a vehicle for "correct" ideas.[4] Influenced by Salama Musa's instrumentalist view of literature, Mahfuz must have felt that, as a writer of fiction, his task was to offer illustrations of those truths assumed to exist, in a fuller and more exact form, at the level of abstract thought.

The supremacy of ideas over the world of experience and the perception of the senses is the hallmark of allegory.[5] Mahfuz's fictional

---

art often contain allegorical or mythical elements. The mythical and the allegorical sometimes converge in a way which makes it hard to define the nature of the work in question (cf. ibid., p. 322). Mythology paints the mythical world in colors which are similar to those used in mimetic art to paint phenomenal reality.

[3] On Salama Musa's influence on Mahfuz see Ghali Shukri, *al-Muntami: Dirasa fi adab Najib Mahfuz* (Cairo, 1969), p. 46 and cf. *al-Sukkariyya*, pp. 108–9; see also an interview with Mahfuz in *al-Majalla* (January, 1963).

[4] For Salama Musa's ideas on literature, see his *al-Adab li'l-sha'b* ("Literature for the People") (Cairo, 1971).

[5] See Fletcher, *Allegory*, pp. 322–23.

writing in this period is the outcome of his desire to reform society, and his primary purpose throughout is to convey ideas. Not all the stories of this early period are allegorical, but the writer's literary approach is, on the whole, didactic. This stage in Mahfuz's literary development was fortunately short, and mimetic art soon prevailed over social ideology.

In his Cairene novels, from *Khan al-Khalili* (1945) to *al-Sukkariyya* (1957), Mahfuz endeavors to grasp social reality as observed directly by him. These stories need not be explained by, nor can they be reduced to, a set of theoretical ideas and moral precepts; they have an artistic existence of their own. Admittedly, many of the characters in these novels represent something beyond their fictional role. Stern patriarch, submissive wife, obedient and dutiful son, rich merchant and other similar characters are social types as well as individual people. Mahfuz has certainly retained the impulse of a social critic and the pathos of a moralist; however, the novelist in him has come into its own.

In *Awlad haretna*, particularly in the story of Adham, we encounter a new approach to reality. It has already been mentioned that *Awlad haretna* is an allegorical book. However, saying that the chapter "Adham" is an allegory on the dawn of human society takes us only so far toward understanding the unique nature of this work. In "Adham" Mahfuz retells the stories of Satan's rebellion and the Fall in close parallelism to the Biblical and Qur'anic traditions. But when we examine Mahfuz's version, we find that the protagonists of the mythical story, as recreated by our author, are modeled on the characters of his Cairene novels, who, in their turn, represent social types.[6] By combining the plots of familiar legends and the human types he had studied for so long in their social context, Mahfuz produced, in the first part of *Awlad haretna*, something essentially new, a Mahfuzian mythology. He has thereby achieved two effects: he has brought sublime mythical figures down to the level of common human experience; and he has invested the fundamental terms of everyday life with an archetypal significance. When *Awlad haretna* is viewed in this fashion, its significance as a turning point in Mahfuz's

---

[6] Mahfuz uses this technique throughout *Awlad haretna*, retelling in turn the stories of Moses, Jesus and Muhammad.

literary development becomes manifest. It has established a mythical level beside the other two levels (the level of abstract ideas and the level of concrete reality), in the light of which Mahfuz's work should be understood. In his subsequent works one must also postulate this mythical level of reference; Mahfuz's language now carries the connotations of his mythology.

PART THREE

MAHFUZ AS POLITICAL CRITIC

CHAPTER 8

A Cunning Art

Mahfuz's achievement of recognition and fame in 1956–57 coincided with the emergence of Jamal 'Abd al-Nasir (Nasser) as the most admired Arab leader in modern times. Hence, it may be instructive to study how Mahfuz perceived Nasser, and how this perception found expression in his stories. This is especially important because of the strict limitations imposed upon freedom of expression during the Nasser years. The historian and political scientist P. J. Vatikiotis points out, in his *History of Egypt*, that during this period "the State ... came to exercise what is virtually total control over all cultural activities in the country; and therefore over intellectual endeavor. It is largely for this reason that writers and artists were impelled to symbolism. Several among them were forced into the role of panegyrists for the solicitation of those in power and authority."[1] Another observer of Egyptian affairs notes: "The authoritarian nature of the system, coupled with the dependence of most intellectuals on government jobs, made the voicing of dissent a rare practice. One major source of criticism was émigré intellectuals such as Ahmad Abu al-Fath and Anwar 'Abd al-Malik, who lost no opportunity to brand the ruling regime from the comfort of a foreign land."[2]

---

[1] P. J. Vatikiotis, *The History of Egypt*, 3rd ed. (Baltimore, 1985), p. 479.

[2] R. Hrair Dekmejian, *Egypt under Nasser: A Study in Political Dynamics* (Albany, 1971), p. 63. Marina Stagh's *The Limits of Freedom of Speech: Prose Literature and Prose Writers in Egypt under Nasser and Sadat* (Stockholm, 1993) offers a careful study of the subject defined in its title.

Narrative fiction as a description and criticism of current events assumes a special significance when other forms of public comment are stifled. Mahfuz's short novel, al-Karnak, published in 1974, nearly four years after Nasser's death, describes the suppression of free thought and the brutality of the secret police during the 1960s. This book appeared at about the same time that Tawfiq al-Hakim published his scathing attack on Nasser's regime, 'Awdat al-wa'y.[3]

These two compositions are very different in mode and style, but both have the same intention – to indict Nasser's regime. Tawfiq al-Hakim criticizes various aspects of the regime: military defeats, economic failures, cancellation of the independent status of the Egyptian judiciary and violation of personal legal rights, and, above all, the personality cult surrounding Nasser. Mahfuz's novel focuses on one subject – the horrible rule of the secret police; other topics such as military failures and economic hardships are mentioned only as background. Tawfiq al-Hakim's booklet is a long essay written as a personal testimony; Mahfuz's book is a dramatic short novel.

The most shocking part of al-Karnak is the story of a young woman, Zaynab, who is arrested by the secret police in order to put pressure on her imprisoned friend, Isma'il, to confess his alleged political crimes. Zaynab is raped by her jailors at the orders of the chief interrogator, the fearsome Khalid Safwan, who watches the scene in order to satisfy his perverted nature. To be sure, al-Karnak came out some three years after Sadat had already publicly condemned the secret police in May 1971. However, the May 1971 reform, for all its significance, did not amount to a total public condemnation of Nasser's regime. And this is precisely what 'Awdat al-wa'y and al-Karnak did signify – condemnation of the regime as a whole. Understandably, the publication of such an indictment of Nasser by Egypt's two most eminent men of letters was a shock to Egyptian and Arab intellectuals, who for nearly twenty years had been accustomed to associate Arab greatness with the person of the admired, almost mythical, 'Abd al-Nasir.

[3] See above, p. 89. Tawfiq al-Hakim's 'Awdat al-wa'y, which was published in 1974 in Lebanon, had been circulating in a typewritten version among limited circles of Egyptian intellectuals for some two years before it came out in print. It should also be pointed out that Mahfuz notes at the end of al-Karnak that he completed the novel in December 1971.

Nasserist writers and journalists counter-attacked, accusing both
Tawfiq al-Hakim and Mahfuz of dishonesty and opportunism.⁴ Muhammad ʿAwda writes:

After Najib Mahfuz had written a long series of novels and
short stories, and not a single line had been crossed out, after he
had accomplished under the protection of the revolution everything that a writer could accomplish, he discovered – after ʿAbd
al-Nasir's death – that Egypt had been no more than an enor-
mous and terrible prison and one huge torture room. . . . But
during that "black" period Najib Mahfuz did not think of pro-
testing in any way. . . . He did not think [then] of publishing the
"testimony" he is publishing now . . . although he could easily
have done so. . . . Najib Mahfuz [suddenly] discovered, after the
death of ʿAbd al-Nasir, that everything which had taken place
[in Nasser's time] was a "crime" – crushing the humanity of the
struggling men [al-munadilin] and violating the honor of the
struggling women [al-munadilat]. Of course, he did not tell [us]
that all this had happened while he had been sitting safely in his
office, or at the very same time that he had been happily receiv-
ing the highest state prizes from the hands of "the chief
executive."⁵

ʿAwda adds that there have always been such Egyptian writers, who,
after the death of a great national hero, attempt to defame the late
leader. Says ʿAwda: "ʿAbd al-Nasir left this world and entered God's
mercy. He now belongs to History and is under its protection. History will give the last and final verdict on him." ʿAwda's argument

---

⁴ Muhammad ʿAwda, al-Waʿy al-mafqud (Cairo, 1975), pp. 283–85; cf. also ʿAbd al-
Rahman Abu ʿAwf, "Misdaqiyyat shahadat Najib Mahfuz ʿala marhalatay ʿAbd al-Nasir
waʾl-Sadat," Majallat al-mawqif al-ʿarabi (October 1986). Ilyas Khuri also presented a
negative evaluation of al-Karnak but, unlike ʿAwda and Abu ʿAwf, whose criticism was
purely political, he tried to justify his negative view of the novel by literary argument; see
"Bayn al-riwaya wa-naqidiha" in his collection of essays al-Dhakira al-mafquda (Beirut,
1982), pp. 110–17. This article was originally published in Shuʾun filastiniyya (August
1974).
⁵ ʿAwda here uses the phrase "al-masʾul al-awwal" which has a double meaning: (a) the
highest ranking official, and (b) the person primarily responsible (the quotation marks are
in the original).

that Mahfuz "did not think then [when Nasser was alive] to protest in any way" is factually wrong. *Al-Karnak* was not the first work in which Mahfuz criticized the Nasserist regime: he criticized Nasser in several of his novels, short stories and plays, both during Nasser's rule and after his death. Admittedly there is a difference between *al-Karnak* and Mahfuz's earlier works which express criticism of Nasser's regime. In all these previous works, the criticism is couched in allegorical or otherwise indirect form. *Al-Karnak*, too, has an allegorical level of meaning (which will be discussed below), but condemnation of the regime is not limited to the covert allegorical level; it cries out from every line of its literal surface. The brutality of the secret police and the resulting atmosphere of terror are realistically described, and the reader is spared no detail of the tortures suffered by Zaynab and Isma'il. In this respect *al-Karnak* is indeed different from those previous works.

Mahfuz's tendency to use the allegorical mode raises a number of intricate questions: did he use allegory in order to hide his meaning from the authorities targeted by it; or did he, rather, want his targets to understand the encoded message, while employing the allegorical cover only to make the criticism less of an affront? In either case his motive would be self-protection against an oppressive regime. Is Mahfuz's predilection for allegory motivated by his desire to achieve didactic effect; or does it simply reflect the fact that he thinks in metaphors?[6] During the years of Nasser's rule – and, indeed, earlier, under the monarchy – fear of the authorities certainly influenced Mahfuz's choice of mode and style. Some years previously, in his novel *al-Sukkariyya* (published in 1957), Mahfuz disclosed (through one of the characters) that he considered allegorical narrative useful for expressing ideas which, due to political constraints, could not be expressed directly. In this novel one of the characters refers to narrative fiction as "a cunning art" which contains "unlimited artifices" and she recommends it as a means of circumventing official censorship. The conversation in question is most illuminating:

---

[6] Cf. Rene Wellek and Austin Warren, *Theory of Literature* (New York, 1956), p. 182, and Angus Fletcher, *Allegory* (Ithaca and London, 1964), pp. 1–23, 321–30.

"You have expressed your thoughts, up to now, through another, in other words, by translation [of articles written by
others]. Haven't you ever thought of choosing a genre that suits
you?"
He was silent, immersed in his thoughts, as if her point had
eluded him, then he asked: "What do you mean?"
"Essays, poetry, short stories, plays."
"I don't know. Essays are the first thing that comes to mind."
"Yes, that's true, but because of political conditions it's not
easy. This is why liberals are forced to publish their views in
underground publications. Essays are outspoken and direct and
therefore dangerous, especially since we are being watched; but
fiction contains unlimited artifices. It is a cunning art and has
turned into a most popular genre. . . ."[7]

The problem with allegory is that it has a paradoxical quality: its
advantage (its cipher-like nature) is also its weakness (its suscep-
tibility to misinterpretation). Furthermore, if the surface story is realistically convincing, the hidden level of meaning may escape detec-
tion altogether, and some readers will not feel the need to decode
the story.[8]

Disappointment with Nasser's regime may already be discerned in
Awlad haretna (*Children of Gebelawi*), Mahfuz's first work to be
published after the 1952 revolution, which appeared in serial form in
al-Ahram in 1959.[9] The philosophical aspects of *Awlad haretna*,
Mahfuz's ambitious allegory on religion, secular power and science,
have been discussed at length in various articles and books, but the
novel's contemporary Egyptian political significance was ignored for
many years.[10]

[7] *Al-Sukkariyya*, p. 248. This particular conversation refers, of course, to conditions
under the rule of King Faruq, but Mahfuz's opinion as to fiction's effectiveness as a vehicle
for "forbidden" ideas is relevant to our discussion. On this matter see my article, "An
Allegory on the Social and Cultural Crisis in Egypt: *Walid al-'Ana'* by Najib Mahfuz,"
International Journal of Middle Eastern Studies 3 (1972), p. 325.
[8] Cf. Jon Whitman, *Allegory: The Dynamics of an Ancient and Medieval Technique*
(Oxford, 1987), pp. 2–3.
[9] See above, pp. 80–82.
[10] The following articles and chapters dealing with *Awlad haretna* contain no reference

The book tells the story of a neighborhood (allegorically representing humankind) in which secular authority has always fallen into the
hands of *futuwwat* (i.e., ringleaders or thugs), who rule the people
with brute force and use their power to satisfy their selfish interests.
A "reliable" narrator describes a typical Cairene quarter in pre-modern times, many generations ago. Ostensibly there is no connection
between the political condition of the *hara* at the time of the narrator
and that of Egypt in the 1950s. However, the narrator speaks for the
author when he compares the conditions of the *hara* in ancient times
with his own days:

> I myself have witnessed this sad situation [that is, the oppres-
> sion of the people by the *futuwwat*] in recent days, [and find it
> to be] a true replica of what the storytellers tell about bygone
> times. However, the poets of the coffee-houses, which are
> found all over our neighborhood – they tell only the stories of
> heroic periods, avoiding any public talk about whatever may
> embarrass the masters (*Awlad haretna*, p. 117).

What we are hearing is not just the fictional narrator complaining
about the *futuwwat* of his time, but also Najib Mahfuz commenting
on the oppressive rule of the latter-day *futuwwat*, the army officers
in Egypt under Nasser. Not only is this a criticism of the officers'
rule, it is also a bleak comment on the role played by the writers and
intellectuals of the period ("the poets of the coffee-houses").[11]

Another reference to contemporary conditions may be found in a
conversation between Jabal (the allegorical figure of Moses) and *al-
mu'allim* Balqiti (Jethro). When Jabal complains that he was forced
to emigrate from his neighborhood, Balqiti remarks, "As long as

---

to its contemporary Egyptian political significance: 'Abd al-Mun'im Subhi's article in *al-Fikr
al-mu'asir* (Cairo, May 1967), pp. 108–9; Mahir al-Batuti's article in *al-Ādāb* (Beirut, July–
August 1967), pp. 81–88; George Tarabishi's article in *al-Ādāb* (Beirut, April 1972), pp. 18–
23; Sasson Somekh, *The Changing Rhythm* (Leiden, 1973), pp. 137–55; Nabil Raghib,
Qadiyyat al-shakl al-fanni 'ind Najib Mahfuz (Cairo, 1975), pp. 225–41. By contrast, Ghali
Shukri appears to have understood correctly the immediate political relevance of *Awlad
haretna*, but alludes to it only in somewhat vague terms. See *al-Muntami: Dirasa fi adab
Najib Mahfuz* (Cairo, 1969), pp. 239–40.

[11] Cf. Vatikiotis's remark above on those writers who assumed the role of panegyrists
for the regime.

there are *futuwwat* there will inevitably be emigrants" (*Awlad haretna*, p. 157). One of Mahfuz's charges against Nasser was that many Egyptians felt compelled to emigrate because of the oppressive nature of the regime. The negative phenomena alluded to in *Awlad haretna* – the emigration of Egyptian intellectuals and professionals, the adulation of Nasser by journalists and writers and the rule of fear – persisted and grew in the following years. In *al-Maraya* (*Mirrors*), a collection of short descriptions of over fifty fictional contemporary Egyptian characters, published in 1972, Mahfuz again refers to these aspects of life under Nasser's regime. One of the young characters explains that he is considering emigration because the Egyptian environment "suffocates [free] thought and justice" (*al-Maraya*, p. 55).

The actual political intention behind *Awlad haretna*, which Mahfuz's commentators failed to point out, was eventually made completely clear by Mahfuz himself. In December 1975, Mahfuz said in an interview:

> I began to feel that there were many faults and shameful things which shocked me, especially the acts of terror, torture and imprisonment. This led me to write my long novel *Awlad haretna*, which depicts the struggle between the prophets and the thugs.... The story of the prophets is the artistic framework, but the intention was to criticize the revolution and the social order which then existed. At that time I saw a new class emerging and becoming exceptionally wealthy. The question which then bothered me was: are we moving toward socialism or to a new kind of feudalism?[12]

In 1983, Jareer Abu-Haidar called attention to the wider political aspects of *Awlad haretna*, noting correctly that it is essentially "a parable of authority and power, not only in Egypt ... but everywhere in the Arab world, or rather in the Middle East."[13] *Awlad haretna*

---

[12] Interview in *al-Qabas* (Kuwait, 31 December 1975). Quoted from Ibrahim al-Shaykh, *Mawaqif ijtima'iyya wa-siyasiyya fi adab Najib Mahfuz*, 3rd printing (Cairo, 1987).

[13] Jareer Abu-Haidar, "Awlad Haratina by Najib Mahfuz: An Event in the Arab World," *Journal of Arabic Literature* 16 (1985), p. 119. This paper was presented at a seminar in Oxford in 1983. Jareer Abu-Haidar apparently reached his conclusions independently, without reference to Mahfuz's explanation of the political intent behind *Awlad haretna*.

thus has three, not two levels of meaning: the surface narrative which serves as a cover – if only a very thin one – for the representation of philosophical, historical and religious problems, which in turn serves as a cover for criticism of contemporary political conditions.

One of the earliest expressions of disenchantment with the 1952 revolution to be found in Egyptian literature is Mahfuz's novel *al-Liss wa'l-kilab* ("The Thief and the Dogs," published in 1961). Although this novel's central theme is not political, as it is concerned primarily with existential problems such as alienation and anxiety, it refers implicitly to the nature of the Nasserist regime.[14] Various Egyptian critics pointed out at the time that there was an element of social criticism in this novel, but this was seen as directed against those opportunists who distorted the true nature of the revolution, not as a negative comment on the regime itself.[15]

The story "*al-Khawf*" ("Fear," 1965) has been rightly seen by one critic as an allegorical comment on the relations between the government and the people.[16] "*Al-Khawf*" is the story of a humble Cairene neighborhood two or three generations ago. At the beginning of the story we hear that the neighborhood is oppressed by two rival gangs. Na'ima, the local beauty, is engaged to be married to Himali (whose name means "meek" or "long suffering"), an honest young man from the same neighborhood, but the rival ringleaders both want to marry her too, and meek Himali is forced to give her up. The whole neighborhood is in a state of fear; everyone is afraid of what may happen in the impending clash between the two thugs and their gangs. Salvation appears unexpectedly in the form of a young police officer who beats up the thugs and scares them off. This story has the aura of a folktale in which the good hero defeats the forces of evil, but the end is very different. The police officer who saves the neigh-

---

[14] See above, p. 82.

[15] See above, p. 83.

[16] "*Al-Khawf*" is included in the collection *Bayt sayyi' al-sum'a* (1965). The interpretation referred to here is that of Mattityahu Peled, "The Views of Najib Mahfuz on the Attributes of Political Power," *Hamizrah hehadash* 16 (1966), pp. 310–18 (in Hebrew). In an interview with Sabri Hafiz in 1972, Mahfuz admitted that he had intended "*al-Khawf*" to be a criticism of the officers' despotic regime. See Sabri Hafiz (ed.), *Attahadath ilaykum* (Beirut, 1977), pp. 110–11.

borhood from the thugs charms Na'ima, and it is rumored that she has secretly given herself to him. Subsequently he loses interest in her. Na'ima is forlorn; the people of the neighborhood now find the rule of the police officer even more oppressive than that of the thugs.

In another story too the police play a major role: "*Hanzal wa'l-'askari*" ("Hanzal and the Policeman," in the collection *Dunya 'llah*, 1963). Like *al-Liss wa'l-kilab*, published two years earlier, and like "*al-Khawf*," published two years later, this story also ends in gloom and despair. But unlike "*al-Khawf*," it has not previously been identified as an allegory.

Hanzal is a wretched drug addict. He has no work and no source of income, he wears rags, and drugs have emaciated his body. After collapsing in the street one night, he is awakened by a policeman who drags him to the police station. Much to Hanzal's surprise, he is not beaten up or shouted at by the policemen. The officer receives him politely and informs him that "things have changed." The officer declares: "Just as we have our military side, we also have our humane side." He further tells Hanzal that the police will now concern themselves with his well-being, and will send him to a clinic to be cured of his drug addiction. Hanzal comes out of the clinic a healthy man. He is again brought before the police officer, who now promises to arrange for him to open a fruit store and to marry his sweetheart Saniyya. Hanzal is overwhelmed with joy. He is, however, worried that the police may not always be so sympathetic: "I am afraid, Sir," he says to the officer, "that the friendship of the police will not be lasting. Although there were many reasons for my misery in the past, the police was one of the main causes... and in regard to Saniyya in particular – it was the police officer Hassuna who first caused her to lose her head." The officer reassures him: "You will not find a single enemy among the police. From now on and for evermore they are your sincere friends. Ask whatever you wish, Hanzal, it's an order!" Encouraged and overjoyed, Hanzal now asks that other poor people be treated in the same manner. This request, too, is granted. Hanzal's wedding celebration is a joyous affair; after much dancing and singing, Hanzal retires to bed with Saniyya. He sleeps, and is again awakened, this time very harshly, by a policeman who drags him to the police station. Looking around, Hanzal sees no trace of celebration, no sign of Saniyya, nothing but a dark and empty street. The whole episode turns out to have been no more than a dream.

"*Hanzal wa'l-'askari*" is a remarkable example of that paradoxical nature of allegory to which I referred above. The story of Hanzal is told with such empathy and is so moving as a realistic story that it has not been seen as an allegory; but it surely is one. The key to the allegorical level of this story is the iconographic quality of "police" and "policemen" in Mahfuz's works.[17] Policemen represent the regime and, more specifically, its brutal, coercive nature. This is the significance of the police in "*Hanzal wa'l-'askari*" as it is in "*al-Khawf*" and *al-Liss wa'l-kilab*. The powerless and artless individual represents the common people who are oppressed by the regime. Hanzal in this story has the same iconographic quality as Himali in "*al-Khawf*" and the thief in *al-Liss wa'l-kilab*: he is powerless and helpless when confronted by the police. Himali, Na'ima's erstwhile suitor who is forced to give her up, is the equivalent of Hanzal; likewise, Na'ima is the iconographic analogue of Saniyya. Once "*Hanzal wa'l-'askari*" is read in this manner, we can see that beneath the surface story of a drug addict's dream, there is yet another story – that of a people which has been led to believe that a military regime will save it from all its ills, and which is now bitterly disillusioned.

The regime, it should be noted, is represented in Mahfuz's works by more than one icon. In the novel *al-Liss wa'l-kilab*, a much more elaborate narrative than the short story "*Hanzal wa'l-'askari*," the regime is represented both by the police – the coercive arm of the state – and by a selfish journalist, who represents those intellectuals who have placed themselves at its service.

The story of Hanzal begins: "Those heavy steps caused a fearful echo in his heart." Further on, Hanzal is described as being in a state of fear. Fear characterizes Hanzal's attitude to the police and thus the people's position vis-à-vis the regime. "Fear" ("*al-Khawf*") is also the title of the other short story in which Mahfuz intimates his views on the relations between Nasser's regime and the people.

Na'ima in "*al-Khawf*" and Saniyya in "*Hanzal wa'l-'askari*" per-

---

[17] On the term "iconography" in relation to allegory, see Fletcher, *Allegory*, p. 6. On the meaning of "police" in Mahfuz's allegories, see above, p. 101.

sonify Egypt and the Egyptian people. This most important icon appears in a number of Mahfuz's allegorical stories: Zahra in *Miramar*, the young woman in *"Yumitu wa-yuhyi,"* the woman in labor in *"Walid al-'ana',"* Qurunfila in *al-Karnak*, Saniyya al-Mahdi in *al-Baqi min al-zaman sa'a*, Randa in *Yawm qutila 'l-za'im*, and other women in other stories, all symbolize Egypt. Some of these stories contain additional secondary female characters. The outstanding qualities of all these women are charm, endurance, hope, and fortitude in adversity.

The male characters who represent the regime in these stories are far less attractive: a corrupt and selfish engineer, a member of Nasser's Arab Socialist Union, in *Miramar*; a womanizing husband (an allusion to Nasser's pan-Arab involvements) in *"Walid al-'ana'"*; a cruel police investigator (Khalid Safwan) and a corrupt official (Zayn al-'Abidin 'Abd Allah) in *al-Karnak*; and the vain and corrupt Sulayman Bahjat (Saniyya's son-in-law) in *al-Baqi min al-zaman sa'a*.

In 1967, a few months before the Six-Day War in June, Mahfuz published the novel *Miramar*, which also paints a negative picture of characters associated with the Nasser regime.[18] Zahra, the charming female character in this novel, is a *fallaha* who comes to the big city to gain education and independence. She is seduced and then betrayed by Sirhan al-Buhayri, a young engineer who is a prominent member of Nasser's Socialist Union. Sirhan, a selfish careerist, participates in a plot to rob the warehouse of the nationalized company in which he is employed. When the plot is discovered he commits suicide. As noted above, Zahra, in Mahfuzian iconography, allegorically signifies Egypt, and Sirhan al-Buhayri – the regime. Another (minor) character who also represents the regime (both literally and allegorically) is a police officer who forces his younger brother, a left-wing intellectual, to give up political activity.

Thus in *Miramar*, as previously in *al-Liss wa'l-kilab*, criticism of the regime is expressed on both the surface literal level and on the allegorical level. The criticism contained in the surface story could, conceivably, be regarded as "constructive" criticism aimed only at those who, like Sirhan, give the revolution a bad name. Hence, it

---

[18] On *Miramar*, see above, pp. 87–89.

could be tolerated. The allegorical meaning, on the other hand, condemns the regime as a whole: Egypt (Zahra) is deceived and betrayed by the regime (Sirhan). This meaning is subversive, and must, therefore, be covert.

"*Yumitu wa-yuhyi*" ("He Causes Death and He Brings to Life") is a one-act play which Mahfuz wrote in the wake of the 1967 war.[19] This obviously allegorical work comments critically on both Nasser's domestic policies and his response to the 1967 defeat. In "*Yumitu wa-yuhyi*" the young man represents Nasser (or his regime), and the young woman, Egypt. When the young man first appears he has just suffered a severe beating, and he declares his determination to avenge himself on his enemy. The young woman – his fiancée – tries to persuade him to stop preparing for war, and to devote himself, instead, to family life with her.[20] A giant (*'imlaq*) appears on the scene, offering the young man help against his enemy. At first the giant presents himself as a volunteer seeking no reward for his assistance, but he soon reveals his selfish intentions and, among them, his desire to share with the hero the favors of the young woman. The indignant hero now faces a new and pressing threat to his honor, far more serious than the mocking laughter of his enemy across the border: he has to find a way to get rid of the giant. A blind beggar (*shahhadh*) now appears on the scene, uttering enigmatic phrases. When asked by the hero why he is not in a home for the handicapped, the beggar has a strange story to tell. He says that he used to be in such a home, but the superintendent of this home was a rude, cruel man and a shameless thief to boot. He and some of his friends rebelled against the superintendent, who was eventually replaced. The new superintendent is honest and compassionate, but is obsessed with a desire to impose strict order and refuses to accept criticism. The beggar therefore fled from the home. When asked by the hero whether the home for the handicapped, for all its faults, was not better than a wander-

---

[19] Published in the collection *Taht al-mizalla* in 1969. The author notes on the back of the front page that the stories contained in this volume were written between October and December 1967.

[20] The young woman's distaste for politics and her indifference to questions of national honor recall the attitudes of the two mothers in the trilogy and in *Bidaya wa-nihaya*. See above, p. 79.

ing life as a beggar, he answers: "Freedom is more valuable than safety."[21]

The giant may be said to represent the Soviet Union, the blind beggar the alienated Egyptian intellectual, the rude superintendent who was replaced, the deposed monarchy. Nasser appears in this play in two forms: he is the hero (the young man) – defeated, humiliated and confused; he is also the "superintendent" who is "obsessed" with strict order and who "refuses to tolerate any criticism."[22] In the final scene of the play we see the dead bodies, who represent the ancestors of the hero, come to life in order to help him expel the giant and face his enemy.

"*Walid al-'ana'*" ("Child of Suffering"), an allegorical story published in May 1970, also ends with a miraculous salvation. In this story a newborn baby, in a display of superhuman powers, kills four threatening giants. The story contains various negative comments on the Nasserist regime.[23] In neither "*Yumitu wa-yuhyi*" nor "*Walid al-'ana'*" is salvation conceived as resulting from the actions of the heroes representing Nasser or his regime.

Nasser is not mentioned by name in *al-Karnak*; there is, however, a very uncomplimentary allusion to him. The corrupt government official, Zayn al-'Abidin 'Abd Allah, tries in vain to seduce Qurunfila (who, it should be recalled, allegorically represents Egypt). We are also told that he once succeeded in buying his way into the bed of

---

[21] *Taht al-mizalla*, p. 164.

[22] Egyptian critics have dealt gingerly with this play. The left-wing critic Mahmud Amin al-'Alim interpreted the image of the giant as follows: "It may signify the United States in our present war against the Israeli and Zionist aggression and existence, or it may signify any intermediary agent coming between man and the humanity of his creative activity." He does not mention the beggar at all. See his article "*Marhala jadida fi 'alam Najib Mahfuz*," *al-Hilal* (Cairo, February 1970), p. 22. Fatima Musa, attempting to steer away from sensitive political issues, interpreted "*Yumitu wa-yuhyi*" as dealing with the spiritual crisis of the young generation at the time, without any reference to specific political circumstances. She mentions the beggar without offering an interpretation; instead she writes: "Perhaps, on another occasion, we shall explore the meaning of 'beggar' in the works of Najib Mahfuz." As for the giant, she says: "Is he the Great Powers or the United Nations or does he represent every powerful agent who uses his power as a means for gangsterism?" Fatima Musa, *Fi'l-riwayya al-'arabiyya al-mu'asira* (Cairo, 1972), pp. 112–13.

[23] See Milson, "An Allegory on the Social and Cultural Crisis in Egypt: *Walid al-'Ana'* by Najib Mahfuz,", *IJMES* 3, pp. 324–47.

Zaynab (a young student, a complementary figure to Qurunfila). The name of this contemptible character evokes the name of Jamal 'Abd al-Nasir (Nasser): *Zayn al-'Abidin* ("the beauty of the worshippers") is the semantic equivalent of *Jamāl* ("beauty"), while *'Abd Allah* is the semantic equivalent of *'Abd al-Nasir* (both mean "Servant of God.")

A direct comment on Nasser occurs in the story *"al-Sama' al-sabi'a"* ("The Seventh Heaven," in the collection *al-Hubb fawq hadbat al-haram*, 1979). The comment, though represented as humorous, is caustic. In this story we hear about a young man whose soul reaches the gates of heaven after his murder by a fellow student. While waiting for sentence to be passed on him, he learns some interesting facts about the procedures of heavenly judgment. He hears that most people cannot be admitted to heaven; only the most virtuous are admitted and allowed to proceed to the second heaven (the ultimate goal being the seventh). All the others are either sentenced to be reincarnated and to suffer life on earth once more, both as a punishment for their past wrongs and as a second chance; or, if they are basically good though not without faults, they are sent back to earth as invisible spirits, to serve as moral guides to others. Each of these spirits is appointed as a tutor (*murshid*) to a particular individual, and the tutor's chance to enter heaven depends on the behavior of his charge, by which his success as a mentor will be judged. While waiting at the gate, the hero has a chance to learn the fate of various famous people. He hears, for example, that Sa'd Zaghlul, founder of the Wafd party (d. 1927), was the only modern Egyptian leader allowed to join the blessed minority admitted directly to the second heaven. He also hears that Mustafa Nahhas, Sa'd Zaghlul's successor as leader of the Wafd (d. 1965), served as Sadat's mentor and was allowed to enter the second heaven after the October 1973 war and the restoration of freedom. It should be recalled here that Nasser, in an attempt to obliterate the Wafd completely, did everything he could to dim the memory of Sa'd Zaghlul as a national hero. Mustafa Nahhas, who in 1952 was prime minister of Egypt, was forced to resign in disgrace by the Free Officers, and was subsequently deprived of his civil rights and banned from public life. Heavenly justice, Mahfuz tells us, does not treat these two leaders as the Nasserist regime did. On hearing of the fate of these two national leaders the young man asks, "What about Jamal 'Abd al-Nasir?" He is told, "He is now the mentor of Qadhdhafi."[24]

Mahfuz did not confine his criticism to Nasser alone. He found fault with Sadat's economic policy in the late 1970s (*al-infitah*, the "open door" policy) which led to steep inflation and created a gap between the beneficiaries of the policy – importers, contractors and corrupt politicians – and the majority of the urban population. Some of the stories in the collection *al-Hubb fawq hadbat al-haram* ("Love on Top of the Pyramid," published in 1979, while Sadat was still in power) describe the hardships encountered by young educated Egyptians in the new economic climate, in contrast with the easy living enjoyed by the *nouveaux riches*. The short novel *Yawm qutila 'l-za'im* (*The Day the Leader Was Killed*, 1985) describes the tragedy of two young people who cannot marry because of economic hardship resulting directly from government policy. Anwar 'Allam, the corrupt high-ranking official in whose department the two young people are employed, dies on the day of President Sadat's assassination. Since this corrupt official and President Sadat share the same first name, the story was understood as a negative judgment on Sadat's regime. Jihan Sadat, the president's widow, was reportedly offended by the story. Mahfuz recounts in an interview how he went to see her to explain that this was "just a novel and not a historical work."[25]

---

[24] *Al-Hubb fawq hadbat al-haram*, p. 110.
[25] Interview with Ghali Shukri, *al-Watan al-'arabi* 46 (January 1988), p. 46.

CHAPTER 9

The Courtroom of History

In 1983 Najib Mahfuz published a book entitled *Amam al-'arsh* ("Before the Throne"). The subtitle defines the book as "a conversation with Egyptian personalities from Mina to Anwar al-Sadat" (*Hiwar ma'a rijal misr min Mina hatta Anwar al-Sadat*). In this book Mahfuz uses elements from Pharaonic mythology as a fictional frame for the expression of his own views on Egyptian history and his evaluation of Egypt's rulers through the ages down to the present. The book consists of an account of a trial presided over by Osiris, the chief deity of the ancient Egyptian pantheon. In Egyptian mythology, Osiris is, among other things, "the judge of the dead." The book is composed of sixty-four dramatic scenes, each representing one "case." Various Egyptian personalities, starting with Mina (that is, Menes, the founder of the first dynasty) and ending with Anwar Sadat, are summoned upon their death to appear before the court of Osiris, who decides who will join the ranks of the "immortals" (*al-khalidun*). Sitting in judgment with Osiris are his sister-wife Isis and their son Horus. Thoth, the scribe of the gods, acts as secretary to the court.

The principles and the criteria of historical judgment in the book become apparent as the trials progress: the ruler is judged according to his dedication to Egypt and his love and kindness towards the Egyptian people. It is Mahfuz's firm belief that the Egyptian people has remained one and the same from time immemorial to the present; the changes of religion – from the old Pharaonic religion to Christianity and then to Islam – have not broken the historical unity of the people, nor have they affected its inherent identity. This conception of Egyptian history is expressed in various ways throughout *Amam al-'arsh*, and is also implicit in the very structure of the book. Politically, the most significant two "cases" judged by the court are Nasser and Anwar al-Sadat. The chapters devoted to them are the longest in the book.

Some details of court "procedure" are necessary, so that we can better appreciate the verdicts and recommendations issued by the court with regard to these two rulers of Egypt. Each person is first invited by Osiris to present his case, that is, to describe his achievements. Once the candidate has introduced himself, the previous leaders, who have already been granted the status of Immortals, can question him, criticize him or bestow praise upon him. Isis, in the role of "counsel for the defense," sums up briefly, emphasizing the candidate's praiseworthy deeds and recommending forgiveness for his faults. Finally, Osiris pronounces his verdict and recommendation.

Two seemingly unimportant cases deserve special attention. A certain 'Ali Sundus, a poor water-carrier, testifies as to conditions in Egypt under Kafur al-Ikhshidi, the black eunuch who ruled Egypt from 946 CE to 968 CE. According to this witness, Kafur was a just and powerful ruler who won the loyalty of the people, despite his low status as a manumitted castrated black slave. This chapter seems to affirm a principle of historical-moral judgement, put here into the mouth of the witness: "A just slave is better than an unjust prince" (p. 148). It is noteworthy that, contrary to what we know of Kafur from historical references to him (which accord with 'Ali Sundus's testimony), the popular image of Kafur is a negative and ludicrous one. The reasons for this are manifold: his dark skin, his degrading physical defect and, last but not least, the fact that he was satirized by the great poet al-Mutanabbi.[1] Hence, there is another important message here, namely: the popular image of a historical figure should not be accepted without question as true, nor should it be allowed to distort our historical judgment.

---

[1] See *EI²*, s.v. "Kāfūr," also cf. Bernard Lewis, *Race and Color in Islam* (New York, 1971), pp. 78–79.

The same message is implicit in the story of Qaraqush, who appears before the court to testify on the Ayyubid period. The historical Qaraqush was a commander and chief minister under Salah al-Din and his successors. Contemporary historiographers bestowed great praise upon him and described him as "the ablest man of his day." There is, however, also a popular image of Qaraqush as a stupid and villainous judge, which is very different from the historical record as we know it.[2] Qaraqush uses his appearance before Osiris's court to protest against this defamation of his name. He says: "Never has a just man been reputed for injustice as I have." No one in court challenges the truth of these words, and Osiris thanks him for his services. Qaraqush is, so to speak, rehabilitated.

In the Qaraqush story, as in the Kafur story, Mahfuz is bent on teaching his readers that it is essential to give up popular notions in order to reach a fair historical judgment. It is important for Mahfuz to establish this point before he reaches the modern era, where he challenges a very formidable popular image – that of Jamal 'Abd al-Nasir.

The "cases" of Nasser and Sadat in Osiris's court are presented here in translation or summary with minimal comments. When his turn comes, Nasser appears before Osiris's court and introduces himself in accordance with the established procedure:

> I am from the village of Bani Murr in the province of Asyut. I grew up in a poor family and endured austerity and hardship. A graduate of the Military College in 1938, I took part in the Palestine war and was among those who were under siege in Faluja. I was deeply affected by the defeat and even more so by its causes, which were rooted deeply in our homeland. I decided, therefore, to transfer the campaign to the home front, where the real enemies of the country were lurking, and so I secretly established the organization of the Free Officers. I observed events, waiting for an opportunity to attack the existing regime, and I achieved my purpose on 23 July 1952.
>
> The accomplishments of the revolution followed in swift succession: the abolition of the monarchy, full independence

---

[2] See *EI*[2], s.v. "Ḳarāḳūsh, Bahā' al-Dīn b. 'Abd Allāh."

[brought about] by complete evacuation [of the British], the end of feudalism through the law of agrarian reform, the Egyptianization of the economy, plans for comprehensive reform in agriculture and industry, intended for the good of the people and designed to remove class differences. We built the high dam and established the public sector [of the economy], heading towards socialism; we created a powerful modern army and propagated Arab unity; we supported every Arab or African revolution; we nationalized the Suez Canal and thus became a beacon and an example to the whole Third World in its struggle against external colonization and internal exploitation. The working people gained in my time a dignity and power which they had not known before. For the first time they were able to enter legislative councils and universities and feel that the land was indeed theirs.

But the colonialist powers were waiting in ambush, and on 5 June 1967 they inflicted a terrible defeat on me. They shook the very foundations of my great work and brought upon me [something] resembling death three years before my day came. I lived as a sincere Arab Egyptian and I died as an Arab Egyptian *shahīd*.[3]

This introduction by Nasser is predictably self-congratulatory; Mahfuz writes with a tinge of irony when he has Nasser praise himself for creating "a powerful modern army" and for "supporting every Arab and African revolution." From Nasser's pan-Arab point of view, supporting revolution throughout Africa and the Arab world is a praiseworthy action; but Mahfuz, who puts Egypt's interests first, intends Nasser's remark to be understood as self-incriminatory.

Ramses II is the first to comment on Nasser's words. Declaring his love and admiration for Nasser, he explains:

My love for you is in fact an extension of my love for myself, as there are many points of similarity between us. . . . Each of us turned his defeat into a victory surpassing all victories. . . . Nei-

---

[3] *Shahīd*, often translated as "martyr," really means "a Muslim who is killed in jihad and who is, therefore, assured of admission into paradise." The claim to admission to paradise implicit in the term *shahīd* is obviously of special importance here.

ther of us was content with his own illustrious achievements, and so he claimed for himself the accomplishments of those who preceded him.

Ramses II alludes here to the fact that he ordered stones and columns to be taken from monuments erected by his predecessors, for use in the construction of temples and monuments built to glorify him; he also had his name carved on monuments erected by his predecessors (*Amam al-'arsh*, pp. 92–93). The analogy with Nasser suggested here refers to Nasser's attempt to obliterate the memory of the heroes of modern Egyptian nationalism who preceded him. It also reflects Mahfuz's opinion that one of Nasser's main claims to fame, the final evacuation of Egypt by the British, was in fact only the final stage of work which had already been carried out for the most part by Nasser's predecessors.[4] Ramses II's praise has, then, an ironic function: behind it lurks Mahfuz's mockery.

Menes criticizes directly: "You were more concerned with Arab unity than with Egyptian unity; you went so far as to erase the very name of Egypt." This latter criticism is directed at Nasser's having changed Egypt's name to the *United Arab Republic*. Another charge is: "You compelled many children of Egypt to emigrate." Nasser does not answer the accusation that he is responsible for the emigration of Egyptian youth. But as for Menes's other charges, his answer is as follows: "It is not my fault that some Egyptians [wrongly] imagined that Arab unity means their perdition. It is not my fault that great achievements were [finally] realized by me, whereas my predecessors had failed to realize them. Indeed, Egyptian history truly began on the 23rd of July 1952." In the context of this trial, this arrogant and presumptuous statement highlights Mahfuz's view of Nasser as a leader whose claims to greatness were disproportionate to his actual achievements.

Thutmosis III charges: "Despite your military education you showed great capability in all areas except the military. In fact you were not an outstanding military commander at all!" Nasser responds: "I was unable to overcome an army which was better equipped and which was supported by the most powerful state in the

---

[4] Cf. Ghitani, p. 80.

whole world." One of the Immortals retorts: "You should have avoided war and stopped provoking the great powers." Nasser answers: "This would have contradicted my aims. I was trapped by deception more than once." Another of the Immortals acidly remarks: "This is an excuse which is worse than the crime."

Sa'd Zaghlul criticizes Nasser for having tried to obliterate Egypt's name.[5] He also criticizes his autocratic manner of government. Nasser's defense against this charge is: "We needed a period of transition in order to lay a firm foundation for the revolution." Mustafa Nahhas, assuming the prosecutor's role, retorts: "This is a feeble argument of dictators which we have heard many times from the enemies of the people." Nahhas accuses Nasser of having governed in a manner which subverted all good intentions.[6] Nasser answers: "For me the meaning of real democracy was to free the Egyptians from colonialism, exploitation and poverty." Nahhas continues his criticism:

> You neglected freedom and human rights. I do not deny that you gave protection to the poor, but you were a disaster for the intellectuals and the educated. You brought upon them arrests, imprisonment, hanging and killing, you debased their dignity and humanity [to the point that] you destroyed their personality, and now only God knows when it will be rehabilitated.... Your dictatorial manner spoiled even your finest decisions. Just look at the deterioration of education and the disintegration of the public sector. Your provocation of the world powers led you into shameful defeats and heavy losses. You did not seek to benefit from the views of others, nor did you learn from the ex-

[5] In 1958, when Egypt and Syria united under Nasser as president, they were jointly renamed the United Arab Republic (al-Jumhuriyya al-'arabiyya al-muttahidda). Nasser retained this as Egypt's official name, even after the union was dissolved in 1961. It was Sadat who restored Egypt's name in 1971, when it was again renamed the Arab Republic of Egypt (Jumhuriyyat misr al-'arabiyya).

[6] For Mahfuz, democracy "is not merely one value among others, but the value which protects all other values. When a person rules as an autocrat, even if he has genius, patriotism and good intentions – they are of no use, because a single error on his part may cause the destruction of the whole building." Mahfuz also regarded the absence of democracy as the main reason for the 1967 debacle. See interview with Amina al-Naqqash in Afaq 'arabiyya, February 1976.

perience of Muhammad 'Ali. And what was the result? Great noise and clamor and worthless myths resting on a heap of ruins.

Nasser:

I led the country from one stage to another just as I led the Arabs [as a whole] and the rest of the oppressed nations. In the course of time the negative phenomena will be taken care of, until they disappear, and that which is beneficial to the people will remain; then people will recognize my real greatness.

Nahhas:

You should have been humbler in your ambitions; you should have devoted yourself to reforming the condition of your country and to introducing progress in all aspects of civilization. Developing the Egyptian village is more important than adopting the revolutions of the whole world, encouraging scientific research is more important than the Yemen war, the fight against illiteracy is more important than the fight against world imperialism. It is a great pity that you caused the country to lose an opportunity it had never had before: for the first time a native Egyptian was ruling the country without opposition from a king or a colonialist [power], but instead of healing his sick fellow compatriots, he pushed them to compete for the world championship, while they were [still] overburdened with disease, and the result was that he lost the championship and lost himself.

Isis intercedes:

My joy at the fact that one of my children returned to the throne is immeasurable. It would take all the walls of the temples to record his illustrious works, but as for his faults – I do not know how to defend him.

Osiris sums up:

If our court had to issue the final verdict on you, justice would require long and difficult contemplation, for only few people rendered to their country as many services as you did, and only a few brought upon it as many evils as you did. However, considering that you are the first native Egyptian to sit on the throne of Egypt,[7] and the first who took special care of the working people, we shall allow you to sit among the Immortals until the end of the proceedings[8] and you will eventually go to your [appropriate religious] court supported by a suitable recommendation.

Seated among the Immortals, Nasser can criticize his successor, Sadat, and when the latter appears before the court, Nasser makes various charges against him. Sadat responds, and Nasser does not come very well out of the exchange. When Sadat presents his own record, he refers to Nasser's serious faults: "... I succeeded him under most delicate circumstances and was fully aware of the decay which had penetrated Nasser's rule to the very bone. I therefore hastened to bring about a new revolution to save the country from the death towards which it was falling" (p. 200). After some words of praise and congratulation to Sadat by various Pharaonic figures, Nasser interjects: "How could you take the liberty of behaving so treacherously toward my memory?" Sadat: "I had to take this position because the main purpose of my policy was to redress the wrongs which I inherited from your period." Nasser: "However, [during my life] I knew you as a friend who consented [to my policies] and supported me."

Sadat forcefully answers the charge of duplicity and disloyalty made here, which reflects real charges made against him by various Nasserist journalists: "It is unjust to blame a person for a position taken by him at a time of black terror, when a father feared his own son and a man his own brother."[9] It has been noted above that similar charges of duplicity and disloyalty were leveled at Mahfuz and

[7] Osiris regards Nasser as the first native Egyptian ruler, because in ancient Egypt the Pharaohs were considered deities.

[8] The phrase "until the end of the proceedings" (li-hin intiha' al-muhakama) means, in fact, until the end of time; "the proceedings" in question – namely, the trial in the heavenly court of Osiris – represent the trial of history.

[9] In the novel al-Baqi min al-zaman sa'a (1982), Mahfuz puts nearly the same words into the mouth of one of his characters, a supporter of the Muslim Brotherhood, who complains within the family circle about the rule of fear. He says: "A man cannot speak frankly even in front of his own son" (p. 60).

Tawfiq al-Hakim in an attempt to discredit them, since in 1974 both published scathing criticisms of Nasser and his rule.[10]

Nasser continues: "Your victory was nothing more than the fruit of my long preparation." Sadat: "A defeated [person] like you could not possibly achieve victory, whereas I restored liberty and dignity to the people, and then I led them to a real victory." Nasser: "And then you gave up everything for a shameful peace; you delivered a mortal blow to Arab unity and brought upon Egypt separation and alienation." Sadat: "I inherited from you a country staggering on the verge of the abyss, and the Arabs did not sincerely stretch out a helping hand to me. I realized that they wished us to be neither dead nor powerful, but to remain prostrated at their mercy, so I did not hesitate to take my decision." Nasser: "And you exchanged a giant [i.e., a Great Power] which had long supported us for a giant which had long been our enemy."[11] Sadat: "I turned to that giant which held the key to the problem, and events have proven me right!"

Nasser further criticizes Sadat for his economic policies, on the grounds that they benefited only the rich, and were a source of corruption. Sadat is also criticized by Nahhas for failing to develop real democracy. Isis sums up: "Thanks to this son, the spirit has been returned to the country,[12] and Egypt has regained the full independence it had before the Persian invasion.[13] He made mistakes as others did, and he accomplished more than many." Osiris: "I welcome you among the Immortals of Egypt. Eventually you will go from here to your other trial backed by an honorable recommendation from us."

Nasser obtains a seat among the Immortals of Egypt, but he does not emerge too well from Osiris's court. This conclusion becomes es-

---

[10] See above, pp, 130–32.

[11] Mahfuz uses the term "giant" (*'imlaq*), in some of his allegorical works as a metaphor for the Great Powers, e.g., in the play "*Yumitu wa-yuhyi*" (1969) and in "*Walid al-'ana*'" (May 1970). See also my interpretation of this figure in "An Allegory on the Social and Cultural Crisis in Egypt: *Walid al-'Ana'* by Najib Mahfuz," p. 342.

[12] The Arabic phrase *ruddati 'l-ruh* evokes the title of Tawfiq al-Hakim's famous novel *'Awdat al-ruh* ("The Return of the Spirit"), in which "the spirit" is the Egyptian national spirit, and its "return" refers to the nationalist upsurge of 1919 under the leadership of Sa'd Zaghlul. This evocative phrase would appear to be used here deliberately, in order to suggest an analogy between Sadat and Sa'd Zaghlul, Mahfuz's favorite leader.

[13] This alludes to the return of the whole of Sinai to Egyptian control as a result of Sadat's peace policy.

pecially clear when we compare the summary of Isis and the verdict
and recommendation of Osiris in the case of Nasser with those in the
case of Sadat. Osiris welcomes Sadat among the Immortals, while
he only "allows" Nasser to "sit among the Immortals." Sadat's recommendation is followed by the adjective *musharrifa* (i.e., giving
dignity, eminence or glory), whereas Nasser's recommendation is described merely as "suitable" (*munasiba*). In this respect Nasser does
not fare well in comparison with Sa'd Zaghlul and Nahhas either,
both of whom are given "the right" to join the Immortals. Nahhas's
recommendation is described as "most honorable" (*akram*).

In contrast to the works described previously, in *Amam al-'arsh*
the form is fictional but the figures of the respondents are not. The
appearance of Egyptian leaders before the court of Osiris is a fantasy
representing an idea which is of supreme importance to Mahfuz,
namely, the existence of a continuous Egyptian history which judges
the nation's leaders. In other words, this fantasy has an allegorical
function. But the contents of the "proceedings" are real; the chapters
dealing with ancient times contain historical information, and the
chapters dealing with Nasser and Sadat reflect both the substance
and the language of contemporary political debate. *Amam al-'arsh*,
therefore, is Mahfuz's most direct, systematic and concentrated attempt to challenge the myth of Jamal 'Abd al-Nasir.

I have attempted to show how Mahfuz commented on Nasser's
regime in a variety of fictional modes: allegory, fantasy and realistic
narrative. In addition Mahfuz has gone on record *in propria persona*
with his views on Nasser and Sa'd Zaghlul:

> Nasser and Sa'd Zaghlul represent two different stages. Nasser
> accomplished remarkable things which should not be over-
> looked, but it is difficult to compare [the two]. Sa'd Zaghlul
> was the first spark. He aspired to independence. Nasser came
> when the country was almost independent, and he brought
> about a real social revolution. Unfortunately, the revolution
> took a hostile attitude toward Sa'd Zaghlul to such a degree
> that his name was banned from books and films, etc. Then the
> circle of time turned. Some days ago I saw a film on Tito's death

and they showed all the world leaders who knew Tito except Nasser. And you know how close the relationship was between Nasser and Tito![14]

Mahfuz also openly admitted that he often feared that his stories would provoke official reprisal:

> After the July 1952 revolution I dealt with very delicate subjects, as [in] *Miramar* or *Tharthara fawq al-nil*. A couple of weeks ago, you [Ghitani] said, "When Najib Mahfuz writes, he does not pay attention to anything and he forgets everything." This is true, [but] sometimes, after I heard the reactions, I would expect frightening things, especially after a story like "*al-Khawf*." Once, in the street, I met someone who asked me what this story meant. It might have been an innocent question, but I was afraid.
>
> Look, I used to criticize the actual situation as a person who was engaged in it [*kuntu anqud al-waqi' naqd al-muntami ilayhi*]. I did not reject the July revolution altogether, . . . I called attention to some negative phenomena which damaged the revolution. You could not find [in my writings] a word against the agrarian reform or the gains of the workers and the fellahin. In *Miramar* [I criticized] the opportunism of the Socialist Union. [What I said] was true. Maybe that was the reason why they did not persecute me. Besides, your sense of innocence gives you courage.[15]

The following anecdote, recounted by Mahfuz, casts some light on the intricate relations between Nasser and the press, and the atmosphere in which Mahfuz created and published his allegories:

> My third meeting with Nasser took place during his visit to the offices of *al-Ahram*, in 1969, if I remember correctly. He spoke to everyone. To me he said: "How are your characters from the old quarters of Cairo doing? It's been a long time since we had

---

[14] Ghitani, p. 80.
[15] Ghitani, p. 78.

a story from you." [Muhammad Hasanayn] Haykal [editor-in-chief of *al-Ahram* and a close associate of Nasser] said: "Actually, there's a story appearing tomorrow. What can I do? His stories will put [him] in prison [one day]." Nasser retorted: "No, they'll put the editor-in-chief in prison!"[16]

---

[16] Ibid., p. 80. Mahfuz recounted this incident again in his interview with Ghali Shukri, *al-Watan al-'Arabi* 46 (29 January 1988), p. 45.

PART FOUR

WHAT'S IN A NAME?

CHAPTER 10

Personal Names in Fiction

> Socrates: Then a name is an instrument of teaching and of distinguishing natures, as the shuttle is of distinguishing the threads of the web.
>
> Plato, *Cratylus*

> Sooner or later, inevitably, we always come back to the question of names.
>
> José Saramago, *A Jangada de Pedra*

Najib Mahfuz chooses the names of his characters very carefully and imbues them with special meaning. In this respect Mahfuz joins a long list of outstanding novelists – Dickens, Melville, Henry James, Gogol, Balzac, E. M. Forster, to mention just a few – who tended to give their characters names which were somehow meaningful or suggestive.

The literary theorist Philippe Hamon writes, "On connaît le souci quasi maniaque de la plupart des romanciers pour choisir le nom ou le prénom de leurs personnages, les rêveries de Proust sur le nom des Guermantes ou sur celui des localités d'Italie ou de Bretagne."[1]

Indeed, the practice of selecting names for fictional characters

[1] Philippe Hamon, "Pour un statut sémiologique du personnage," in R. Barthes et al., *Poétique du récit* (Paris, 1977), p. 147.

which are more than just a "linguistic sign" for the personage has been the subject of some scholarly attention, both theoretically (in the context of the poetics of narrative fiction) and practically (by interpreting the names of characters in the works of specific authors).[2] Joseph Ewen and Shlomith Rimmon-Kenan call this device "a means of characterization by analogy." Rimmon-Kenan regards it "as a reinforcement of characterization rather than as a separate type of character-indicator ... because its characterization capacity depends on the prior establishment, by other means, of the traits on which it is based."

It should be stressed at the outset that the literary phenomenon which concerns us here is something other than the naming of personages in allegories, where the names of the dramatis personae are totally identical with the characters (as in medieval morality plays)[3] or closely correspond to the characters' roles (as in philosophical and didactic novels).[4] We are dealing with works in the realistic mode, where characterization is accomplished by various means other than naming, the name being mainly a linguistic sign for the personage.[5] Therefore, when we find in such works a personal name which seems

[2] For general theoretical treatment of this subject see Hamon, pp. 147–50 and Shlomith Rimmon-Kenan, *Narrative Fiction: Contemporary Poetics* (London and New York, 1989), pp. 67–69. See also Joseph Ewen, *Character in Narrative* (Tel Aviv, 1980, in Hebrew), pp. 102–107. For the study of this feature in the works of specific authors, see e.g., Elizabeth H. Gordon, *The Naming of Characters in the Works of Charles Dickens* (Lincoln, Nebraska, 1917). Joseph Ewen discusses in some detail the use of personal names as means of characterization in modern fiction, giving examples – primarily from Hebrew literature – of various techniques and particular purposes behind the choice of names. On "meaningful names" in Russian literature see J. B. Rudnyckyj, "Function of Proper Names" *Stil- und Formprobleme in der Literatur* (Vorträge des VII. Kongresses der Internationalen Vereinigung für moderne Sprachen und Literaturen in Heidelberg, Heidelberg, 1959), pp. 378–83. Cf. also David Lodge, "Names," in his book *The Art of Fiction* (London, 1992), pp. 35–40.

[3] The names Lust, Envy, Justice, etc., in medieval morality plays said all that could be said for "characterization."

[4] Voltaire's *Candide* is a famous example. An outstanding example from medieval Arabic literature is *Hayy ibn Yaqzan* ("Alive, son of Wakeful"). *Hayy ibn Yaqzan* is in fact the name of two different philosophical allegories, one by Ibn Sina (Avicenna, d. 1037) and another, better known, by Ibn Tufayl (d. 1185).

[5] That characters' names in such works of fiction are mere linguistic signs which could be easily dropped or exchanged becomes apparent when we consider how novels are read in translation. Readers of translated novels containing unfamiliar names which they find hard to pronounce tend to forget or disregard these names and, instead, they identify the characters

to be more than just a suitable linguistic sign for the personage (and this, as has already been noted, is not uncommon), we need to ask what special meaning the author intends by it. It is surprising that this significant feature of Mahfuz's narrative art has not so far been given the critical attention it deserves. Although various scholars have suggested interpretations for names in Mahfuz's allegorical works, there has been very little treatment of the phenomenon as it occurs in his realistic novels.[6]

'Abd al-Muhsin Taha Badr, who, in his study of Mahfuz, did note the writer's tendency to use "meaningful" names in his realistic novels, considered this a regrettable flaw.[7] The interpretations suggested by Badr for some of these names are trivial and philologically inadequate; it is on the basis of this faulty understanding that he dismisses Mahfuz's careful choice of meaningful names as nothing more than a sign of artistic immaturity.[8]

In this section of the book I attempt to explore the special significance of personal names in the realistic works of Najib Mahfuz. I deal here with the names of characters in Mahfuz's short stories and novels set in contemporary Egypt; I exclude his historical novels and those of his stories which have an obvious philosophical and allegorical nature. The reason for the exclusion of the historical novels is evident: in these novels the names of the main characters (actual names of ancient Egyptian kings and queens) were not chosen by Mahfuz, but dictated to him by the historical subject matter underlying these works. The reason for excluding his allegorical works is

---

by means of other more essential attributes: "the mother," the father," "the son," "the daughter," "the thief," "the policeman," etc.

[6] For treatment of Mahfuz's use of names in his allegorical works, see Tarabishi, *Allah fi riḥlat Najib Maḥfuz al-ramziyya* (Beirut, 1980), passim, and especially pp. 73 n., 77 n.; Raja' 'Id, *Qira'a fi adab Najib Mahfuz: Ru'ya naqdiyya* (Alexandria, 1989), p. 215, and Sasson Somekh, *The Changing Rhythm: A Study of Najib Mahfuz's Novels* (Leiden, 1973), p. 141.

[7] 'Abd al-Muhsin Taha Badr, *Najib Mahfuz: Al-Ru'ya wa'l-adāh* (Cairo, 1984), pp. 248–49, 259–60, 326.

[8] See below, pp. 189–90. Mohamed Mahmoud, on the other hand, in his study of *al-Liss wa'l-kilab*, calls attention to the symbolic meaning of the names in this novel, and offers adequate interpretations. See "The Unchanging Hero in a Changing World: Najib Mahfuz's *al-Liss wa'l-kilab (The Thief and the Dogs)*," in Trevor Le Gassick (ed.), *Critical Perspectives on Naguib Mahfouz* (Washington, 1991), p. 126.

different but, in the light of what has been said above, equally obvious: the meaning of names in allegories is inseparable from the
meaning of each allegory as a whole, hence, one cannot speak of a special meaning of the personal names in it.

Before proceeding to interpret the personal names in the works of
Najib Mahfuz, we should briefly review the conventions which gov-
ern the naming of characters in modern fiction and which, needless
to say, reflect cultural attitudes. The essential fact here is the preva-
lence in our culture of the assumption that there is no special analogy
between a person and his name. Hence, those modern authors who
imbue the names of their characters with a special meaning also attempt to make their intentions in the choice of names covert, so that
it should not appear to deviate from the prevalent cultural attitude.[9]

In life we do not expect a person's name to disclose anything
about that person's moral and physical qualities, let alone about his
past or future; a John or a Jane can be handsome or ugly, wise or stupid, fortunate or ill-fated. Of course, a name is usually distinctively
male or female; it is also taken for granted that a personal name may
implicitly indicate the linguistic, ethnic and religious affiliation of its
bearer. In modern realistic literature, as in modern life, this is, more
or less, what a personal name may be assumed to convey. Hence, the
standard literary convention in modern realistic fiction with regard
to the names of characters is that the name should "fit" the character
in terms of gender and the name's intrinsic implicit social content,
but it should not have, or rather, it should not appear to have, any
particular significance otherwise. The name should look as though it
has been picked at random from the available stock of suitable
names, that is, names which are standard in that character's social
setting.

The nature and the influence of the modern convention concerning names in fiction are well illustrated in the following passages
quoted from Elizabeth Hope Gordon's study on the naming of characters in the works of Charles Dickens (1917). Referring to "the

---

[9] The "obsessive concern" of many novelists with the choice of names (*le souci quasi
maniaque*) to which Hamon refers may be the result of precisely this – the desire to choose
a name which will be analogous to the character in a special way and, at the same time, to
keep this intention covert.

names of characters in the works of the majority of nineteenth- and twentieth-century novelists," Gordon writes:

> The growing tendency toward the commonplace in realism has necessitated the selection of neutral names or names taken outright from actual persons.... [With] the contemporary novelists, there is usually nothing in a name to denote an intimate correspondence between it and the character to which it belongs.[10]

She emphasizes the difference between the modern and pre-modern approaches to the naming of characters:

> Such names as appear in the morality plays and in the early Elizabethan drama have fallen into disrepute as a feature of literature. It was doubtless a great convenience in the ante-program days for the audience to be able to conjure from the name of a character whether to applaud him as a hero or to execrate him as a villain. The early novelists made use, with more or less freedom, of this custom of descriptive nomenclature.... Modern literature is marked by a nearly complete disappearance of the names that give a clue to the occupation or nature of the character to which they pertain....[11]

Gordon notes:

> Except for Trollope's individualized portraits, many of them catalogued with descriptive names, the last noteworthy appearance in fiction of names that pertinently distinguish the characters is in the works of Charles Dickens, especially in his early books.

We see that although Gordon was evidently enthralled by Dickens's ingenuity in the choice of his characters' names, she believed that his approach to the naming of characters was somehow a residue of the past and that it did not quite conform to the conventions of "realism" and "the modern novel." But, in fact, this does not seem to be the case.

---

[10] Elizabeth H. Gordon, *The Naming of Characters*, p. 3.
[11] Ibid., p. 4.

There would appear to be a gap between the literary convention regarding the names of characters in the modern novel and the actual practice of many, if not most modern novelists. These writers quite often choose for their characters names which they intend to be somehow "meaningful," besides being realistically suitable. In doing this they neither defy the realistic convention nor disregard it; rather, they operate behind it, using it as a screen: the names they give their characters may appear to be chosen at random, but in fact they are not. The realistic convention with regard to names has thus enhanced the significance of those names of fictitious characters which a modern novelist might have chosen with a special meaning in mind. The realistic convention forms, as it were, a protective shell for the special inner meaning; the shell, however, is not hermetically sealed, and its very existence turns its contents into "privileged information."

CHAPTER 11

A Note on Egyptian Personal Names

Some basic information on the common characteristics of Egyptian personal names will be useful for the discussion of names in Mahfuz's novels.

Egyptian names are, of course, Arabic names. For Egyptian Muslims (the overwhelming majority of Egypt's population), Islamic tradition is a major influence on the choice of personal names.[1] Most Egyptians do not have a family name, and a man is usually called by his own personal name followed by his father's name. Thus, "Ahmad Amin" would signify "Ahmad the son of Amin." The same procedure is followed with regard to women: "Zaynab Amin" denotes "Zaynab, daughter of Amin." (On official papers or in the telephone directory, a tripartite name would be used, i.e., the person's name followed by his father's name followed by the grandfather's name, e.g., in the name Ahmad Amin 'Abdallah, 'Abdallah would be the name of the grandfather.) Occasionally, however, one does find a family name attached to the name, most commonly in the form of *nisba*, a relative adjective indicating a connection to a place, a tribe, or any other general concept, e.g., al-Manfaluti (from a town called Manfalut), al-Asyuti (from Asyut).[2] Another common type of family name de-

---

[1] On the stucture of Islamic names see Annemarie Schimmel, *Islamic Names* (Edinburgh, 1989), pp. 1–13.

[2] On *nisba* see ibid., pp. 10–13. It should be noted that some personal names look like *nisba* names although they are not: Zayni, Fahmi, Rushdi, Qadri are not real *nisbas*, but abbreviated forms contracted respectively from Zayn al-Din ("the beauty of religion"), Fahm al-Din ("the understanding of religion"), Rushd al-Din ("the guidance of religion"),

rives from professions (on the pattern of *fa'āl*), e.g., Najjār (carpenter), Ṣabbāgh (dyer). Both these types of name are normally preceded by the definite article (*al-*).

There is in Arab tradition a form of appellation known as *kunya* which consists of the word *abu* ("father") followed by the name of that person's eldest son, thus: Abu Ahmad is "the father of Ahmad." In some parts of the Arab world, it is customary to address a man by his *kunya* instead of by his personal name; this form is not normally used in Egypt as a substitute for the first name. Its feminine equivalent (Umm Ahmad, "the mother of Ahmad") is, however, prevalent in traditional circles. In such company it would be highly impolite to address an adult woman by her own first name.

While the stock of personal names is very large indeed, some types of name are especially preferred in Muslim society. The name "Muhammad" is clearly the most popular. "Ahmad" and "Mahmud," which derive from the same root and are traditionally believed to be variants of "Muhammad," are also popular. "'Abd Allah" ("servant of God") is only one of many names constructed on the pattern: *'abd* ("servant") followed by any one of the many titles of God, e.g., 'Abd al-Hakim ("servant of the Wise One"), 'Abd al-Rahman ("servant of the Merciful One"). According to Islamic tradition, God has ninety-nine names known as *al-asmā' al-ḥusnā* ("the most beautiful names"),[3] and any one of them can be used in this manner. Predictably, names constructed on this pattern are very popular among Muslims. The dictum ascribed to the Prophet: "The best names are those derived from the root *ḥ-m-d* or constructed with the word *'abd*" (*khayr al-asma' ma ḥummida wa 'ubbida*) reflects a traditional Muslim preference which is still current.

The list of popular, specifically Islamic names also includes the names of the Prophet's son-in-law and grandsons, 'Ali, Hasan and Husayn, and those of his companions, 'Umar and 'Uthman. For Muslim women, the names of his daughter, granddaughter and

---

Qadar Allah ("God's decree") or Qadr Allah ("God's power"). Some of these names appear also in the feminine as women's names (e.g., Qadriyya). On these pseudo-*nisba* names, see Schimmel, p. 63.

[3] On Allah's "most beautiful names" see *EI*[2], s.v. "al-Asmā' al-Ḥusnā."

favorite wives – Fatima, Zaynab, 'A'isha and Khadija – are very popular choices. The names of Biblical figures mentioned in the Qur'an (such as Ibrahim, Musa, Yusuf, etc.) are very common in Egypt; since they are not distinctively Islamic, they are used by Copts (Egypt's indigenous Christians) as well as by Muslims. Names such as Butrus (Peter) or Murqus (Marcus), which are clearly Christian, distinguish their bearers as Copts. There is also a host of Arabic adjectives and nouns which are used as personal names: Jamīl ("beautiful"), Amīn ("trustworthy"), Najīb ("noble," "excellent"),[4] 'Ādil ("just"), Maḥfūẓ ("protected [by God]"), Fu'ād ("heart"), etc. Such names are common among Muslims and Copts alike.

---

[4] In the Egyptian colloquial usage, *najib* also has the meaning of "smart," "bright."

CHAPTER 12

Two Early Short Stories

In the story "*Yaqzat al-mumya'*" ("The Mummy's Awakening," 1939),[1] we find that Mahfuz uses the names of the main figures as "a means of characterization by analogy." The story relates a miraculous event witnessed by a certain Professor Dorian, a French Egyptologist working in Egypt. Professor Dorian is invited to the estate of a well-known Egyptian personality, Mahmud Pasha al-Arna'uti, a very rich man with considerable influence in government circles, known not only for his wealth, but also for his great love of French art and the French language. He owns a large collection of French art which he has promised to bequeath to the French people after his death.

When Dorian and other French guests gather in the palace of al-Arna'uti, their host informs them he has agreed to the request of a certain local saint, Shaykh Jadallah, to search for hidden treasure in the grounds of the estate. Al-Arna'uti does not really believe that the shaykh has any secret knowledge, but gives his consent to the search and to digging for the treasure as a kind of joke, thinking to entertain his guests. Much to the surprise of all those assembled, the workers find an ancient Egyptian tomb, and the whole group goes to see what it contains. The tomb turns out to be that of Hur, a great military leader from the Pharaonic era. Hur's sarcophagus opens miraculously, and the mummy of Hur rises as a living person. In the ancient

[1] This story, originally published in *al-Riwaya*, Cairo, April 1939, is included in the collection *Hams al-junun*.

Egyptian language (which Professor Dorian, of course, understands, but the others, including al-Arna'uti, do not), Hur scolds and rebukes the pasha for robbing and oppressing his children, the native Egyptians. Hur speaks to the pasha in anger, believing him to be a former slave of his, Shanaq by name, whom he brought as a captive from the north – an assumption attested to by Arna'uti's fair complexion. Enraged, Hur asks how a former slave could oppress the free people of Egypt. The pasha, not understanding a word of what the revived mummy says, drops dead from fear. Dorian, like everybody present there, is completely astounded, but, as he says, he has to believe what he sees with his own eyes: "Even Descartes himself, had he been in my place, would not have laughed at his senses."

The names of the main characters are significant; they underline and specify the allegorical meaning of the story. The pasha's name is Mahmud Pasha al-Arna'uti. *Mahmud* ("Praiseworthy") is of course a standard name, but in this case it clearly has an ironic meaning. The pasha is praised lavishly by his friends, including the French professor, Dorian, but the qualities for which they praise him – his great love and dedication to France and French culture at the expense of Egypt – are nothing but cause for contempt and indignation in the eyes of Mahfuz and his Egyptian readers of the 1930s, imbued as they are with Egyptian nationalism. *Al-Arna'ūṭī* means "the Albanian" and is a thinly disguised allusion to the Albanian origin of the royal Egyptian family at the time – the family of Muhammad 'Ali. The pasha's name highlights the social and political significance of the story, as though the author wanted to make sure that the political and social intention would not be missed.

The name of the professor, who narrates the story as a witness, is Dorian. In Arabic spelling this can read *Darian*[2] which may be construed as an adjective derived from the Arabic root *darā*, "to know." Dorian/Darian is the person who knows things: he knows Egyptian history and the ancient Egyptian language, but his knowledge does not enable him to understand the miraculous event.

The saintly shaykh's name, *Jādallāh*, means "God's gift" or "God's munificence." It reflects the shaykh's own belief and that of his fol-

[2] With one exception, the name is spelled throughout the story without the letter *waw*.

lowers that man's accomplishments are actually nothing more than
the result of God's munificence. The French Egyptologist Dorian refers to him as *al-shaykh al-mu'min* (i.e., one who believes in God)
and describes him as "having supernatural powers and ... being
guided toward his goal by his divine knowledge." It is important to
note the contrast between the professor and the shaykh. The shaykh
is *al-mu'min* – a man of faith and one guided by his divine knowledge
(Arabic: *'ilmuhu al-ilahiyy*). He goes on with the digging despite the
jokes of the pasha and his friends. Professor Dorian notes: "neither
of us [the pasha or myself] knew what Fate had in store for him"
(*Hams al-junun*, p. 90). The verb he uses to signify his lack of knowledge, *la-yadri*, has the same root as his own name.

The name of the Pharaonic commander whose tomb they discover
is Hur. The choice of this name is highly significant: in Egyptian mythology, Hur (Horus) is the name of the deity king of Egypt, son of
Osiris and Isis.[3] The name Hur highlights the allegorical function of
this figure – to represent the idea of indigenous Egyptian nationalism
rising against the Turko-Albanian oppressors.

Shanaq – the name of Hur's slave who, in Hur's eyes, is none other
than the pasha Mahmud al-Arna'uti – evokes a number of pejorative
meanings. *Shanaqa al-ba'ir* means "to curb a camal [by means of a
nose-rein]." The adjective *shaniq* (when applied to a man) means
"cautious" or "fearful." *Shaniq* means "one whose origin is suspect." *Shinniq* is "a man evil in disposition" or "a self-conceited
young man."[4]

In "*al-Ju'*" ("Hunger"),[5] another story from Mahfuz's early period, a
rich young man returns late at night from an evening of drinking
and gambling during which he has lost a large sum of money. His

---

[3] In the most famous myth associated with his name, Hur succeeds Osiris when the latter
is murdered and avenges him by defeating the murderer. Hur, who is usually portrayed as a
hawk or as hawk-headed, is thus identified with the living king, and Osiris with the dead
king. See Anthony S. Mercantante, *Who's Who in Egyptian Mythology* (New York, 1979),
s.v. "Horus."

[4] See, Lane, *Lexicon of the Arabic Language*, s.v. "*sh-n-q*."

[5] This story is included in Mahfuz's first published collection of short stories, *Hams al-
junun* (1948). The date of its original publication is not known, but it was probably written
in the late 1930s.

gambling losses apparently do not bother him, but he feels that he needs a walk to overcome the effect of the alcohol that he has absorbed. On his way he encounters a poor man who is about to throw himself from the bridge into the Nile. He grabs him and prevents him from committing suicide; as he talks to him he learns that this man is desperate because he is poor and cannot support his hungry wife and children. He has been dismissed from his job in a factory, after losing his arm in a work accident. His sorrows became unbearable when he found out that the owner of a bakery, who in the past had tried to seduce his wife, was again trying to seduce her by sending bread to his home. In despair and anger, he tries to take his life. Upon inquiry, the young man learns from the poor man that the owner of the factory from which he was unjustly dismissed after the accident is none other than his own father. Feeling pity for the poor man, the young man gives him a note and instructs him to go back to the factory where suitable work will be found for him so that he can resume an honorable life. The story ends with the rich young man asking himself: "Who knows how many suffering families like that of Ibrahim Hanafi could be made happy by the amounts that I lose every night at the club?"

The names of the characters in the story are interesting. The rich young man is Muhammad 'Abd al-Qawiyy, that is, Muhammad son of 'Abd al-Qawiyy. Muhammad is the name of the Prophet and 'Abd al-Qawiyy is a name constructed from a combination of the word *'abd* ("slave," "servant") and one of the adjectives signifying God (*al-asma' al-husna*). 'Abd al-Qawiyy, his father's name, means "the servant of the powerful," and is therefore analogous to the power and authority his father possesses. His own name, Muhammad, has an ironic intention here, because the young man, we are told, violates the Islamic prohibitions against drinking and gambling.

The name of the poor man who is about to kill himself is Ibrahim Hanafi and that of the rich young man's father is 'Abd al-Qawiyy Shakir. Ibrahim Hanafi, the name of the poor worker, comprises two elements. The surname, *Hanafi*, is derived from the same root as *hanif*, a name by which the prophet Ibrahim is designated a number of times in the Qur'an (3:67, 30:30 and 16:120). In giving the family name Hanafi to the poor invalid Ibrahim, Mahfuz clearly invites

comparison between this person and the Qur'anic Ibrahim al-Hanif.[6]
In the Qur'an, Ibrahim (the Biblical Abraham) is associated with the
quality of thankfulness and gratitude to God. He is described as
shakir, grateful to God for his kindness (Qur'an 16:120–21 and
14:37). The name Shakir ("grateful") is given as a second name to
the owner of the factory, the father of the rich young man, whose
name is 'Abd al-Qawiyy Shakir. We learn, though, from the poor
worker, Ibrahim, that the rich owner of the factory did not live up to
his name. The poor man says: "I used to be much more persevering
than the bey, the owner of the large factory, because I used to be content and satisfied, whereas he would *complain and show discontent*
with his [supposedly] hard circumstances and find all sorts of excuses
to reduce the livelihood of some and to treat others in a miserly way.
I never lived in comfort or wealth, but my life was full of hope" (my
emphasis).

We see here that the poor man, Ibrahim Hanafi, like his Qur'anic
namesake, was content with and grateful for what he had. However,
unlike the Qur'anic Ibrahim whom God protected and saved (Qur'an
21:71), poor Ibrahim Hanafi does not seem to have enjoyed God's
protection. By contrast, the rich man, whose very name is Shakir
("grateful"), did not show gratitude to God for his wealth. All three
characters have names which are ironically contradicted by their
behavior. The young man, Muhammad 'Abd al-Qawiyy, though
bearing the name of the prophet of Islam, flouts all Islamic prohibitions against wine and gambling. His father is 'Abd al-Qawiyy
Shakir, whose second name means "grateful," but who is ungrateful.
Lastly, the poor man who bears the name of Ibrahim, the grateful
servant of God whom God protected, is, indeed, grateful, but does
not seem to have enjoyed God's grace.

Even the name of the relatively insignificant figure in the story was
not chosen at random. The baker, who is mentioned as the man who
had in the past tried to seduce Ibrahim's wife and who renews his efforts at seduction, is Sulayman. "Sulayman" occurs in a number of

---

[6] Grammatically, the *nisba* form derived from *ḥanif* is *ḥanifi* not *ḥanafi* (which is derived
from *ḥanifa*), but since *ḥanafi* is a fairly common name whereas *ḥanifi* is not, it is not
surprising that the author chose the form Ḥanafi (rather than Ḥanifi) so as to give the name
a familiar sound.

Najib Mahfuz's stories as the name of a man who sexually exploits women. The reason for this choice would seem to originate in the legends adduced by the Qur'an exegetes in relation to the phrase "We tempted Sulayman" (Qur'an 38:34). According to one of these legends, Sulayman (the Biblical Solomon) once said that he was planning to have seventy women in one night. I believe that Mahfuz had this legendary image of Solomon in mind when he chose the name Sulayman for characters associated with sexual exploitation.[7]

---

[7] Cf. the character of Sulayman Pasha Sulayman in *al-Qay'* (above, pp. 62–63); see also below, pp. 180–81, 208–9.

CHAPTER 13

Khan al-Khalili

Khan al-Khalili (1945) is the first of Mahfuz's novels to be set in contemporary Egypt. It tells the story of a family – father, mother and son – who, in September, 1941, move from their apartment in the Sakakini quarter of Cairo to an apartment in the Khan al-Khalili quarter, for fear of the German air raids. They believe that Khan al-Khalili, which is in the vicinity of the revered al-Husayn mosque, will be safe, since the Germans, who supposedly want to win Muslim support against the British, would be reluctant to bomb a place so sacred to Muslims.

The son, Ahmad 'Akif, a bachelor nearing forty, is a low-ranking official in the government service and the family's main financial support, the father having retired from work some twenty years before. Ahmad falls in love with Nawal, the neighbors' sixteen-year-old daughter, and cultivates hopes of marrying her. His much younger brother, Rushdi, a bank clerk in Asyut in Upper Egypt, returns home for a holiday. He brings good news: he is being transferred to the bank's central offices in Cairo and will remain in the family's new home. He, too, falls in love with the same girl. A young man in his twenties, Rushdi is dashing and handsome, and it is he who wins the heart of Nawal. Rushdi, who does not know of his brother Ahmad's love for the girl, tells Ahmad of his love for her, and the latter, who is very devoted to his younger brother, "gives up" his love for his brother's sake. Ahmad, who has not only financed Rushdi's education, but has also cared for him like a father, is torn between his love for Rushdi and his jealousy of his younger brother's capacity to indulge in pleasure – and especially of his success with women. Rushdi has great personal charm and he succeeds in befriending Nawal's father to the extent that the latter invites him to his home and introduces him to his wife and daughter, a sign of unusually intimate friendship and trust in that conservative milieu. He also asks him to give private lessons to his daughter and younger son. Although Rushdi and Nawal are not formally engaged, both families happily consider them a couple.

There is, however, no happy ending. The younger brother is a pleasure-seeker who spends his nights drinking and gambling. He contracts tuberculosis, but because of his unrestrained character he pays no heed to the doctor's advice and continues his reckless way of life. His condition deteriorates and he has to go to a sanatorium for treatment. When Nawal's parents learn of his serious illness, they order their daughter to stop seeing him. Rushdi dies. A few months later, the family decides to leave Khan al-Khalili. Ahmad 'Akif rents another apartment in the house of one of his colleagues at work; at the end of the story we find him nurturing a vague hope that in this new home he may find the right match for himself, in the person of his colleague's widowed sister.

The name of the main character, Ahmad 'Akif, is composed of both the name of the person himself, Ahmad, and the name of the father, 'Akif. The name of the father is 'Akif Ahmad. The word 'ākif is the active participle from the verb 'akafa, suggesting behavior characteristic of both the father (a minor figure in the novel) and the hero. The Arabic verb 'akafa 'ala signifies usually "to apply oneself [to reading or prayer]," "to devote one's time [to one matter] exclusively while ignoring and avoiding other subjects." The idiom 'akafa fi means "to seclude oneself within [a place]."

The father of the hero, 'Akif Effendi Ahmad, who is about sixty years old, was dismissed from his post as a government official and forced into retirement some twenty years before the novel opens. The initial reason for his suspension was a false accusation of corruption, but what finally led to his dismissal – even after his innocence had come to light – was his insolence towards the administrative investigators who found that he had been negligent in carrying out his responsibilities at work. After his forced retirement he became very reclusive, staying at home, devoting all his time to prayer and reading the Qur'an (see pp. 24–25). In describing the behavior of the father, 'Akif Effendi, the author uses a number of expressions which are close in meaning to or which partially overlap the verb *'akafa fi*. Thus, for example, the mother tells her son, in reference to the father (p. 4): "Your father has secluded himself in his room as he usually does." The author also writes of him (pp. 24–25): "He imposed upon himself strict seclusion following his retirement while still in his physical prime, and appeared to devote his life to worship and Qur'an recitation. He would leave the house only rarely, to take a walk by himself or to visit the tombs of saints." The author adds: "He removed himself from men and from the world and regarded worship as refuge and rest" (p. 25).

As the eldest son, Ahmad 'Akif was compelled to assume responsibility for supporting the family and paying the tuition and other expenses incurred by his young brother Rushdi's studies. The author says of him that he has inherited from his father his responsibility (as the family provider) and his disease (p. 26). What is this disease? One can only speculate, because the author does not mention anywhere in the book that the father suffered from physical illness. But he does mention certain personality traits that caused him a great deal of damage: arrogance on the one hand and incompetence on the other (see p. 14 and p. 25). The father is not capable of realizing that he has faults and that his behavior is flawed, and tends to put all the blame on "the injustice of the world." These same qualities appear in the son, Ahmad 'Akif. Ahmad 'Akif, too, is a low-ranking government official, in the Ministry of Public Works. He regards himself as a victim of external circumstances beyond his control. He had wanted to study law, hoping to advance and reach a high position like Sa'd Zaghlul, the famous Egyptian leader (p. 14). When he had to break off his studies to provide for the family (after his father had been dismissed) "he became convinced, deep in his heart, that he was an oppressed martyr and a hidden genius, the wronged victim of blind Fate." His complaint about blind, unjust Fate becomes a kind of "sickly hallucination." This, then, is the illness or the disease which he inherited from his father.

While the father devoted himself to prayer and Qur'an reading, the son devoted all his spare time to secular reading. First he tried to prepare externally for the law school examination, but after failing he decided to start reading in order to broaden his general knowledge, not in an attempt to acquire any diploma, because he was afraid of another failure. However, he claims to others that the reason for this was that he does not attach any importance to diplomas and examinations (p. 16). His reading is unsystematic and casual (p. 20): "He used to read without thinking." "His mind became a utensil containing a mixture of all sorts of information instead of being a thinking head" (p. 20). For a while he read books on magic, hoping to acquire mysterious forces through which he could gain wisdom and power (p. 21). Ahmad 'Akif is described as a man who "gave himself up to persistent mental and emotional seclusion" (p. 19). His temporary addiction to books on magic is described by the idiom *wa 'akafa 'aleyha* ("he diligently applied himself to them," p. 21), that is, a repetition of the verb *'akafa*. Ahmad 'Akif's mother "felt sorry whenever she saw her husband immersed in reading the Qur'an and her eldest son secluded near his desk" (p. 92).[1]

Ahmad 'Akif's skewed psychological make-up is apparent in his attitudes towards marriage, sex and the status of women, which Mahfuz describes in the course of the story. Because of his own failure to find a suitable marriage partner, Ahmad entertains a very low view of women, regarding them as lustful creatures who maintain modest manners only as a mask. "He persuaded himself that the real woman is the whore ... because she has removed from her face the mask of hypocrisy" (p. 39). It is clear that Mahfuz considers these views to be completely perverted, a symptom of the immature and unbalanced personality of Ahmad, whom he describes as "a child at the age of forty" (p. 35).

Another character, a young man called Ahmad Rashid, is presented in juxtaposition to the hero. Ahmad 'Akif meets Ahmad Rashid in the local café and establishes a sort of friendship with him – a relationship of conversation and debates – because this young man,

---

[1] Here again the active participle *'ākif* occurs; see also the expression *khala ila nafsihi fi hujratihi* ("secluding himself in his room") on p. 92 and again on p. 100.

unlike the others who frequent the café, is educated, and Ahmad 'Akif regards him as worthy of his company. The meeting between the two is described as follows: "Afterwards he turned his eyes to Ahmad Rashid with special interest. This was a man in his full strength. His face was round, his head large. He wore dark glasses. This young man aroused his interest because he was a lawyer, that is to say, an educated person. The practice of law was the profession which he had desired when he was still at the age of hopes and aspirations. But he had failed to achieve it, even though he had never admitted this failure and continued to feel rancor toward every lawyer, just as he felt rancor toward every writer and intellectual, because he felt toward them as a man feels toward someone who has married his sweetheart" (pp. 51–52). Ahmad 'Akif's jealousy of Ahmad Rashid intensifies when he learns that his "rival" serves as private teacher to Nawal, his secret love.

The contrast between these two men is conspicuous. Ahmad 'Akif is a frustrated man, his education is not organized or systematic, and his thoughts and ideas are mixed and confused, whereas Ahmad Rashid is described as a man with progressive social views who believes in socialism and science, and attempts to examine logically every subject he deals with. Ahmad Rashid's views on education for girls are the antithesis of Ahmad 'Akif's conservative opinions; he clearly considers girls to be equal to boys in their capacity for study and in their right to education. His name, Rashid (that is, "intelligent," "one who chooses the right path," "one who exercises *rushd*, i.e., reason, sensible conduct"), clearly indicates that Mahfuz prefers the personality and ideas of Ahmad Rashid over those of Ahmad 'Akif. During a debate between the two on attitudes to the past, to cultural traditions, to religion and science, Ahmad Rashid maintains a very radical approach which totally negates the legacy of the past and religion itself. He speaks mockingly about the use which Ahmad 'Akif makes of quotations from classical Arabic poetry in order to back up his arguments (see pp. 58–59).

Although Mahfuz would seem to prefer Ahmad Rashid's progressive views to the confused and reactionary ideas expressed by Ahmad 'Akif, he is critical of the former's one-sidedness. Mahfuz expresses his criticism indirectly, in his description of Ahmad Rashid as blind in one eye. This detail may be understood metaphorically: the person who views all phenomena exclusively with the eye of reason (p. 53) is in fact partly blind.[2]

Mahfuz has chosen to give both protagonists – Ahmad 'Akif and Ahmad Rashid – an identical first name, thereby making the second name of each even more salient, and highlighting the difference between the two. Ahmad is a very common Muslim name and thus can be used for two protagonists in one novel without creating the impression of lack of verisimilitude.[3] It is, of course, a "good" name; Ahmad is derived from the root *ḥ-m-d*, the same root from which the name Muhammad is derived, and Ahmad itself is traditionally regarded as one of the names of the Prophet Muhammad. It should be noted that Ahmad is a common name and is often used by Mahfuz as a neutral name which does not, in itself, indicate any special quality or attitute. The adjective *aḥmad* poses an interesting problem of morphological ambiguity: it may be understood as a comparative or superlative adjective derived either from *ḥāmid* "giving praise," "thankful [to Allah]" or from *ḥamīd* "praiseworthy," "laudable." Typically, Najib Mahfuz chooses this inherently ambiguous name for characters who are neither wholly positive nor wholly negative, and who can be therefore alternately praiseworthy and blameworthy. Thus grammatical ambiguity is used here as a metaphor for moral and psychological ambiguity.[4]

Ahmad 'Akif's younger brother, Rushdi, is a debauched young man who spends his nights playing cards and drinking heavily. His name, Rushdi 'Akif, belies his character and behavior. Whereas in the case of the two former protagonists, Ahmad 'Akif and Ahmad Rashid, the parallelism between the meaning of the name and the person bearing it is a parallelism of analogy, in the case of Rushdi 'Akif it is a parallelism of contrast, and so the effect is one of irony. The younger brother is not at all reclusive, nor does he apply himself

---

[2] See *Khan al-Khalili*, pp. 63, 98 and 99. Cf. Mahfuz's short story "*Qaws quzah*" ("Rainbow") in the collection *Bayt sayyi' al-sum'a* (1965), in which the parents of the young hero, who insist on viewing everything rationally, are unable to understand their adolescent son.

[3] See above, p. 166.

[4] Cf. the function of the name Ahmad in the novel *al-Qahira al-jadida*, below, p. 187.

to reading, praying and Qur'an recitation (as suggested by the name 'Akif). He spends his nights outside the house and does not behave at all reasonably (he does not behave with *rushd*), and he is completely unrestrained. His gambling companions admiringly name him "the Lionhearted" (*qalb al-asad*) for his daring in gambling, and he feels very proud of this epithet. Mahfuz, however, has no respect for his foolhardiness. Rushdi himself tells his brother: "You are a wise man, brother, whereas I am a crazy young man and this [i.e., having no restraints] is the philosophy of madmen" (p. 117).

As I have already mentioned, Mahfuz often adds the title "devil" or "diabolic" to the term madness (*junun*), almost to the point of causing the two, madness and the devil, to be inextricably combined.[5] And, in fact, in this story the father, 'Akif Effendi, says to his son Rushdi, "you are undoubtedly like the devils" (p. 172). So the ironic intention of the name Rushdi 'Akif is disclosed not only indirectly, in the description of his reckless and irrational behavior, but also directly, by labelling him "madman" and "devil" – terms which express the very opposite of reason, sobriety and proper conduct.

The girl who is the object of the love of the two 'Akif brothers is Nawāl, meaning "gift" or "favor." Her name is derived from the verb *nāla*, meaning "to give," and is closely related to the verb *nāla* meaning "to gain," "to receive," or "to attain."[6] But neither of the two brothers gains Nawal.

One very minor character (one of those whom Ahmad 'Akif meets in the local café) deserves to be mentioned because of the special meaning of his name – Sulayman 'Itta. He is dwarfish and hunchbacked with an ape-like face; because of his ugly looks he is nicknamed "the monkey" (p. 51). More than fifty years old, he is about to marry a young and beautiful girl, who reportedly has agreed to marry him because she expects, upon his death, to inherit his handsome retirement pension (he is an inspector of elementary schools). This matching of contrasts – the woman's youth and beauty, the man's advanced age and ugliness – occasions the indignant comment of the progressive-minded Ahmad Rashid: "Their

---

[5] See above, pp. 101–3, 108.
[6] *nāla, yanūlu*: "to give"; *nāla, yanālu*, "to gain," "to receive."

coming together will not be a marriage but a double crime – it is thievery on one side and rape on the other" (p. 104). Sulayman's surname 'Itta ("moth worm"), suggests decrepitude and decay; it is clearly intended as an analogous means of characterization.[7] The name Sulayman links him to a series of characters in Mahfuz's stories who bear this name, all of whom share a common trait: they sexually exploit women.[8]

The mother of the hero is Sitt Dawlat. In contrast to the lethargic father, she is a vivacious and energetic person, and is the real head of the family. The name Dawlat (which the author spells in the Turkish fashion), meaning dynasty, government or state (Arabic: *dawla*), alludes to her dominant role in the family.[9] At fifty-five she manages to keep up her appearance, and is displeased with her older son's negligence about his clothes. She scolds him, "You're turning your mother into an old woman and damaging her good reputation. There's a laundry over there. So why should your suit be wrinkled and sagging? And there's the barber shop. So why should your chin be stubbly? The world is full of happy events: why do you shut yourself up among yellowing books? Why did you let your head go bald on top and grey on the sides? You're really making an old woman of me!" Ahmad smiles and teases her by answering, "Admit it: I am forty, aren't I?" This blunt statement of the frightful truth shocks her and she rebukes him: "Shut that big mouth of yours! Has the world ever seen a son who claims to be the same age as his mother!" She has suffered sorrows in her life – her husband's dismissal, the death of a child in infancy many years before – but she manages to keep up her good spirits. "Praise be to God! The [natural] cheerfulness of Sitt Dawlat, Ahmad's mother, covered up her sorrow just as henna covered up her grey hairs" (pp. 26–27).

---

[7] 'Itta is the colloquial form of 'uththa.

[8] Cf. above, pp. 172–73 and below, pp. 208–9.

[9] The Turkish pronounciation is "Devlet"; it is transliterated here according to the standard Egyptian pronounciation.

CHAPTER 14

Al-Qahira al-Jadida

The plot of *al-Qahira al-jadida* ("The New Cairo," 1946) revolves around a young man, Mahjub 'Abd al-Da'im, who attempts to make a career for himself in Cairo. Mahjub, who comes from a relatively poor family, is a fourth-year student at the university. His father is a low-ranking official in some commercial firm and can only meagerly support his son. Mahjub is a cynical and selfish person: he cares only about himself. Moreover, he is rather unattractive, and is frustrated by his inability to establish romantic contacts. His only experience with women has been a passing contact with a low-class prostitute. Mahjub is jealous of his handsome friend, 'Ali Taha, who has won the heart of the beautiful Ihsan, whose father owns a cigarette kiosk near the student hostel and who is in her last year of high school. Ihsan and her family live in an apartment facing the student hostel. (It should be noted that, at the time of the story, relations between young men and women in Egypt were extremely restricted by social convention. They could meet either by prior arrangement with the consent of their families, with marriage in mind, or clandestinely, after establishing contact following the exchange of secret glances.)

A great misfortune befalls Mahjub's family when the father suffers a stroke and is forced to retire on a limited pension. Mahjub must now subsist on an even more meager monthly allowance than before. When he finally graduates, he seeks a position in the government bureaucracy but finds this difficult to achieve without political or family connections. Seeking assistance, he resorts to one Sālim al-

Ikhshidi, a native of his hometown who has made good in the government service. This Salim used to be among the student leaders who protested against the oppressive rule of the pro-Palace government, but he has abandoned his former democratic nationalist ideals for a good position in the government bureaucracy. Salim does not help Mahjub find work in the government service, but he does arrange for him to become a free-lance reporter for a magazine covering social affairs and entertainment. This can bring in only a very limited income but is better than nothing. It also gives the author the opportunity to describe an aspect of the social life of Egypt's elite. As the "reporter" Mahjub covers a charity ball organized by a rich lady of the Turko-Egyptian aristocracy, the author shows us the vanity of Cairo's elite and their superficial aping of French culture.

Unexpectedly, Salim offers Mahjub a job as private secretary to a certain Qasim Bey, director general of a ministry. Salim informs the overjoyed Mahjub that there is, however, a condition which he must fulfill: he must marry Qasim Bey's young mistress, and must consent to continued intimate relations between them. The cynical careerist Mahjub accepts the ignominious offer. He discovers that the woman he has to marry is none other than the beautiful Ihsan, who, under pressure from her parents, has severed her relations with 'Ali Taha to become the mistress of the rich Qasim Bey. In this corrupt manner, Mahjub advances quickly in the bureaucracy, and, in fact, overtakes Salim on the career ladder by becoming chief assistant to Qasim Bey, who has himself become a member of the cabinet. Both he and Ihsan are sucked into a dissolute milieu, and there is clearly no domestic happiness between them.

One day, when Qasim Bey comes to Mahjub's apartment to have his pleasure with Ihsan, two unexpected visitors show up. One is Mahjub's father, who has not heard from his son for a long time. Mahjub has not informed his parents of his marriage, nor has he sent them any financial help. Naturally, the father is very angry, and scolds his son sharply. The second visitor is much more troublesome: she is Qasim Bey's wife. Salim al-Ikhshidi has, apparently, informed Mahjub's father of his son's address and tipped off Qasim Bey's wife, as a cunning way of getting even. As a result of the exposure, there is a public scandal: Qasim Bey has to resign from his cabinet position and Mahjub, his chief assistant, is exiled to a provincial post in Aswan.

In this early realistic novel by Mahfuz, we find that the names of the main characters have meanings that underline their characterization. In the first pages of the novel the author presents the main character and his three friends. All four are university students in their last year of studies and each has a different world view.

The hero, Mahjub 'Abd al-Da'im, is mainly concerned with achieving a position in public service, so that he can enjoy a comfortable life and economic security. He does not believe in any ideal, is not committed to any ideology, and scoffs at both the scientists and the religious scholars (p. 25). He has only one response to any question concerning problems of ethics and society: *tuzz!* ("Garbage!"). Only one thing matters to him, and that is the satisfaction of his desires and lusts; he does not value friendship and would not hesitate to destroy his friends if it suited his purposes. He views the devil as the model of perfection, saying, for example, "Let me take an example from Iblis, the absolute model of perfection, he represents real rebellion, real pride, real ambition and revolution against all principles" (p. 31). Among his friends is Ma'mun Ridwan, an able and hardworking student who is very strict in observing religious ordinances and ethical precepts. He is tall, strong and very handsome, but avoids involvement with women because of his religious principles. For him, Islam is the answer to all the problems of both the individual and society (p. 46). "Islam is the balm (*balsam*) for all our pains," he says. He is a loyal friend and is ready to help his friend Mahjub when the latter asks for a loan (p. 70).

The second friend is 'Ali Taha. 'Ali Taha is also a man of high moral principles but, unlike Ma'mun, he is an atheist and secularist. He regards religion as something of the past; in modern times, he believes, ethics and public order should be based on science. He is a model of true social consciousness and idealism. After losing his religious faith, he was for a while confused and perplexed, but once he became acquainted with the positivist philosophy of Auguste Comte, he found an answer to the problem of ethics. He dreams of the possibility of realizing paradise on earth and considers himself a socialist. "His spirit, having begun its journey in Mecca, arrived in

Moscow" (p. 23). He is neither cynical nor debauched, and therefore befriends the pious Ma'mun Ridwan, despite the contrast between their world views. "He did not conceal the fact that he admired Ma'mun Ridwan for his sincerity and courage." 'Ali Taha, like Ma'mun, helps Mahjub with a loan, when he is pressed for money (p. 91).

The third friend is Ahmad Budayr. In his political and social views, he is close to the ideology of the Wafd party but avoids taking a stance on matters of society and ethics, in the debates in which his friends frequently engage. He explains his reluctance to take a position by saying that he is a journalist. Responding to the question "But what is your opinion?" he answers, "The journalist should listen and not speak, especially in days like these" (p. 8). Ahmad Budayr more or less represents the political positions of Najib Mahfuz, who is known to have been a supporter of the Wafd party.

The similarity between author Najib Mahfuz and Ahmad Budayr, the character in this novel, is not limited to the Wafdist political position, but may be found also in the fact that they both lack a clear world view responsive to the problems of social order and personal morality. The state of lacking a firm opinion is a condition which Najib Mahfuz likens to a state of darkness (*zalam*). In an interview, Mahfuz once said: "You can be sure that if God were to save me from darkness by an opinion [*ra'y*, i.e., opinion, view] of my own, I would not hesitate for one minute to publish it in writing in the most suitable, indeed, the only way, in an article ... but what can I do, I have no new vision."[1] Ahmad Budayr, lacking a clear opinion of his own, is the observer who, in his capacity as a journalist, reports what he sees and hears, and reflects the reality to which he is a witness. Thus, he is analogous to the writer Mahfuz, who announces that he has no clear doctrine and prefers to express himself in narrative fiction which reflects complex reality in its totality.

Let us now consider the names of these four characters, starting with Ma'mun Ridwan. The word *ma'mūn*, the passive participle of the verb *'-m-n*, means "one who is trusted," "trustworthy." This name is derived from the same root as the word *īmān* ("faith," "religious belief"), and *mu'min* ("a believer," "a Muslim"). The name

---

[1] Muhammad 'Afifi, *al-Hilal* (February 1970), p. 39.

suits the character of the bearer, and is related through its root to
words signifying religious faith in general and Islam in particular.
And thus the name Ma'mun combines two elements which seem to
be appropriate to the man: trustworthiness and religious faith. The
word *ridwān*, his second name, means God's contentment with man
and man's contentment with his lot, that is, with God's decree. In
Muslim legend, Ridwan is the name of the angel who is the treasurer
of paradise (*khazin al-jinan*).[2] In Egyptian folklore, Ridwan (colloquial: Radwan) is known as the doorkeeper of paradise (*haris al-
janna*).[3] The association of the name with God's contentment, and
specifically with paradise, makes it a very suitable Mahfuzian choice
of name for a pious character. Not surprisingly, Mahfuz uses it elsewhere for ironic purposes.[4] The name Ma'mun Ridwan, with its two
components, is therefore a means of characterization by analogy:
there is a correspondence between the name and the person who
bears it.

'Ali Taha, the second friend – Ma'mun Ridwan's companion and
ideological rival – also bears a name which matches his character and
attitudes. 'Ali means lofty, high, superior, and this is indeed appropriate to a person described as having excellent personal qualities and as
upholding high ideals. The second component of the name – Taha –
is taken from the Qur'an, sura 20. The letters *ta* and *ha*, which open
this chapter, belong to a group of mysterious combinations of letters
which appear at the beginning of some of the suras of the Qur'an and
which are known in Islamic literature as "the openings" (*fawatih*),
such as *ya sin, alif lam ra, alif lam mim*, etc. The traditional Qur'an
commentators suggest various interpretations for these combinations
of letters. One of those proposed for the combination *ta ha* is that

---

[2] See Abu Ja'far Muhammad b. Jarir b. Rastum al-Tabari, *Dala'il al-Imama* (Najaf 1963/
1383), p. 12. I am indebted for this reference to Prof. Etan Kohlberg of the Hebrew University
of Jerusalem.

[3] In Abu al-'Ala' al-Ma'arri's *Risalat al-ghufran*, Ridwan figures as the angel in charge of
entry to paradise. Ma'arri refers to Ridwan as *khazin al-jinan*. See *Risalat al-ghufran*, ed.
'A'isha 'Abd al-Rahman (Cairo: Dar al-ma'arif, 4th printing, n.d.), pp. 249–50.

[4] See below, pp. 214–15, Ridwan, Yasin's son in the trilogy. That Mahfuz had precisely
this connotation of the name Ridwan in mind becomes eminently clear in the case of
Muhammad Ridwan, the paralyzed neighbor of Ahmad 'Abd al-Jawad (*Bayn al-qasrayn*,
pp. 152, 392). See below, p. 219–20.

taha was a command given to the Prophet Muhammad at the beginning of the revelation contained in this chapter. The imperative form,
ṭāhā, is, according to these commentators, a secondary derivation
from *ta'hā*, meaning – "tread on it," or "stand on it," that is: "stand
on the ground with both your feet." The reason for the order, according to this exegesis, was that Muhammad, while waiting to
receive the revelation, stood on one foot, or, according to another
tradition, on his toes, and so the order was given to him to stand
firmly on the ground with both feet. According to other interpretations, *ta ha* means "O man!" in Syriac, Nabatean, or Ethiopian.[5]
Following the exclamation *ta ha* comes the verse which says: "We did
not reveal the Qur'an to you in order for you to suffer." The expression *ta ha*, whether understood as "stand on the ground with both
your feet" or "O man!" is inextricably bound to this subsequent
verse, which is, therefore, associated with the name Taha. Thus
Mahfuz's choice of Taha ("tread on the ground") as the second name
of our character, suggests that his idealism – alluded to in his first
name 'Ali ("superior") – is focussed on the achievement of happiness
for man in this world.

Ahmad, the first component of the name of the journalist, Ahmad
Budayr, is, as we have already noted, a very common name. Although the name Ahmad itself has a positive meaning, Mahfuz often
uses it to indicate a certain ambiguity in the character's moral stance,
or in his own attitude to the character who bears it. Ahmad is thus a
fitting name for this journalist who refuses ever to take a stand.
Budayr is a diminutive form of the Arabic word *badr*, meaning "the
full moon"; hence, Budayr means "a small moon." The journalist's
name reflects his main characteristic: he does not express any opinion of his own, nor has he any vision of his own. He only records and
reports what he hears and sees. Therefore, a comparison to the
moon, which has no light of its own, is apt.

The name of the hero is Mahjub 'Abd al-Da'im. The word *maḥjūb*
usually means "protected," "covered" or "shielded." But in the

---

[5] On this verse, see Baydawi, *Anwar al-tanzil wa-asrar al-ta'wil*, and Jalal-al-Din al-
Suyuti, *Lubab al-nuqul fi asbab al-nuzul*. See also s.v. "*Ṭaha*" in the dictionary *Lisan al-
'arab*.

Qur'an, the word *mahjub* has another quite different meaning: in
sura 83:15, *mahjubun* are the sinners who are denied God's grace
and are prevented from seeing Allah's face in paradise. Here Mahfuz
is clearly hinting at the ironic contrast between the conventional
meaning of the name Mahjub and the Qur'anic meaning of the word.
Earlier in this same chapter of the Qur'an, it is said that the list of the
sinners is kept in *sijjin*. *Sijjin*, according to some commentators, is the
book in which the bad deeds of the sinners are recorded. Other commentators say that *sijjin* is the name of the place, at the very bottom
of hell, where Satan (Iblis) and all his cohorts – demons and men
alike – will be imprisoned until they are brought to the last judgment.
The hero of the novel, Mahjub, who regards Iblis as a model for his
behavior, is appropriately given the name Mahjub (that is, one of
Iblis's cohorts), evoking all these traditional Qur'anic connotations.
The second component of the name, 'Abd al-Da'im, is one of many
proper nouns containing the names of Allah ("the most beautiful
names," *al-asma' al-husna*); al-Da'im ("the eternal," "the one who
exists forever") is one of these names. Mahjub, however, is not a
servant of God the Eternal, as his name 'Abd al-Da'im would seem to
define him, but an admirer of Satan and a slave to the eternal Tempt-
er's seductions.

Mahjub 'Abd al-Da'im's wife is called Ihsan Shehata. Ihsan, a
beautiful young woman with seven younger brothers, is the daughter
of poor parents. Her father, who now owns a small cigarette shop
near the students' dormitories, has a dubious past, as does her
mother. The mother was a prostitute and the father, Shehata Turki, a
gigolo. Ihsan's parents want to use their daughter as a source of income and are therefore ready to give her as a mistress to a rich man
(pp. 20–21). Ihsan loves the student 'Ali Taha, but her parents put
pressure on her to sever her relations with 'Ali because he is not rich
and because, as they argue, "she had to think of her parents and her
hungry brothers." She is in a quandary for a while, pulled between
her feelings and her sense of responsibility to her family: "Two important matters were pulling her heart in two opposite directions
from the very first minute: the life of her heart and the life of her family" (p. 20). Ihsan's father and mother help Satan seduce her and turn
her away from the right path. After hesitation, she submits to the will

of her parents (p. 90): she becomes the mistress of a rich man, Qasim Bey, director general of a government ministry.

The name Ihsan is a verbal noun derived from *ahsana* ("to do good," "to give charity"); *ihsān* means the performance of good acts, the giving of alms, charity.[6] *Ihsan*, the act of donating alms to beggars, is associated linguistically and experientially with the beggars' typical phrase of supplication, *hasana*. Shehata, the name of Ihsan's father, is the Egyptian colloquial form of *shihādha* which means beggary. Ihsan ("charity") and Shehata ("beggary") are closely connected, except that *shehata* suggests the vulgar, demeaning and contemptible nature of beggary, while *ihsan*, the generous response to the beggar's supplication, suggests virtue. The fact that *shehata* is linguistically "vulgar" (being a colloquial form) intensifies the contrast. The name Ihsan Shehata thus alludes to the sad and perplexing paradox that one of the highest virtues is inextricably linked to one of the most demeaning situations.

The word *ihsan* occurs twelve times in the Qur'an and in six of these instances it appears within the phrase *wa-bi'l-walidayn ihsan* (once *wa-bi-walidayhi ihsan*) meaning "[it is obligatory] to treat [one's] parents kindly" (Qur'an 2:83, 4:36, 4:62, 6:151, 17:23, 46:15). In all of these instances, the commandment to be kind to one's parents follows immediately upon the commandment to worship God alone. It is clearly a duty of the highest religious value. The irony in Ihsan's name is therefore extremely sharp: in obeying her parents and, as it were, in compliance with the Qur'anic commandment *wa-bi'l-walidayn ihsan*, Ihsan prostitutes herself.

'Abd al-Muhsin Taha Badr, who takes exception to Mahfuz's practice of investing his characters' names with special meaning, offers the following interpretation for some of the names discussed above: "Ma'mun Ridwan is trustful (*amin*) and content (*rad^{in}*) just as the author trusts him and is content with him. 'Ali Taha has high aspirations (*dhu himma 'aliya*). Ahmad Budayr sets out (*yubadir*) to discover secrets, he is indeed a journalist; his moral character is on the

---

[6] In some Sufi writings *ihsan* signifies the highest level of human behavior and faith, ranking above *islam* and *iman*: "Islam is the external aspect, and *iman* [faith] is the internal aspect, and *ihsan* is the real essence of both the external and the internal." Sarraj, *Kitab al-luma'*, ed. R.A. Nicholson (Leiden and London, 1914), p. 6.

whole praiseworthy. Ihsan ... is a beautiful woman (*hasna'*). ..."[7]
Badr tries to demonstrate the triviality and triteness of Mahfuz's
choice of allusive names, but he ignores the references to the Qur'an
and to Islamic tradition, and so fails to perceive Mahfuz's intention.

The family name of Shehata, Ihsan's father, is Turki, "Turk." By
naming this corrupt character "Turki" in allusion to his Turkish origins, Najib Mahfuz recalls the corruptive influence of the Turkish
Ottoman rule on Egyptian life.

Ihsan's rich lover, Qasim Bey, is a married man who has no intention of marrying Ihsan, preferring to keep her in an apartment where
he can visit her discreetly at his pleasure. To keep up appearances she
has to be married off to a complacent husband. This ignominious
deal is arranged by Qasim Bey's secretary, Sālim al-Ikhshidi, to whom
Mahjub has turned for help in obtaining a job in the government.

Sālim is an ordinary name meaning "whole," "unblemished,"
"faultless," which is obviously ironic in this case. His family name al-
Ikhshidi is rather unusual, although it is well known in Egyptian
history. Kafur al-Ikhshidi was a black eunuch who ruled Egypt for
twenty-two years (946–968 CE). Najib Mahfuz does not intend to
compare the fictitious al-Ikhshidi of the novel with the historical
Kafur al-Ikhshidi, who was a remarkably effective ruler and whom
Mahfuz evidently holds in high esteem.[8] Kafur al-Ikhshidi is chiefly
remembered, however, due to a satirical poem written about him by
the poet al-Mutanabbi who ridiculed him for being a eunuch.[9] In
folklore particularly, the eunuch, as the servant of the harem, is associated with the demeaning task of bringing concubines to his master's
chamber. Salim, of course, is not a eunuch; he is physically "whole"
(*sālim*), but, like a eunuch in the harem, he slavishly serves the lusts
of his master.

This novel is set in Cairo in 1934, when pro-Palace politicians
were running the government, having replaced the more popular
Wafd cabinet in 1930. Liberal intellectuals felt frustrated and oppressed during this period; the Constitution of 1923 had been abo-
lished in 1930, and freedom of expression had been seriously curbed.

---

[7] 'Abd al-Muhsin Taha Badr, *Najib Mahfuz: al-Ru'ya wa'l-ada* (Cairo, 1984), p. 259.

[8] Najib Mahfuz, *Amam al-'arsh*, p. 148.

[9] *Diwan al-Mutanabbi*, vol. 2 (Beirut: Dar al-Kitab al-'Arabi), pp. 139–48.

In describing the corrupt behavior of the Turko-Egyptian aristocrat Qasim Bey, Mahfuz passes judgment on the social class and ethnic group to which this politician belongs.

As previously noted, this novel contains themes anticipated in two of Mahfuz's short stories: *"Mahr al-wazifa"* ("The Price of Office") and *"al-Qay'"* ("Vomit").[10] *Al-Qahira al-jadida* combines the themes of both these short stories.

[10] See above, pp. 62–63.

CHAPTER 15

The Beginning and the End

In *Bidaya wa-nihaya* ("The Beginning and the End," 1949), the three sons are Hasan, Husayn and Hasanayn, and the daughter is called Nafisa.[1] The boys' names are all derived from the same root – *ḥ-s-n*. The adjective *ḥasan* means "beautiful," "handsome," "good." This is the name of the eldest son. The next son is called Husayn, the diminutive form of Hasan, and the third is Hasanayn, a dual form meaning "two Hasans." Hasan and Husayn are the names of the grandsons of the Prophet, the sons of 'Ali and Fatima. As such they are very common Muslim names. The dual form, Hasanayn, is used in various traditional sources as a reference to both grandsons of the Prophet: the older (Hasan) and the younger (Husayn). It, too, is a fairly common name. The use of three names from the same root is not unknown in Arab families: to all outward appearances, the author is following an accepted custom of no particular significance. Later on in the novel we encounter other characters with names from this same root. The chief secretary of the school in Tanta where Husayn, the second brother, is employed, is called Ḥassān Ḥassān Ḥassān (i.e., Hassan son of Hassan son of Hassan). Introducing himself to Husayn, his new assistant, the chief secretary explains: "It is customary in our family to name the eldest son after his father. Haven't you heard of the Hassan family of the Buhayra province? The students, those dogs, they call me 'Hassan to the power of

---

[1] For a summary of this story, see above, pp. 104–6.

192

three'" (*Bidaya wa-nihaya*, p. 205). Mahfuz, whose choice of names is rarely accidental, has given this rather comical character a ridiculous name. The secretary's daughter is called Ihsan, also derived from the·root *ḥ-s-n*.

The name of the sister, Nafisa ("precious") is related to the word *nafs* ("soul"), which in Islamic literature, especially in the Sufi tradition, designates the desirous soul, the seat of desires and evil inclinations. This meaning of the word is based on the Qur'anic phrase (12:53): "*Inna 'l-nafsa la'ammara bi'l-su'*" ("Indeed, every soul is prone unto evil"). The obvious contrast between the meaning of the name Nafisa ("invaluable," "precious," "priceless") and the wretched reality of Nafisa's life gives a constant ironic ring to the name in the novel. The author deliberately highlights this contrast in various instances. Thus, for example, in one of the final chapters, when Nafisa's younger brother discovers that his sister is a prostitute, he tells her that she will not be able to save her "contemptible" life (p. 369, *ḥaqīra*, an antonym of *nafisa*). Elsewhere the girl's misery is heightened by the fact that she is paid only trifling wages for her work. The Arabic word *zahīda* – "trifling," "paltry," "insignificant" – is again an antonym of *nafisa*. To Cairenes the name Nafisa is inevitably associated with Sayyida Nafisa (d. 824), the great-granddaughter of Hasan, the Prophet's grandson. The mosque built on her tomb is visited by many who seek her blessing and intercession.[2] This suggests yet another ironic juxtaposition.

In one passage in the story we encounter an interesting discussion of the name Nafisa within the narrative. This occurs when Nafisa allows a man to pick her up as a prostitute for the first time. "He asked her, 'What is your name?' [She answered] 'Nafisa.' The name did not seem to please him and he asked her, 'Why didn't you choose a more elegant name?'" The reader is given to understand that the client, taking her for a professional prostitute, assumes that the name Nafisa is a "professional name," and he does not like it. (No explanation is given for his dislike of the name Nafisa, but we may conjecture that he objects to its meaning "precious" and hence "high-priced," and to its association with piety, since it may well remind

---

[2] Richard Parker, Robin Sabin and Caroline Williams, *Islamic Monuments in Cairo: A Practical Guide* (Cairo, 1985), pp. 137–39.

him of the saintly Sayyida Nafisa mentioned above.) "She did not grasp his intention. Misunderstanding him and offended, she answered, 'I like it.' [He answered:] 'Well, long live the names – Miss Nafisa – no offense intended'" (p. 167).[3]

The author makes full use of the possibilities inherent in the connection between the name Nafisa, the noun *nafs* ("soul," "psyche") and the root *n-f-s*. Nafisa recalls how her father used to comfort her for not being good looking: "To be amiable is more valuable than to be handsome" (repeated on pages 48, 49 and 70). The word used in this phrase is *anfas* ("more precious," "more valuable"), which is the comparative form of the adjective *nafisa*. This highlights the contrast between the girl's name and her wretched condition.

The author uses the word *nafs* ("soul," "self"), in many instances when Nafisa thinks of herself, and in this manner he further underlines the connection between the name Nafisa and the various qualities of the person, "the self" (*nafs*) who bears it. Thinking of her irresistible attraction to the grocer's son Salman Jabir, Nafisa says to herself: "He is not a man. If he were a man he would not depend on his father in such a ridiculous manner and would not be so much afraid of him. Still, I love him and want him. I belong to him, soul and body [*nafsan wa-jasadan*]. I have no one apart from him. Why do I have this soul that torments me so?" (p. 116).

When the mother reflects sadly on the unfortunate condition of her eldest son, the criminal, who is hiding from the police, she thinks that perhaps her family has been stricken by the evil eye: "They envied her the government official and the officer." The phrase used for "they envied her" is *nafasu 'alayha*. Here again, the word used is from the same root *n-f-s* (p. 311). The sad contrast between Nafisa's name and her misery as a poor seamstress is also underlined in the scene where Nafisa is asked to prepare dresses for a bride. Nafisa looks at the material from which she will make the dresses and says: "What precious silk" (*Ya lahu min harir nafis*) (p. 70).

It is clear that the name Nafisa is not at all suitable for the girl. She is unattractive and her life is miserable. Adjectives that would suit her

---

[3] It should be noted that Mahfuz refers in a number of his stories to prostitutes who change their names; see below, pp. 213–14, 231–32.

are, indeed, "miserable" and "wretched"; the Arabic equivalent of these adjectives is *ta'isa*, rhyming with *nafisa*. The mother – speaking to her son Husayn and referring to her daughter – says, "Nafisa is an unfortunate girl [*Nafisa fatāh ta'īsa*]" (p. 221). The abstract noun from the same root *ta'āsa* appears a number of times in connection with Nafisa, who says to herself "misery [*ta'āsa*] pierces our flesh, just as this needle is piercing this piece of material" (p. 48). And in another passage the writer describes her feelings: "It increased her misery [*ta'asataha*] that she was paid only very insignificant wages for her work." He has Nafisa thinking of her unfortunate past (*madin ta'is*) (p. 281). When the words *nafisa* and *ta'isa* are written in Arabic script without diacritical marks on the two first consonants, they look the same.

The full significance of the fact that the three brothers' names are from the same root may be grasped by comparing the brothers with the three characters in the story "*al-Wajh al-akhar*" ("The Other Face").[4] This story would appear to be an allegory in which the three characters represent both social and psychological forces.[5] On the psychological level, the three characters represent the psyche, and the struggle between them represents internal strife within the self, which would appear to be perceived by Mahfuz in Freudian terms: the criminal is the id; the police officer the superego; and the educator the ego. In one of the key sentences in the story, the narrator says: "We are three and we are one." In *Bidaya wa-nihaya*, the choice of the names of the three brothers – Hasan, Husayn and Hasanayn, derived as they are from the same root – would appear to allude to the same concept: the different qualities displayed by each one of the brothers are all inherent in human nature, which is essentially one.[6]

The names of the minor characters in this novel are also chosen carefully to serve as analogous means of characterization. Thus, for example, the name of the father who dies at the beginning of the

---

[4] In the collection *Taht al-mizalla* published in 1969.

[5] See above, pp. 100–101.

[6] One can hardly perceive the younger brother, the army officer Hasanayn, as representing the superego in a real sense. But the key notion here is that the brothers' basic characteristics are all part of the human psyche – good and evil are both rooted in the same psyche and this psychological interpretation connects all three brothers to the notion of *nafs* – psyche or soul.

novel is Kamil Effendi 'Ali. (The title *effendi* indicates that its bearer does not belong to the working class, but is a government official.) He is a low ranking official and a weak person, and his weakness has had adverse effects on the education of his first son, Hasan. "Hasan bore miserable witness to the weakness of the father and his spoiling," whereas the mother "was the real hub of the house. Indeed, she used to play the role of the father, who was weak and closer in character to the tenderness and weakness of mothers" (p. 18). The father's name, Kāmil Effendi 'Ali, is made up of two adjectives which are the very opposite of the kind of person he seems to have been. Kamil ("perfect") is certainly contradicted by his defects of character, and 'Ali ("high" or "lofty"), is belied by his low official rank and humble social status.

The good neighbor of the family, the only person who gives them real support and visits them when they move to a new apartment, is Farid Effendi. *Farīd* means "unique." Indeed, the mother refers to him as "the best of all people" (p. 326).

The young grocer who seduces Nafisa is called Salmān Jābir Sālman. The name Salman, from the root *s-l-m* is close in meaning to *salim* ("sound," in either the physical or moral sense). However Salman the grocer suffers from poor eyesight, and he cruelly deceives Nafisa, thus contradicting both aspects of his name.

Salman's father's name, Jabir, suggests various analogies between name and character with regard to both father and son. Salman dreads his father, who treats him oppressively; he says to Nafisa, "My father is a tyrant [*abi rajul jabbar*]" (p. 115). *Jabbār* ("oppressor," "tyrant," also "almighty"), one of the divine names, is from the same root as Jabir. The verb *jabara* means "to set (broken bones)," "to restore," "to help up," but also "to compel, force"; this last meaning is usually expressed by the form *ajbara*. The phrase *jabara khatirahu* means "to comfort, console (someone)," "to treat (someone) kindly." The noun *jābir* means "bonesetter."

Nafisa is emotionally shattered when she hears that Salman Jabir, to whom she submitted some days before, is going to marry another woman. She pours out her anger on him, "Do you take me for a doll that you play with when you wish, and smash when you wish?" (p. 131). As a result of Salman Jabir's conduct, Nafisa becomes a shattered woman. Salman Jabir's destructive behavior contradicts the salubrious meaning of *jabir*. When Nafisa, in her rage, attacks him, he cries, "Don't touch me! I didn't force you to do anything [*lam ujbirki 'ala shay'!*]" (ibid.).

Another minor character in the novel is an aristocratic, high-ranking official who knew the father and whom the family approaches for help after the father's death. His name is Ahmad Bey Yusri. Yusri is derived from the word *yusr*, meaning "wealth," "easy circumstances."

The names of the two young officers, classmates of Hasanayn who are mentioned in the story, seem again to have been chosen with an ironic intention. The haughty and aristocratic officer who gossips about Hasanayn's failure to obtain Ahmad Yusri's daughter's hand in marriage, is Ahmad Ra'fat. The noun *ra'fa* means "mercy," "compassion." This meaning, of course, contrasts sharply with Ahmad Ra'fat's malicious comments about Hasanayn (p. 343). The family name Ra'fat is spelled in the Turkish fashion, which highlights the family's affiliation with the Turko-Egyptian ruling class. Such affiliation carried, in itself, negative connotations for Najib Muhfuz.[7]

The other classmate is 'Ali al-Bardisi, who tells Hasanayn about Ahmad Ra'fat's insults and claims to have defended him against them. The name 'Ali suggests, of course, high status – which may refer both to this character's aristocratic origin and to the high moral stand which he claims to have taken. The name Bardisi may be viewed as relating him to the town of Bardis in Upper Egypt, which would suggest a genuinely Egyptian origin (in contradistinction to the Turko-Egyptian Ahmad Ra'fat). It may also allude to some moral qualities; *bardis* is interpreted in the classical dictionaries as "cunning," "arrogant," or "an evil man."

---

[7] On Mahfuz's negative view of the Turkish element in Egyptian society, see above, pp. 63, 190; and below, p. 210, n. 10.

CHAPTER 16

The Cairene Trilogy

The trilogy tells the story of a middle-class Cairene family in the years between 1917 and 1944. The first part (*Bayn al-qaṣrayn*, 1956) takes place between 1917 and 1919, the second (*Qaṣr al-shawq*, 1957) between 1924 and 1927 and the third (*al-Sukkariyya*, 1957) between 1935 and 1944.

Bayn al-qaṣrayn

The family lives in the Jamaliyya quarter, in Bayn al-Qasrayn alley (whence the book's title). The head of the family, Sayyid Ahmad 'Abd al-Jawad, who owns a local grocery store, demands – and receives – implicit obedience from his wife and children (three sons and two daughters). He does not allow his wife to leave the house even for prayers in the mosque, and allows her to visit her mother only if he escorts her. His strictness in this regard is considered extreme even among his friends, who share the moral norms and attitudes of traditional Muslim society, in which respectable women are not expected to be seen by men who are not members of their immediate family. Sayyid Ahmad is a devout Muslim who prays regularly and is known for his charity. But this highly respected merchant is also a pleasure seeker who spends his nights partying with his friends in the company of women of pleasure. His children know nothing of this aspect of their father's life. His wife, Amina, a very pious woman, knows, of course, about his parties and drinking habits because she

198

waits for him nightly, and on his return removes his shoes and socks and pours water on his hands for him to wash his face. The fact that her husband violates the Islamic prohibition against alcohol upsets her, but she dare not protest. She also suspects that her husband keeps company with women but this, too, she submissively accepts, having been told by her mother shortly after her marriage that this is a husband's privilege. Yasin (21 years old) is Sayyid Ahmad's eldest son, not by Amina, but by his first wife whom he divorced, while she was pregnant with Yasin, because she refused to submit to his despotic rule. Yasin was brought up by his mother until the age of ten when Sayyid Ahmad took him back. The kind-hearted Amina treats Yasin as a son, and he regards her as a mother. Yasin, who did not finish elementary school, is employed as a secretary in a school. Like his father, he is a tall, broad-shouldered, handsome man. He also resembles his father in his unrestrained pursuit of women. Amina's four children are Khadija (20), Fahmi (18), 'A'isha (16) and Kamal (10). Khadija is a strong-willed, lively and industrious girl, but she is not particularly beautiful. It is the fair-haired, blue eyed 'A'isha who is the beauty of the family. Unlike Khadija, 'A'isha does not like to help in the house, and has to be reminded of her duties. Khadija and 'A'isha are both waiting for their father to arrange the right match for them. In preparation, they both concentrate on eating as much as possible, because the taste of the time dictates that women should be plump. Khadija teases the beautiful and slender 'A'isha for her failure to gain weight. Fahmi has just started studying law and Kamal is in elementary school. At the beginning of the novel Sayyid Ahmad has recently terminated his affair with Jalila, a professional singer ('ālima), and is about to embark upon a new relationship with Zubayda, another well-known 'ālima.

Yasin, who is in the habit of ogling and pursuing any woman who looks available, is attracted to Zannuba, the young lute-player in Zubayda's band. After energetic pursuit, Zannuba, who knows Yasin only by his first name, invites him to her room in Zubayda's house, and while he is there, tells him they can enjoy themselves without fear of interruption because her mistress is busy with her lover and patron, one Sayyid Ahmad 'Abd al-Jawad, a merchant from the Jamaliyya quarter. Yasin is horrified. Zannuba, noticing his reaction, asks: "What's the matter with you? What are you making such a fuss about, like a girl whose virginity is being taken?" Thus Yasin learns about the hidden aspect of his father's personality, which he will soon reveal to his brother Fahmi.

Fahmi falls in love with Maryam, the neighbors' beautiful daughter, whom he stealthily watches each time she appears on the adjacent roof. He reveals to his mother that he would like to marry her and asks her to obtain his father's approval. Amina broaches the matter to Sayyid Ahmad, who angrily rejects the idea that his son should make his own decisions about whom to marry and when.

The sexually-obsessed Yasin one night enters the room of the middle aged maid, and makes advances to her. Her cries of protest wake Sayyid Ahmad, who angrily rebukes Yasin and concludes that the time has come to marry him off. He arranges a marriage for him with Zaynab, the daughter of one of his friends. Although Zaynab is a very attractive young woman, Yasin quickly tires of her and one night gets into bed with his wife's black maid. His pregnant wife catches them in the act, leaves the house and goes back to her parents. She demands a divorce and he has no choice but to comply, as her father supports her. Yasin's son, Ridwan, is born after the divorce.

One day, when Sayyid Ahmad is away on a business trip, the children prompt their mother to fulfill her long standing wish to pray at the al-Husayn mosque. Kamal, the youngest of the children, takes her to the mosque, but on the way home she is hit by a car, breaks her collarbone, and has to take to bed. The children decide to conceal the nature and the circumstances of the injury; they are in the habit of lying and covering up in order to protect themselves from their father's anger. But Amina cannot lie to her husband, and she tells him what has happened. As soon as she is well enough to get out of bed, Sayyid Ahmad banishes her to her mother's house. His children's pleas to bring their mother back go unheard. The neighbor, Umm Maryam (Maryam's mother) comes to intercede on Amina's behalf, but Sayyid Ahmad remains unmoved. Finally he gives in when Mrs. Shawkat, a highly respected friend of the family and the widow of an influential and wealthy aristocrat, comes to plead with him.

Each of these two visitors has an ulterior motive. Mrs. Shawkat wants 'A'isha as a wife for her younger son, Khalil. Although Sayyid Ahmad is not very happy that the younger daughter should marry before the elder, he cannot refuse. 'A'isha marries and moves into the Shawkat mansion in Sukkariyya Street. In due course she gives birth to a daughter, after a very difficult labor. The doctor informs the family that the baby's heart is very weak, and that she will not live beyond her teens. Some time later Khadija is married to Khalil's older brother, a widower. Thus the two sisters find themselves once more living in the same house.

The hidden motive behind Umm Maryam's visit to Sayyid Ahmad is far less respectable. Her husband has been bedridden for a number of years and the beautiful and sensuous Umm Maryam hopes to arouse Sayyid Ahmad's interest in her. Although he is not indifferent to her charms, he does not respond. However, some months later, after her husband's death, she tries again, successfully. One night, when Sayyid Ahmad is on his way home after an evening with her, he is stopped by British soldiers, dragged off together with other men from the neighborhood, and forced to fill in a ditch dug by young nationalist Egyptians in order to hinder the passage of British military vehicles. Thus, in a comical and unheroic way, Sayyid Ahmad becomes an unwitting participant in the nationalist struggle. Fahmi is actively involved in anti-British demonstrations; defying his father's orders to stay away from political activity, he has become one of the leaders of the student nationalist movement. In the demonstration held to celebrate Sa'd Zaghlul's return from exile, he is shot and killed.

Qasr al-shawq

The second part, Qasr al-shawq, takes up the story some five years later. This volume takes its name from the street in which Yasin's mother lived, in a house which he inherited upon her death.

Kamal, now seventeen years old, has just finished high school, and Amina holds a family celebration. The writer uses this as an opportunity to bring us up to date on family news. Sayyid Ahmad 'Abd al-Jawad has mellowed somewhat and is now less distant and harsh with his wife and children. 'A'isha now has three children, two boys and a girl, and Khadija has two sons. Both sisters and their families still live in the Shawkat family house in Sukkariyya Street, but while 'A'isha manages to get on very well with her mother-in-law, Khadija is in perpetual conflict with old Mrs. Shaw-kat. Kamal, who is studious and reflective, has been experiencing a secret, intense, romantic attachment to 'A'ida, the sister of one of his classmates.

Kamal now has to decide how to continue his education. His fa-ther would like him to go to law school, but Kamal has decided to go to teachers college because he wants to study the humanities, "in or-der to understand the origin of life and its purpose." Sayyid Ahmad is deeply disappointed and angry, but does not impose his will on his son.

Kamal unwittingly angers his father, when the latter comes to know that his son has published an article on Darwin's theory of the origin of species. Sayyid Ahmad is beside himself with rage when he reads that his son has written that man is descended from the apes. When Kamal attempts to defend himself by arguing that these are not his views but those of a certain Englishman, his father answers: "You should reject their learning as you do their occupation of Egypt."

Kamal's love for 'A'ida is a frustrating and bitter experience. This daughter of a rich and aristocratic family leads him to believe that she is attracted to him, while in fact she is making use of him to tease the young man in whom she is really interested, and whom she soon marries. Her husband, also of aristocratic family, receives a diplo-matic appointment and they leave together for France. Kamal learns from another friend that his feelings for 'A'ida were common knowl-edge, and that 'A'ida had poked fun at his naive and romantic yearnings. This same friend takes Kamal for his first taste of alcohol and his first visit to a brothel. Kamal begins to frequent the brothel, where, during one of his visits, he encounters his brother Yasin, who takes advantage of the occasion to tell Kamal about the secret aspect of their father's personality.

Yasin, who for a number of years has lived as a bachelor, catches a glimpse of Maryam (the girl Fahmi previously wanted to marry) and is attracted to her. After a short flirtation she tells him that if he wants her he has to marry her. When he tells Amina that he plans to marry Maryam, she is deeply hurt, considering this a desecration of Fahmi's memory. Yasin, therefore, has to leave the family home and move into his house in Qasr al-Shawq. Sayyid Ahmad, unlike Amina, does not dare to object to Yasin's marriage because of the clandestine affair he once had with Umm Maryam. Umm Maryam happily agrees to the marriage, but during the course of their interview Yasin finds himself attracted to the mother, and she encourages him to start an affair with her. After a few days Yasin tires of Umm Maryam and marries her daughter as planned.

Since Fahmi's death, Sayyid Ahmad has stopped having extra-marital affairs. But, now, five years later, he accepts an invitation to spend an evening with his friends on Zubayda's houseboat (Zubayda is now supported by one of Sayyid Ahmad's friends). Sayyid Ahmad is attracted to Zannuba, the young lute-player (formerly Yasin's mistress). When he approaches her, she refuses him, deeply wounding him and undermining his self-confidence. He now finds himself obsessed with her, and in order to win her, he gives in to her demands and rents a houseboat for her.

Yasin happens to meet Zannuba by chance and their previous attraction revives. They spend the evening drinking together, and Yasin takes Zannuba home with him for the night. Maryam, his wife, is outraged, and leaves the house. Yasin divorces her and offers to marry Zannuba, unaware that she is his father's mistress. Zannuba now presents Sayyid Ahmad with an ultimatum: marriage or separation. She lets him know that a respectable man, who had an affair with her a few years previously, is now offering to marry her. Sayyid Ahmad sees this as a way out. Yasin marries Zannuba secretly, but after a while Sayyid Ahmad hears of the marriage from his friends.

For a period, Sayyid Ahmad stops going to his friends' parties on Zubayda's houseboat. But a year later he goes back. He is on the point of going to bed with Zubayda when he suffers a heart attack. He recovers, but is ordered to lead a very quiet life. The book ends sadly. 'A'isha's husband and two sons are dying of typhoid. While Kamal sits grief-stricken at home, he hears the news of Sa'd Zaghlul's death. Yasin, that same evening, in his house in Qasr al-Shawq, is waiting for Zannuba to give birth to his child.

Al-Sukkariyya

Eight years later, the bereaved 'A'isha – already an old woman at thirty-four – is living with her daughter Na'ima at her parents' home. Amina, who is nearing sixty, also looks older than her age. Na'ima, now sixteen, is strikingly beautiful and is the very image of her mother at the same age. Sayyid Ahmad, although retaining his elegant appearance, has lost his strength and has to sell his grocery store. Kamal, still a bachelor living with his parents, teaches English in an elementary school. He has retained his interest in philosophy and publishes articles on various Western philosophers. He befriends a young Coptic writer, Riyad Qaldes, and the two start to meet regularly to discuss literature, art and philosophy. One day he chances to meet Budur, the younger sister of his former love 'A'ida. A serious attachment develops and, although Budur is many years younger than he is, she expects the relationship to lead to marriage. Kamal, however, is hesitant, and the relationship comes to an end.

Sayyid Ahmad's grandsons are growing up. Ridwan, Yasin's son, is very handsome and intelligent. He has studied law and, through his connections with a government minister who shares his homosexual proclivities, he attains a high position at a young age. Khadija's two sons differ greatly from each other in their political orientation: 'Abd al-Mun'im is very religious, and joins the Muslim Brotherhood, whereas Ahmad is a left-leaning secularist. Kamal is very attached to both his nephews; he feels a special affinity with Ahmad, but feels uncomfortable with 'Abd al-Mun'im's Islamic fervor. 'Abd al-Mun'im marries his cousin Na'ima; the marriage, however, ends tragically when Na'ima dies in childbirth.

Ahmad, a student of sociology, plans to become a journalist. He is in love with a fellow student, but she refuses him when she learns that he is not as wealthy as she would like. Ahmad starts to write articles for a progressive magazine where he meets Sawsan, the assistant editor, and they are mutually attracted. Sawsan, the daughter of a poor worker, is a communist. Despite his mother's vehement protests, Ahmad marries her. Yasin's marriage to Zannuba, the former lute-player, has turned out well. Zannuba has become a respectable housewife and has gradually been accepted into the family. The young widower, 'Abd al-Mun'im, makes a second marriage to his cousin Karima, the daughter of Zannuba and Yasin.

When the Second World War breaks out, Sayyid Ahmad is already very much enfeebled and finds it difficult to walk to the shelter during air raids. One night, when the all-clear sounds and the family are about to go back to the house, Sayyid Ahmad suffers a stroke from which he does not recover. Khadija's two sons are arrested for their political activities. Amina falls ill and the doctor tells Kamal she is dying. When Yasin learns of Amina's grave condition, he comes to keep Kamal company for the night. Kamal, however, sends him home to wait for his daughter Karima to give birth.

The Characters' Names

The father of the family is called al-Sayyid Ahmad 'Abd al-Jawad. Al-Sayyid is of course a standard title – "Mr." But in the case of al-Sayyid Ahmad 'Abd al-Jawad, the term *sayyid* (which means "lord," "chief," "master") seems to be an integral part of the name. The author usually refers to Ahmad 'Abd al-Jawad as "al-Sayyid," and some characters address him as Si al-Sayyid, that is "Mr. Sir" (e.g., *Bayn al-qasrayn*, pp. 101, 259). This emphasis on the title *Sayyid* in relation to Ahmad 'Abd al-Jawad underlines his authoritarian character and patriarchal position. The name Ahmad, as previously noted, indicates a degree of moral ambiguity in the nature of the character who bears it; it is the second name, that is, 'Abd al-Jawad (the name of Ahmad's father) that carries interesting connotations. This name is one of many Muslim names constructed from the word *'abd* ("servant") and one of the ninety-nine names of Allah (*al-asma' al-husna*). Mahfuz would appear to intend the second component of names composed in this way (in this case – *jawād*) to suggest a quality or an aspect of the person named. *Jawād* means "generous," and indeed, al-Sayyid Ahmad is praised for his generosity (*Bayn al-qasrayn*, p. 283). In another instance he is addressed as *al-Sayyid al-karim Ahmad 'Abd al-Jawad*, i.e., "the generous Mr. Ahmad 'Abd al-Jawad" (*Bayn al-qasrayn*, p. 98, cf. also pp. 102, 256).

Karīm is a much more common word for "generous" in Arabic than *jawād*, which has the additional meaning of "racehorse." I tend to think that the author intentionally chose the name 'Abd al-Jawad rather than 'Abd al-Karim because he wanted the name to have this additional connotation. When Sayyid Ahmad's wife awaits his return from his nightly party, she hears "the sound of the hooves of a race-horse [*jawad*]" which announces the arrival of her husband (*Bayn al-qasrayn*, p. 11). In this allusive manner the author creates a con-nection between Ahmad 'Abd al-Jawad, who is known among his friends for his sexual prowess, and the image of a racehorse, *jawad*. This is an indirect allusion to the parallelism, but we also find an explicit simile. When Sayyid Ahmad takes the tambourine to ac-company his mistress as she sings, he is "like a racehorse rearing up and ready to rush forward" (*Bayn al-qasrayn*, p. 116). On a number of occasions Sayyid Ahmad is also likened to a camel, because of his size and strength (*Bayn al-qasrayn*, p. 118, *Qasr al-shawq*, pp. 89, 91). Umm Maryam, trying to revive her affair with him, says, "You are a camel as beautiful as the full moon" (ibid., p. 155).

The importance of the racehorse simile may be more fully ap-preciated when we compare it to the various similes and refer-ences likening Sayyid Ahmad's eldest son, Yasin, to a mule, a bull, a camel or even an elephant. Yasin physically resembles his father: he has a large frame and a handsome face and, like his father, an insatiable sexual appetite. Unknown to his father, he conducts a life of debauchery, drinking and womanizing. In this inclination too he resembles his father, but unlike Sayyid Ahmad, who is known for his elegance and discriminating taste (*Bayn al-qasrayn*, p. 446), Yasin does not discriminate between pretty and ugly, clean and dirty, rich and poor (*Bayn al-qasrayn*, pp. 81–82). Like his father, he is sometimes called "camel," but the difference be-tween him and his father is noticeable even in these small jokes. His mistress Zannuba – who will become his wife – says to him: "You, honorable sir, resemble a camel in height and breadth" (*Bayn al-qasrayn*, p. 281). She further teases him, "A child's brain in a camel's body, isn't it so, my dear camel?" (ibid., p. 286).

The author compares him to a violent bull (*thawr ha'ij*) (*Bayn al-qasrayn*, p. 81). This is also how his father thinks of him: "You would like to be like your father, you bull!" (*Bayn al-qasrayn*, p. 326; *Qasr al-shawq*, pp. 364, 365). Zannuba says to him: "It seems that you would like to be a bull in a cowshed, that's what you are!" (*Qasr al-shawq*, p. 301). When he jumps in passion upon his mistress, he is described "as an elephant coming down upon a gazelle" (*Bayn al-qasrayn*, 289). His father calls him "mule," alluding to his physical strength and, by the same token, to his brainlessness (*Bayn al-qasrayn*, p. 326; *Qasr al-shawq*, pp. 123, 124, 154). Attempting to excuse Yasin for his decision to marry Maryam, Sayyid Ahmad says to Amina, "He has good intentions, although he is a mule" (*Qasr al-shawq*, p. 188). Yasin is described once as a racehorse, in a way which reminds us of his father: "He rushed forward like a bolting racehorse" (*Qasr al-shawq*, p. 144). However, one word – "bolting" – highlights the difference between the unruly son and the dignified father.

The name Yāsīn is derived from the thirty-sixth sura of the Qur'an which opens with the letters *yā'* and *sīn* and is therefore named *Ya Sin*. This two-letter combination is one of the mysterious *fawatih* ("openings") mentioned above whose precise meaning is unknown;[1] however, according to some exegetes, *ya sin* means *ya insan*, that is, "O man."[2] The sura of *Ya Sin* is popularly held in special reverence, and a number of *hadith*s proclaim its distinctive merit. The Prophet is reported to have said: "Everything has a core, and the core of the Qur'an is [the sura of] *Ya Sin*."[3] Repeated recitation of this chapter is believed to be an especially efficacious means of invoking God's mercy.[4] The name Yasin is therefore associated with piety.

One of Yasin's drinking companions is in the habit of addressing him as Hajj Yasin; "He insisted on giving him the title 'Hajj' out of respect for his blessed name" (*al-Sukkariyya*, p. 68). Zannuba his mistress says to him, "I sometimes doubt that your name is really Yasin" (*Qasr al-shawq*, p. 301). Zannuba's remark is directed at the outrageous contrast between the pious name and the debauched conduct of the man who bears it. However, the name Yasin was not chosen merely to suggest an ironic contrast between Yasin's impious

---

[1] See above, pp. 186–87.

[2] See Baydawi's commentary on Qur'an 36:1.

[3] Al-Tirmidhi, *Sunan* (Homs, 1967), vol. 8, p. 101, no. 2889.

[4] Such repeated recitation is known as *'addiyyat yasin*, cf. Ahmad Amin, *Qamus al-'adat* (Cairo, 1953) p. 284.

behavior and his name; such a contrast would have been achieved had he been called Muhammad (the Prophet's name) or Salih ("pious"). Yasin's name suggests also an ironic contrast between the meaning "man," "human being," which is supposedly inherent in it, and his animal-like behavior highlighted by the many references to him as an animal. Thinking about him, his father says, "What an animal!" (*Bayn al-qasrayn*, p. 326); and on another occasion, "That's just like Yasin, a man – or rather an animal – who always causes trouble" (*Qasr al-shawq*, p. 123). Kamal thinks of the "animal-like qualities of Yasin" (*Qasr al-shawq*, p. 74).

The contrast *insan* (human being) – *hayawan* (animal) appears clearly in the following words of Kamal, Yasin's younger brother; its relevance to our discussion will be clear: "I view sexual desire as a base instinct and I loathe the thought of surrendering to it. Perhaps it was created in us only to inspire us to resist it and to rise above it so as to deserve the rank of true humanity [*al-insaniyya al-haqqa*]. I should either be a human being or an animal [*imma an akuna insanan wa-imma an akuna hyawanan*]" (*Qasr al-shawq*, p. 83).

Sitting one day in a café, Yasin lets himself sink into erotic daydreaming ("naked dreams"), a frequent habit of his. "He was abruptly awakened by the voice of a donkey driver shouting *yiss* at his donkey" (*Bayn al-qasrayn*, p. 83). Yasin here is indirectly likened to an ass. It is noteworthy that the author spells the interjection used by the driver to stop his donkey in the rather unusual form *y-s*, which is identical with the Qur'anic spelling of Yasin's name, instead of the usual rendering, *h-s* (pronounced *hiss*).[5]

Sayyid Ahmad's wife is called Amīna (which means "trustworthy" or "faithful"). Derived from the same root as *iman* (faith) and *mu'min* (believer), the name Amīna cannot fail to evoke the connotation of piety as well as its actual sense of trustworthiness.[6] The name fits her well, for she is indeed the very paragon of faithfulness, and of many other laudable qualities. The semantic content of the adjective

[5] Cf. Hinds and Badawi, *A Dictionary of Egyptian Arabic* (Beirut, 1986), s.v. *hss*.

[6] See above, p. 185, my remarks on Ma'mun in *al-Qahira al-jadida*. The name *Amina* should not be confused with the name *Āmina* (safe, peaceful) – the name of the Prophet's mother.

amina in itself would make this name "a means of characterization by analogy," to use Ewen and Rimmon-Kenan's term. It seems, however, that Najib Mahfuz had a special reason for choosing this name for her apart from the suitability of its semantic content and its connection to *iman*: the name Amina occurs in the traditional Islamic legends related to the Qur'anic story of Sulayman (Biblical Solomon). Al-Kisa'i's *Qisas al-anbiya'* has the following account: "Sulayman had a handmaid (*jariya*) called al-Amīna, who never left him, and when he would enter the bathroom or would want to seclude himself with his [other] women, he would hand her his seal for safe keeping."[7]

Like her Mahfuzian namesake, this Amina, the trusted handmaid of Sulayman, patiently awaits her master when he goes to take his pleasure with his other women.[8] This analogy not only reinforces the characterization of Sayyid Ahmad's wife, but discloses Mahfuz's critical attitude towards the womanizing man, be he the canonized Solomon or a contemporary Cairene.

That the name Sulayman carries for Najib Mahfuz a pejorative connotation has already been noted above (in relation to the occurrence of this name in "*al-Ju'*" and in the story "*al-Qay'*"). We have seen that this connotation is derived from the image of Sulayman (the Biblical Solomon) as a man who boasts of his sexual prowess.[9]

The two daughters of Sayyid Ahmad and Amina are named after the Prophet's two most famous wives, Khadija (bint Khuwaylid) and 'A'isha (bint Abi Bakr). The older daughter is named Khadija, after Muhammad's first wife, the younger 'A'isha, after his third and much younger wife, whom he married a few years after Khadija's death. The analogy between Sayyid Ahmad's daughters and their historically famous namesakes is not limited to correspondence of seniority by age. Khadija, Muhammad's wife, is known to have been a strong-willed, independent woman, engaged in commerce. The Kha-

---

[7] Muhammad ben 'Abdallah Kisa'i, *Qisas al-anbiya'*, ed. I. Eisenberg (Leiden, 1923), p. 293.

[8] In some sources (e.g., Baydawi) she is called Amina and in others (e.g., Kisa'i and Jalalayn) al-Amina.

[9] See above, p. 173.

dija of Mahfuz's story is described as strong willed and pragmatic. The historical 'A'isha is reputed to have been exceptionally beautiful, with a fair complexion (*ḥumayrā'*) and long hair. She reportedly was Muhammad's favorite wife. Her namesake in the Cairene trilogy is described as having a fair complexion, blue eyes and long golden hair; she is the beauty of the family. Her physical charm is often contrasted in the story with her sister's rather unattractive appearance. 'A'isha of the trilogy is known in the family for her beautiful voice and her love of singing. This is reminiscent of a well-known Islamic tradition describing 'A'isha as fond of listening to songs. Perhaps the most important point of analogy is this: Khadija was the only wife by whom the Prophet Muhammad had living children, whereas 'A'isha bore him no child. In Mahfuz's story, 'A'isha has no living offspring; her two sons die as infants and her daughter dies in labor without giving birth.[10] Her sister Khadija has two sons, one of whom presents her with a granddaughter towards the end of the novel.

The combination of so many details in the characterization of Sayyid Ahmad's daughters, corresponding to well known characteristics of their historical namesakes, clearly points to Najib Mahfuz's special interest in elaborating this analogy.

The husbands of the two sisters are the Shawkat brothers, Ibrahim and Khalil ("friend"), sons of a highly respected upper-middle-class family of Turkish origin. The family name Shawkat is typically Turkish; although *shawkat* is originally an Arabic word, the family name is spelled in the Turkish fashion (with a *ta'*, not *ta' marbuta* at the end). *Shawka* means bravery, valor, verve, élan, might, power. Najib Mahfuz describes the two Shawkat men as meek and lethargic; they clearly are devoid of the personal traits suggested by the name; the ironic intention in the choice of the name is obvious.[11] The family as

---

[10] Mattityahu Peled suggests a possible explanation as to why Mahfuz would not allow 'A'isha's offspring to survive. According to his interpretation, the blue-eyed 'A'isha represents the Turkish element in Egyptian society, and the fate her family meets is Mahfuz's verdict on this alien ruling class. See Mattityahu Peled, *Religion, My Own: The Literary Works of Najib Mahfuz* (New Brunswick and London, 1983), pp. 109–18.

[11] The qualities which now distinguish the Shawkats are *khumul* (obscurity; apathy), *ḍa'a* (lowliness), *faragh* (idleness), see *Bayn al-qasrayn*, p. 335.

such, though still economically comfortable, "has retained nothing of its past power and high rank ... *except the name.*"[12] In this double entendre Najib Mahfuz again points to the covert ironic meaning of the name.

Although there is an age difference of some fifteen years between them, the two Shawkat brothers are described as having the same physical and mental characteristics: "they were more like twins...." (ibid., p. 335). Aptly, Najib Mahfuz gives them names which in Islamic tradition signify the same personage – the Qur'anic Ibrahim whose epithet is Khalil (Qur'an 4:125, *wa-'ttakhadha 'llah ibrahima khalilan*, "Allah chose [Abraham] to be His friend"). In Mahfuz's stories either one of these two names, Ibrahim or Khalil, is usually applied to an ill-fated man (as noted above, in the section on the story "*al-Ju'*"). Khalil Shawkat dies of illness together with his two infant sons. His older brother Ibrahim had his share of misfortune before he married Khadija: his first wife and children had died.

'A'isha's daughter is Na'ima, a name related etymologically and semantically to *ni'ma* ("grace," "benefaction," especially God's) and *na'im* ("the abode of the righteous in the hereafter"). It is also akin to *nā'im* ("tender," "fine," "delicate"). Na'ima, who has inherited her mother's beauty and good singing voice, is the darling of the whole family. She is devout to a degree unusual in a teenager. She is in love with her handsome cousin 'Abd al-Mun'im, Khadija's elder son, who is also attracted to her. 'Abd al-Mun'im ("the servant of the Benefactor") is himself very religious and is a member of the Muslim Brotherhood. He asks his parents to arrange for him to marry even before he has graduated from high school, because, as he candidly explains to them, he fears that he may not be able to resist the temptations of desire. He marries his cousin Na'ima, but the two are not blessed with happiness for long. Na'ima, whose name alludes to God's benefaction, dies in labor. This terrible blow does not, however, shake 'Abd al-Mun'im's faith in the Benefactor.

'A'ida Shaddad is the name of the rich aristocratic girl who is the object of Kamal's unrequited love. Adoring her and viewing her as an

---

[12] My emphasis. *Bayn al-qasrayn*, p. 331: "*wa'in lam yabqa lahum min 'izzat al-qidam ... illa 'l-ism.*"

angelic creature, Kamal, to himself, calls her "the worshipped one."
He is shocked when one of his friends (the young man who will
eventually marry 'A'ida) pronounces her name in the course of conversation. "The name that is too awesome for him to utter in his heart,
let alone in public, this misguided young man pronounces carelessly
as though it were a name of one of the swarming masses" (*Qasr al-
shawq*, p. 233).

'Ā'ida means "she who returns" or "she who visits the sick." In ancient Arabic poetry the verb *'āda* (from which *'ā'ida* is derived) is
associated with the theme of *tayf*, the image of the departed woman
haunting the heartbroken lover. The connection between the verb
'ada and the concept of the beloved's image is obvious: the image
keeps returning to the mind of the lover. A very famous line of Arabic poetry, which Mahfuz probably had in mind, brings together the
concept of *tayf* and a synonym derived from the verb *'āda* – *'īd*. The
line reads: "O return of remembrance! how with thee come longing
and wakefulness, and the passing of a phantom darkling, spite of ter-
rors by the way!"[13] The word *'īd* (rendered here by the translator as
"return of remembrance") is explained by the classical lexicogra-
phers as "a recurring trouble, anxiety, or desire."[14] At one point,
Kamal, in his mind, associates his beloved 'A'ida with the concept of
tayf. When 'A'ida asks him whether he plans to become a poet or a
prose writer, he thinks to himself, "I have exhausted all poetry in silent conversations with your image [*tayf*]."[15]

At two significant points of the story of Kamal's love for 'A'ida, he
uses the verb *'ada* ("to return") in relation to her. When we first learn
about Kamal's love, through a long interior monologue (when Kamal
is expecting 'A'ida's return from summer vacation), even before we
know the name of his beloved, we hear him say, "When will you return?"[16] At his last meeting with 'A'ida, Kamal, who has a premo-

---

[13] This is the first verse of Ta'abbata Sharran's poem: *ya 'idu ma laka min shawqin wa-
iraqi, wa-marri tayfin 'ala 'l-ahwali tarraqi. The Mufaddaliyyat*, ed. Charles James Lyall
(Oxford, 1921), translated by Lyall (Oxford, 1919).

[14] Mahfuz mentioned that the villa of his beloved's family was in a street called "Hasan
'Id" (Ghitani, p. 107). In view of Mahfuz's predilection for musing on names, it would seem
plausible that this street name inspired his choice of the name 'Ai'da for Kamal's love.

[15] *Istanfadtu al-shi'ra fi munajati tayfiki, Qasr al-shawq*, p. 204.

[16] *Mata ta'udina?* ibid., p. 19.

nition that he and his beloved will never meet again, says to her, "It seems that you will never return."[17] Thus, the story of Kamal's love for 'A'ida ("she who returns") is enclosed by sentences dealing with her return and making use of the verb from which her name is derived – at the beginning, a question inspired by yearning and hope; at the end, an expression of sad recognition of failure.

Another meaning of the word *'a'ida* in classical Arabic is "gift, favor, or compassion." All of these meanings sound bitterly ironic in view of 'A'ida's attitude toward Kamal. It is worth noting that the name of the girl who is the object of the frustrated love of the hero of *Khan al-Khalili* is Nawal, which also means "gift."[18] It should also be noted that in one of Mahfuz's early stories from the 1930s the name of the unfaithful, attractive young woman is 'A'ida.[19]

Shaddad ('A'ida's family name) is an adjectival form derived from *shadda* which means "to tie," "to tighten" or "to pull"; the adjective *shaddad* itself is of the pattern *fa''al* signifying intensity of action. Used as a common noun, *shaddad* signifies any of a number of devices the purpose of which is to pull or tighten. The name Shaddad describes well the powerful attraction that 'A'ida exerts on Kamal, and his attachment to her.

'A'ida's name becomes the subject of Kamal's ruminations when he goes to a brothel for the first time. The passage in question throws interesting light on Kamal's attitude to women but, more important for our present analysis, it reveals Mahfuz's interest in name symbolism. Having chosen one of the women, Kamal asks the experienced friend who is escorting him whether he knows her name. The friend answers, "Here she is called Warda, but her real name is 'Ayyusha." Warda means flower or rose; 'Ayyusha is an Egyptian colloquial form for 'A'isha, common among lower-class Egyptians. Upon hearing his friend's answer, Kamal muses: "'Ayyusha – Warda! If only one could change one's nature as one changes one's name! In 'A'ida herself there is something similar to this combination of 'Ayyusha – Warda" (*Qasr al-shawq*, chap. 35, p. 392).

---

[17] *Yabdu annaki lan ta'udi*, ibid., p. 282.

[18] See above, p. 180.

[19] See "*Khiyana fi rasa'il*," *al-Riwaya* (Cairo, 15 July 1937). The story is included in the collection *Hams al-junun*.

One should note, however, that the name 'A'ida is composed of syllables from the names 'A'isha and Warda, rather than from a combination of 'Ayyusha and Warda. To be sure, 'Ayyusha is a colloquial form of 'A'isha, but this is precisely the point: the two names are in fact one. 'A'isha is also the name of Kamal's beautiful sister. The dichotomy between the standard form 'A'isha and the colloquial 'Ayyusha parallels the disparity in social status between Kamal's wellborn sister and the wretched prostitute he frequents.[20] Kamal's erotic fantasies as a ten-year-old were associated with the image of this sister. Every day, on his way back from school, he would stop to look at a billboard advertising cigarettes which showed a picture of a woman reclining on a sofa and smoking. "In his thoughts he used to call her 'sister 'A'isha,' because of the resemblance between them – the golden hair and the blue eyes. Although he was barely ten, still he was absolutely fascinated by the woman in the picture and many a time he would fantasize her enjoying a life of luxury, and himself sharing that life with her" (*Bayn al-qasrayn*, pp. 56–57).

Budūr is 'A'ida's much younger sister, who was just a toddler at the time Kamal fell in love with 'A'ida. Kamal used to show her the signs of affection and tenderness which he could not show to her sister. Sixteen years later he accidentally recognizes her in the university lecture hall and, for a while, they become friends. The word *budūr* has two lexical meanings: the *masdar* (verbal noun) of *badara*, "to appear suddenly or unexpectedly" and the plural of *badr*, "the full moon." *Badr* is a standard simile and metaphor in Arabic, both literary and colloquial, for a beautiful face. Specifically, the plural form *budūr* is used in Egyptian colloquial as an epithet for a good looking youth or girl. Both meanings are pertinent. Budur is described as a very lovely young woman and she makes a sudden appearance in Kamal's life.

Yasin's son from Zaynab, his first wife, is called Riḍwān. Born after his parents' divorce, he grows up for a few years in his mother's care.

---

[20] The same idea is reflected in Mahfuz's use of the names Zaynab and Zannuba. Zaynab is the standard form of the name; Zannuba the colloquial form. Zaynab is Yasin's wellborn first wife; Zannuba is the lute-player who becomes his third wife.

Upon reaching school age, he comes to live with his father. His parents' divorce causes the sensitive Ridwan a great deal of emotional pain. By the time he graduates from high school he has become aware of his homosexual inclinations. He is introduced by a friend to an influential politician who privately indulges his homosexual desires and who cultivates a group of young protégés. With the help of this politician, 'Abd al-Rahim Pasha 'Isa, Ridwan obtains a government position and enjoys quick promotion. The family apparently does not suspect the homosexual nature of Ridwan's close relations with the pasha. He is well liked by the whole family; even his aunt Khadija, who sees faults in everybody, regards him as an exemplary young man, and she urges her two sons to emulate him. The irony is clear: the young man who behaves in a manner regarded in Qur'anic law as an abomination has a name meaning "God's contentment." Ridwan, it should be recalled, is, in Egyptian folklore, the "doorkeeper of paradise," who admits the blessed to the heavenly abode.[21] Thanks to his political contacts, young Ridwan is able to help his father obtain a promotion; moreover, he manages to cancel a plan to transfer his uncle Kamal to a provincial town. Ridwan's ability to "open doors" for members of his family, that is, to secure favors for them, would seem to warrant his name, admittedly with a sly ironic twist.

Ridwan's patron, 'Abd al-Rahim Pasha 'Isa, is described as a capable and highly respected politician. He is dedicated to the ideals of Egyptian nationalism and upholds high standards of public service. He explains to Ridwan and his other disciples that people in politics or in public service must excel in hard work and display impartiality, but that private life remains private. Mahfuz's picture of 'Abd al-Rahim Pasha 'Isa and the description of his meeting with his young admirers is remarkable for its combination of frankness, objectivity and irony (al-Sukkariyya, pp. 80–88).

Both components in the pasha's name suggest compassion and tolerance. Rahim means "compassionate" or "merciful." We have already noted that Mahfuz often uses construct names of 'Abd and

---

[21] On Ridwan as the "guardian of paradise," see above, p. 186.

one of God's epithets in order to establish a correspondence between
that particular attribute and the person bearing the composite name.
'Isa is the Qur'anic name of Jesus. It may be noted in this connection
that, in the chapter of *Awlad haretna* about Rifa'a, who is meant to
represent Jesus, Mahfuz describes Rifa'a as a very delicate young
man who is ridiculed by his neighbors for his effeminate appearance
and manner. His sexual abstinence arouses suspicion, and ugly
rumors begin to circulate. The choice of the name 'Isa (Jesus) for the
high-minded homosexual politician is reminiscent of Mahfuz's depiction of the character allegorically representing Jesus in *Awlad haretna*,
as a man of ambiguous sexual inclination.

In portraying 'Abd al-Rahim Pasha 'Isa, Mahfuz apparently drew
on a real political figure of the decades preceding the 1952 revolution. Egyptians familiar with the political scene of those years
specifically remember a top-ranking Egyptian politician who was
rumored to be homosexual, but who was highly esteemed for his in-
tegrity and cultural sophistication. During the thirties and forties, he
served a number of times as minister of education, precisely the same
post as that held by 'Abd al-Rahim Pasha 'Isa in the novel.

The names of two foreign characters (in fact the only non-Egyptian
fictional characters in this or any other of his novels) are carefully
chosen with a covert special meaning; their choice displays that
combination of whimsicality and serious intent so typical of Najib
Mahfuz. Kamal, as a twelve-year-old boy, befriends the British
soldiers encamped near the family's house during the period of
political unrest in 1919. Although he fully identifies with the
Egyptian nationalist attitudes of his family and environment, he likes
to visit the British encampment. Kamal's encounters with the British
soldiers are depicted in a way that subtly make us aware of the
ambivalence which the sensitive young Kamal (and the young Najib
Mahfuz) must have felt toward the British.[22] Only one of these
soldiers – Kamal's "best friend" – is mentioned by name. Kamal is
attracted to this particular soldier because he is especially good
looking, has gentle manners and knows a few words of Arabic. His

---

[22] *Bayn al-qasrayn*, pp. 456–63, 502–3; see the incident with Maryam pp. 504–5.

name is Jolyon, an extremely uncommon English name. It is, however, the given name of several members of the Forsyte family in Galsworthy's *Forsyte Saga*, which Mahfuz read and admired.[23] Is this Najib Mahfuz's way of paying tribute to a favorite English writer, the author of the famous English family saga, in his, the Cairene family saga? I think so; the name of the only other English character in the trilogy – a professor of sociology at the University of Cairo – would appear to have been selected from similar motives. We encounter the professor at the tea party which he and his wife give for the students before they go to England on vacation for the summer. Although the students are all intensely anti-British, they like and respect the professor. Ahmad, Khadija's second son, one of his best students, is at the party. Ahmad's thoughts show the ambivalence toward the British professor: "The personal qualities of the English are seductively charming" (*al-Sukkariyya*, p. 218); "there is a clash between our love for our professor and our hatred for his people" (ibid., p. 219). The British professor's name is Mr. Forster, which would appear to be a covert tribute by the Egyptian novelist to the English novelist and author of *Aspects of the Novel*, E. M. Forster (ibid., pp. 216–17).[24]

Sayyid Muhammad Ridwan, his wife and daughter are the neighbors of Ahmad 'Abd al-Jawad and his family. At the beginning of the story, Sayyid Muhammad Ridwan is paralyzed and bedridden, having suffered a stroke some years before. In fact he has no role to play in the novel, but his wife and daughter do, as does his name. Both the wife and the daughter are objects of erotic interest to all the male members of Sayyid Ahmad's family.

As a child, Kamal frequently visits these neighbors and feels very much at home in their house, where mother and daughter alike welcome him warmly, joke with him and tease him. The cheerful manner of the two women is in sharp contrast to the sorry condition of the head of this household. The mother, an attractive woman in her early

[23] See above, p. 36.

[24] *Aspects of the Novel* first appeared in 1927. Mahfuz's interest in E. M. Forster may equally have been aroused by his other works – particularly his book on Alexandria (*Alexandria: A History and a Guide* [Alexandria, 1922]).

forties, greets Kamal with kisses and asks him, "When will you be grown-up so I can marry you?" She even lets the boy watch her put on her make-up and feel the smoothness of her face. The daughter Maryam, about twenty years old, invites Kamal to sit on her bed, challenging him to "tickling matches." She instructs Kamal to greet her with a kiss whenever he comes to visit; to his kiss on her cheek, she responds with a kiss on his mouth. The atmosphere surrounding Muhammad Ridwan's wife and daughter is charged with erotic sensuality; their uninhibited behavior differs appallingly from the modest demeanor of Kamal's mother and sisters (*Bayn al-qasrayn*, pp. 152–54).

Fahmi, Kamal's older brother, a law student, is passionately attracted to the beautiful Maryam. Normally, a young man like Fahmi would not be allowed to look at a young woman of his class (other than his sisters); a well bred young woman would not appear before men and would be expected to hide herself quickly the moment she noticed a man looking at her. Fahmi, however, avails himself of the proximity of the flat roofs of his and Maryam's houses and he goes to the roof of his house to watch Maryam as she comes to hang laundry on her roof. Much as Fahmi is aroused by the sight of Maryam, he cannot avoid the disturbing thought that she does not behave as a respectable young woman should: she does not hide promptly upon his appearance on the roof but goes on with her work as if she has not noticed him, although she most certainly has (*Bayn al-qasrayn*, p. 69). Fahmi dismisses this thought and asks his mother to obtain his father's permission for him to become engaged to Maryam. Sayyid Ahmad 'Abd al-Jawad is outraged by his son's request, as he considers it most impertinent for Fahmi even to think about engagement before completing his studies; he angrily rejects the suggestion, and thus puts an end to the matter (ibid., pp. 146–49).

About a year later, Kamal is witness to a scene that irreparably tarnishes Maryam's reputation: he sees her smiling from the window to an English soldier signaling to her from the street. The soldier, Kamal's "friend" Jolyon, asks him to carry a package to her. Kamal refuses and reports the event to his mother, sisters and brother, who are all shocked by the revelation that Maryam is not the virtuous girl they have taken her to be, but a licentious woman (*Bayn al-qasrayn*, pp. 503–8). The irony in the name Maryam is obvious. Maryam (Mary), mother of 'Isa (Jesus), is presented in the Qur'an as the very model of chastity (Qur'an, 66:12).

Five years after Fahmi's frustrated attempt to become engaged, and about four years after his death in an anti-British demonstration, Yasin, the eldest of Sayyid Ahmad's children, decides to marry Maryam (*Qasr al-shawq*, pp. 66–73). By this time Yasin has already been divorced from his first wife for several years, and Maryam has recently divorced her husband. When Yasin asks his father's consent to his marriage with Maryam, Sayyid Ahmad is shaken, for he has had a secret affair with Maryam's mother some years before: he cannot argue strongly against Yasin's choice because he cannot reveal the true cause of his objection (and he has not been made aware of the English soldier incident). Reluctantly, he must therefore give his consent (*Qasr al-shawq*, p. 123). What the father does not know (and what will remain a secret) is that Yasin will have his own brief affair with Maryam's mother shortly after asking for her daughter's hand in marriage. Kamal, who witnesses Yasin's approaches to Maryam, recalls that for a long time she was the subject of his own erotic dreams (*Qasr al-shawq*, p. 74). Yasin's marriage to Maryam ends in divorce: she leaves him when Yasin returns home one night drunk, with another woman. Some twenty years after this, Kamal again sees Maryam; the period is that of the Second World War, and Kamal sees her serving drinks to English soldiers in a bar. He remarks to himself, "Thus, Maryam began with the English and she ended up with the English" (*al-Sukkariyya*, p. 228).

Maryam's mother, Bahija (usually referred to as Umm Maryam),[25] makes a pass at Sayyid Ahmad some time after he refuses Fahmi's request to become engaged to Maryam. Even though he is attracted to this woman with her "ample body and swaying buttocks," he ignores her invitation because he has a rule "not to transgress on the sacred rights of a neighbor or a friend" (*Bayn al-qasrayn*, pp. 256–59). However, some months later, when her husband is dead and she again approaches Sayyid Ahmad, he no longer feels constrained. The conversation in which Sayyid Ahmad and Umm Maryam agree on a

---

[25] *Bahija* means beautiful, joyous or delightful.

secret meeting at her house is a remarkable example of Mahfuzian
humorous double entendre and irony. Umm Maryam rebukes Sayyid
Ahmad for ignoring her earlier approach, for which he apologizes
with polite excuses. Toward the end of the conversation, he says to
her,

> "Forgiveness is often the secret password to paradise.... The
> paradise I mean is at the junction of Bayn al-Qasrayn [alley]
> and al-Nahhasin [alley]; fortunately its door opens on to a side
> path hidden from watchful eyes and it has no keeper."
>   It then occurred to him that the doorkeeper of the heavenly
> paradise had the same name as the deceased [man] who was the
> guard of the earthly paradise that he was now seeking to enter.
> He was momentarily worried, fearing that the woman might
> have noticed the same ironical fact, but he saw her abstracted
> as if in a dream. He sighed [in relief] begging in his heart God's
> forgiveness (*Bayn al-qasrayn*, p. 392).

"The deceased [man] who was the guard of the earthly paradise" is
the woman's husband, the late Muhammad Ridwan, whose second
name, Ridwan, is indeed the name of the angel guarding the entrance
to paradise or in charge of the treasures of paradise (*khazin al-
jinan*).[26]

Kamāl, Sayyid Ahmad's youngest son, is described as devoid of the
physical charm of his father and the beauty of his mother. He is
painfully conscious of his unattractive appearance. The irony in the
choice of his name, which means "perfection," seems all too obvious.
Perfection is a divine quality which mortals do not possess.
"Perfection belongs to God alone" (*al-kamāl li-llah wahdah*), asserts
Sayyid Ahmad to excuse himself for his moral laxity (*Bayn al-
qasrayn*, p. 50). 'Abd al-Rahim Pasha 'Isa also quotes this dictum,

---

[26] See above, p. 186, the use of the name Ridwan in *al-Qahira al-jadida*. It should be
noted that in the case of Sayyid Muhammad Ridwan, Ridwan is actually the person's name
rather than his father's name. In many Egyptian families it is customary to add the name of
the Prophet to the given name, e.g., Muhammad Anwar, Muhammad Hasanayn; in such
cases the distinctive name of the person is the second component of the given name: Anwar
or Hasanayn and, in our case, Ridwan.

while explaining to his young protégés how one should judge the conduct of public persons (al-Sukkariyya, p. 84).

Kamal is made aware of his physical imperfections even as a child, because the children of the neighborhood mock him for his unusually big head and protruding forehead. They call him *abu ra'sayn* ("two-headed"). His mother comforts the crying Kamal, who reports this insult to her, and tells him that there is no greater honor than to have a feature similar to that of the Prophet Muhammad (*Bayn al-qasrayn*, p. 57). She is referring to a well-known tradition that the Prophet Muhammad had a large head.[27]

The nickname "Two-Headed" is of great significance. It alludes to Kamal's "two minds": his attraction to Western thought and literature on the one hand, and his attachment to his own cultural heritage on the other.

Mutawalli 'Abd al-Samad, the wandering Sufi holy man who appears a number of times throughout the novel, bears a name closely corresponding to his vocation. *Mutawalli* means "one who has undertaken or aspires to *wilaya*," that is, the role of *waliyy* ("holy man"). *'Abd al-Samad* means "the servant of the Eternal." Allah's epithet *Samad* ("everlasting," "eternal") alludes to a characteristic of the holy man himself, for although he is very old, he appears to defy age; at seventy-five he is "in a state of health which arouses envy" (*Bayn al-qasrayn*, pp. 45–46).[28]

Shaykh Mutawalli 'Abd al-Samad knew the late father of Sayyid Ahmad 'Abd al-Jawad and he is still alive when Sayyid Ahmad dies. However, his continuing good health and supposed agelessness are no more than a legend; in reality the old Sufi shaykh is not immune to the ruinous effects of time. Najib Mahfuz points subtly to this reality: in his first appearance, at the shop of Sayyid Ahmad, he is described as "rushing in" (*Bayn al-qasrayn*, p. 45); some ten years later, coming to visit Sayyid Ahmad who is in bed recuperating from a heart attack, he walks "leaning on his cane" (*Qasr al-shawq*,

---

[27] *Kana salla 'llahu 'alayhi wa-sallam dakhm al-ra's*, al-Tirmidhi, *Sunan* (Homs, 1967), vol. 9, p. 254, no. 3641.

[28] Apart from his supposed agelessness, Mutawalli 'Abd al-Samad would appear to possess other divine attributes (cf. Somekh, p. 132, n. 6).

p. 445). More than a decade later, at the time of Na'ima's wedding, the old shaykh is in an extremely pitiful state – he can no longer control his bladder and Kamal sees him wetting his clothes (al-Sukkariyya, p. 148).

The mental decline of the Sufi shaykh is likewise significantly noted by Mahfuz. During his first appearance in Sayyid Ahmad's shop, the shaykh prays for the latter's children whom he mentions by name, one by one, in order of age (Bayn al-qasrayn, p. 48). When he arrives at Na'ima's wedding he asks the names of Sayyid Ahmad's children and grandchildren so that he can pray for them. When Sayyid Ahmad is told of this, he thinks, "What a pity, he forgot your names. May God forgive old age" (al-Sukkariyya, p. 147). A couple of years later, the shaykh sees the funeral of Sayyid Ahmad and asks whose funeral it is. When a man answers him that this is the funeral of Sayyid Ahmad 'Abd al-Jawad, he asks, apparently not recognizing the name, "Where [is he] from?" The man says to him, "He is from this quarter, how come you don't know him? Don't you remember Sayyid Ahmad 'Abd al-Jawad?" But the shaykh does not remember anything (ibid., p. 270). The once energetic, alert and authoritative holy man is now senile.

When Shaykh Mutawalli visits Sayyid Ahmad during his illness, the latter thinks admiringly, "You are very dear to me, Shaykh Mutawalli, you are one of the landmarks of time [anta min ma'alim al-zaman]" (Qasr al-shawq, 448). Obviously, this thought occurred to Sayyid Ahmad while he still believed the holy man to be as formidable and unchanging as Time itself. However, he was eventually to find out how much the holy man was ravaged by age. Sayyid Ahmad's words "You are one of the landmarks of time" appear to have two quite different meanings. When they first occur to Sayyid Ahmad, as an expression of admiration of the shaykh's putative capacity to withstand time, "one of the landmarks of time" is construed as "one of the unchanging and ever recurring marks of time." However, when the same phrase is considered in the light of what we come to know about the shaykh's deterioration to a state of decrepit senility, "one of the landmarks of time" means "one on whom time has left its marks." There is every reason to believe that the ambiguity of this phrase is intentional and therefore ironic.

Nicknames are also significant, because they disclose how a character is perceived by others. We have already noted the significance of the nickname "Two Headed" given to Kamal as a child, because of his unusually big, protruding forehead. Later, when he falls unhappily in love with 'A'ida, she and her friends call him behind his back, "the distracted lover."

Other nicknames are also revealing. The women of the neighborhood call the mother Amina "the Bee" (al-naḥla), on account of her diligence and her constant activity around the house (Bayn al-qasrayn, p. 14). This same bee image has another function when Kamal applies it in his mind to his beloved 'A'ida: "The bee is by nature a queen; the garden is her domain, the nectar of flowers her drink, her spittle honey, and the reward of the person who moves around her throne is a sting" (Qasr al-shawq, p. 204).[29]

The stern father Sayyid Ahmad 'Abd al-Jawad is known to his intimate friends as "the Master of Joking" (Bayn al-qasrayn, p. 380, al-Sukkariyya, p. 53).[30] His wife and family, of course, are ignorant of this nickname just as they are ignorant of the frivolous side of his personality.

Khadija is especially prone to nicknaming people. She is quick to observe the peculiar defect in everyone and to invent a nickname that underscores it. She is so good at inventing such names that these are regularly used in the family circle (Bayn al-qasrayn, p. 34–35). Their parents' long-time friend, the widow of Mr. Shawkat (who will become her mother-in-law), she calls "the machine gun," because she squirts saliva when she speaks. She calls their neighbor, Umm Maryam, "In God's name, Milords" (li-llah ya asyadi), because she often comes to their home to borrow household utensils, and invariably uses this formula of request. She refers to the teacher of the neighborhood Qur'an school as "the worst of God's creation," for a dual reason: because he repeatedly pronounces this phrase (the epithet of Satan, Qur'an 113:2) "due to his profession, and also because

---

[29] The Arabic word used here for him "who moves around" is ta'if, which is the term usually applied to those who perform the rite of circumambulating the holy Ka'ba in Mecca (called in Arabic tawaf).

[30] The Arabic phrase used in the first instance, rabb al-daḥk, is in literary Arabic, while the second, dahkaji agha, is a colloquial expression influenced by Turkish.

he is extremely ugly."[31] The *ful* vendor she calls "Baldy," and the milkman, "One-Eyed." She is somewhat kinder to members of her own family. She calls her mother *al-mu'adhdhin* ("the muezzin"), due to the mother's habit of rising early from sleep. Her brother Fahmi she calls "Bedpost" because he is thin, and for the same reason she calls her sister 'A'isha "Bamboo Reed."

Events must also be named so that they can be remembered. Sayyid Ahmad and his friends celebrate a special event: following the violent death of his son, Sayyid Ahmad has avoided having intimate relations with women of pleasure for five years; now he has come to make merry with his friends and their mistresses. Greeting Sayyid Ahmad on his arrival, one of his friends says: "This is a historic night in your life and in ours. We should give it a suitable name to celebrate it, 'the night of the old man's return.' What do you say?" Putting his hand on his friend's shoulder, Sayyid Ahmad answers, "I'm no old man. Old man, your father!" (*Qasr al-shawq*, pp. 85–86). The name suggested for the event, "the night of the old man's return," besides its teasing of Sayyid Ahmad, includes a humorous reference to an Arabic book, called *Ruju' al-shaykh ila sibah fi 'l-quwwa 'ala 'l-bah* ("The Old Man's Return to His Youth in Sexual Potency"), a famous sixteenth-century composition containing advice on strengthening or regaining potency and arousing desire.[32]

I should like to close this chapter on names in the trilogy with the description of a short scene from *al-Sukkariyya* (p. 292): Kamal, now a bachelor in his mid-thirties, is accosted by a worn out old beggar-woman, while sitting in a café with his friends Riyad Qaldes and Isma'il Latif. When the waiter tells them that this miserable beggar is

---

[31] The penultimate sura of the Qur'an, in which the phrase occurs, is one of the most popularly recited, as it is a prayer for God's protection. It was one of the first chapters learned by children in the Qur'an school. Satan is popularly believed to be hideously ugly.

[32] The book is usually attributed to the Ottoman religious scholar Shams al-Din Ahmad ibn Sulayman, known as Ibn Kamal Pasha or Kemal Pasha Zade (d. 1534). See *EI*², s.v. "Kemāl Pasha-Zāde." An anonymous English translation of the book, entitled *The Old Man Young Again*, appeared in Paris in two volumes in 1898–9. This book, under its abbreviated title, *Ruju' al-shaykh* ("The Old Man's Return"), is mentioned again in the trilogy, *al-Sukkariyya*, p. 53.

the once famous and beautiful singer Zubayda, their curiousity is aroused, and they introduce themselves. When Isma'il Latif gives his name, Zubayda laughingly responds: "Long live the names, even though yours is a name which has no meaning." The first part of Zubayda's response is conventional;[33] the second, however, requires explanation. When Zubayda says that the name Isma'il Latif "has no meaning," she is probably saying that it has no associations for her. Kamal and his friends, however, are amused by the remark, possibly because Zubayda's response conceals a private joke planted by Mahfuz for the linguistically erudite: Zubayda has unintentionally echoed the classical Arabic dictionaries' definition of *Isma'īl*. *Lisan al-'arab*, the most famous of the medieval Arabic lexicons, defines *Isma'īl* as "a name," and attributes no meaning to it.[34] Thus, an apparently casual remark by the illiterate Zubayda reveals the meticulous attention which Mahfuz devoted to the names of his characters.

[33] "Long live the names" (*'āshat al-asmā'*) is a colloquial expression of blessing used, mainly by women, on hearing a name.

[34] See *Lisan al-'arab*, s.v. *'sm'l*. A modern Arabic dictionary of names notes that Isma'il is "a name for which no explanation is given," *Mu'jam al-asma' al-'arabiyya*, p. 32.

CHAPTER 17

The Thief and the Dogs

The plot of *al-Liss wa'l-kilab* ("The Thief and the Dogs") has already been summarized in the chapter on Mahfuz's works. The hero of this novel, Sa'id Mahran, is ironically named. *Sa'id* means "happy," "fortunate" – the very opposite of Sa'id's condition. The Sufi shaykh in whose house he finds temporary refuge says to him, "You are very miserable, my son [*anta ta'is jiddan ya bunayya*]" (p. 84). *Mahran*, the second component of the name (Sa'id's father's name), is derived from the verb *mahara* – "to be skillful, dexterous, adroit." In fact, Sa'id is described on one occasion as "climbing up the wall with the dexterity of an acrobat [*bi-maharat al-bahlawan*]" (p. 50). In another instance, Sa'id, recalling the times that he practiced with his pistol in the desert, says to himself: "This desert witnessed your skill [*wa-shahida hadha al-khala' maharataka*]. They said that you were [the angel of] death himself and that your shot never missed" (p. 62). But however much Sa'id may congratulate himself on his extraordinary dexterity and skill (*mahara*) at shooting, he nevertheless fails miserably in his attempts to avenge himself on those who have betrayed him, precisely when the time comes for him to prove his presumed qualities. Thus, ironically, he also fails to live up to the name Mahran.

Upon his release from prison Sa'id seeks refuge and help from the Sufi shaykh, 'Ali al-Junaydi, the spiritual guide of Sa'id's late father many years before. The shaykh's house is open to Sa'id as a refuge, but the shaykh's mystical utterances cannot give solace to his troubled soul; much less, practical help in satisfying his immediate needs. Shaykh 'Ali is truly sublime (*'aliyy*) as his name indicates, but he is also out of touch with the world and with real life. The second part of his name, the *nisba* al-Junaydi, is a reference to the great tenth-century mystic of Baghdad, al-Junayd (d. 910).

Sa'id's mentor-turned-enemy is the journalist Ra'uf 'Alwan. His surname 'Alwan, like the Sufi shaykh's first name, is derived from the root *'-l-w* signifying highness, excellence and sublimity. Sa'id regards Ra'uf 'Alwan as much more than an ideological mentor: "His [own] life was nothing but an extension of the ideas of this man ... and if he [Ra'uf 'Alwan] has betrayed them, woe unto him!" thinks Sa'id (p. 41). Sa'id compares the left-wing journalist Ra'uf to his own father's mentor: "You are not less sublime than Shaykh 'Ali" (p. 34).

It should be recalled here that the names *Ra'uf* ("compassionate") and *'Ali* ("lofty," "sublime") are both among the epithets of God (*al-asma' al-husna*). Both bearers of these names in the novel appear in some way "godlike," the one to Sa'id's father, the other to Sa'id. The godlike role of Ra'uf vis-à-vis Sa'id can be discerned in the following: When Sa'id realizes that Ra'uf has changed and is no longer the man he once admired, he says, "You *create me* and then you withdraw, you simply change your ideas after they have become embodied in my person" (p. 47, my emphasis).[1]

Najib Mahfuz artfully emphasizes how these two clashing ideologies – religion and Marxist revolutionary doctrine, represented respectively by Shaykh 'Ali and Ra'uf – compete for control over Sa'id's mind. When Sa'id seeks help and advice from the shaykh, the latter orders him, "Take a Qur'an and read!" Then he repeats five times, "Purify yourself and read [*tawadda' wa-'qra'*]" (pp. 28–29). The allusion to God's command to Muhammad (in sura 97), "'*qra*'," cannot be missed. In another scene we hear Sa'id recalling how Ra'uf used to order him, "Train yourself [to use the pistol] and read [*tadarrab wa-'qra'*]!" (p. 62). The reading intended by Ra'uf is of course that of Marxist doctrine, but his phrase closely resembles the shaykh's order.

Ra'uf 'Alwan's name, like that of Sa'id Mahran, means the very

---

[1] The Arabic word translated here as "withdraw" is *tartadd* which also means to commit an act of apostasy, to be an apostate.

opposite of what he is. Ra'uf is not compassionate as his name denotes, but is totally pitiless and devoid of empathy for his former
disciple. The revolutionary intellectual who used to agitate in the
name of socialist ideals now lives in luxury in a sumptuous villa; he
has become a base opportunist. Intending to kill the journalist, Sa'id sarcastically thinks, "Ra'uf 'Alwan – the excellent lofty traitor [*ra'uf 'alwan,
al-kha'in al-rafi' al-mumtaz*]" (p. 78). Mahfuz very nearly spells out here
the irony of the contrast between Ra'uf's name and his true nature.

Sa'id's other adversary is his one-time henchman – 'Ileish Sidra,
who deceived him with his wife Nabawiyya and took Sa'id's place as
Nabawiyya's husband and head of the gang. This is something that
Sa'id could not have imagined: "How could she incline to the dog
and abandon the lion?" (p. 104). To Sa'id, 'Ileish is "a dog," a base
and servile creature (pp. 8, 31), and he calls him "dog mange" (p.
14). *'Ileish* is not a very common name, and is to be found mostly
among people in rural areas. Its meaning and derivation are not commonly known. 'Ileish is phonetically reminiscent of the word
'illawsh, meaning jackal or wolf.[2] Be it jackal or wolf, it is a close
relative of the dog. Similarly, the name of the corrupt engineer in
Miramar is Sirhan which means "wolf." In that novel, Sirhan betrays
both the ideals of Arab Socialism, which he hypocritically professes,
and the woman whom he promised to marry.[3] Both 'Ileish and Sirhan
are criticized as traitors; traitors are called "dogs" in *al-Liss wa'l-
kilab*. The fact that they are both named after animals from the
Canidae family would seem to fit Mahfuz's purpose and method of
naming. The name 'Ileish has some phonetic similarity to 'Ali although there is no etymological connection between the two. Thus,
the name of the vilest character in this story and the name of the most
sublime are reminiscent of each other.[4]

---

[2] See *Taj al-'arus*, s.v. "'-l-sh," and Damiri's *Hayat al-hayawan*, vol. 2, p. 211. The
possible connection between the name 'Ileish and *'illawsh* was noted correctly by Mohamed
Mahmoud in his article "The Unchanging Hero in a Changing World: Najib Mahfuz's *al-
Liss wa'l-kilab (The Thief and the Dogs)*," in Trevor Le Gassick (ed.), *Critical Perspectives
on Naguib Mahfouz* (Washington, 1991), p. 126.

[3] The name Sirhan occurs also in Mahfuz's *Afrah al-qubba* (*Wedding Song*, 1981) as the
name of the theater director who exploits his position of power to get the women he wants.
See *Afrah al-qubba*, pp. 23–24, 92 (where he seduces the young Halima).

[4] This phonetic similarity between 'Ileish and 'Ali was employed by Tawfiq al-Hakim in

'Ileish's second name, *Sidra*, appears to be a nickname alluding to
his figure: he is described as having a body "like a barrel" (*jism
barmili*) (*al-Liss wa'l-kilab*, p.13). In Egyptian colloquial, *sidra* or
sidriyya is a large bowl.[5] The name *Sidra* alludes also to 'Ileish's conduct and destiny. *Sidra*, meaning lote tree (Zizyphus lotus, or lotus
jujube) in literary Arabic, is mentioned in the Qur'an 53:13–16. The
traditional understanding of this Qur'anic passage is that Muhammad saw the angel sent to reveal God's message to him standing
by the *sidrat al-muntaha* – "the lote tree of the final reach." Hence,
the lote tree is regarded as a sacred tree which should not be felled.
The heavenly *sidra* is believed to be located in the seventh heaven
to the right of the Throne; it is at or adjacent to *jannat al-ma'wa*,
"the paradise refuge," where the souls of the pious and martyrs rest.
Near the heavenly *sidra* a large throng of angels worship God; even
the angels are not allowed to go beyond it. The name Sidra is therefore associated with the notion of sanctity, piety, and divine grace
and protection.

What irony that this should be the name of 'Ileish "the dog." What
irony within irony that 'Ileish escapes Sa'id's vengeance as though
miraculously protected. Sa'id thinks, "He [Sa'id] will be hunted by
the hangman's rope while 'Ileish is safe" (p. 86).

The third connotation of this name has to do with its ostensible
derivation from the same root as the verb *sadara*, "to be heedless or
carefree." Najib Mahfuz uses the adjectival form *sadira* to describe a
heedless bird, an image alluding to Sa'id's carelessness when 'Ileish
Sidra was stealthily plotting with Nabawiyya against him. Irony
again.[6]

The irony in the choice of the name Nabawiyya is clear: *nabawiyya*, a feminine adjective derived from *nabiyy* ("prophet"), sug-

---

his short story "*Tarid al-firdaws*," where the hero 'Ileish re-names himself 'Illewi (a colloquial
nisba from 'Ali); "*Tarid al-firdaws*" in *Qisas Tawfiq al-Hakim, al-majmu'a al-ula* (Cairo,
1949), pp. 47–84.

[5] See Hinds and Badawi, *Dictionary of Egyptian Arabic* (Beirut, 1986) s.v. "*sidriyya*,"
and "*midra*."

[6] The word *sadir* also occurs in *al-Sukkariyya*, p. 250, in a negative comment on Kamal's
journalistic writing. The speaker, a young communist activist, criticizes Kamal for his total
absorption in his quest for the "absolute," while remaining politically uncommitted. She
says, "He is passing by without paying attention [*yamurru sadiran*] to the real sufferers."

gests that the bearer of this name is expected to emulate the virtues of the Prophet's womenfolk: to display chastity and loyalty, and to enjoy his blessing. Instead, however, Nabawiyya deceives Sa'id with his treacherous henchman 'Ileish, and later marries him. Indignantly, Sa'id thinks, "Nabawiyya, 'Ileish – how have these two names become one?" (p. 8). Here again Mahfuz actually calls the reader's attention to the names of the characters.[7]

Sa'id, attempting to avenge himself on 'Ileish, shoots at the door of his apartment, supposing him to be standing behind it. In fact, he kills an innocent person who had come to occupy the apartment, which the cautious 'Ileish has left. The man whom Sa'id kills by mistake is one Sha'ban Husayn, a simple worker in a warehouse. *Sha'bān*, the name of the eighth month of the Muslim year, is quite a common personal name. In the pre-Islamic tradition of Arabia, Sha'ban was one of the four sacred months during which all fighting and killing was forbidden; the notion of Sha'ban as a month of special religious importance was carried over to Islam. According to popular belief, on the night preceding the 15th of Sha'ban it is decreed who will die in the coming year. Sanctity and immunity as well as death are thus associated with the month of Sha'ban, and are evoked by its name. The personal name Sha'ban may suggest two more meanings: the first (and more easily recognized) is related to *al-sha'b*, "the people," especially "the common folk"; the second (intended for the linguistically erudite) is related to *sha'ūb* – Death.[8] Sha'ban's second name (i.e., his father's name) is Husayn, which relates him to the most famous of those who were wrongly killed – Husayn, the Prophet's grandson.

Indeed, *Sha'ban* seems to be Mahfuz's chosen name for those who are wrongly killed. In *Awlad haretna*, Sha'ban is an innocent man

---

[7] The name Nabawiyya appears also in the novel *al-Tariq* (*The Search*, 1964). Sabir, the hero of *al-Tariq*, is engaged in a search for his father, whom his mother left before he was born. The mother was a "madam" running brothels. As he has no money, he sells his furniture to his mother's closest friend, also a brothel keeper. This woman is never to appear again in the story, but she is mentioned by name: Nabawiyya (*al-Tariq*, p. 22). Here also, the contrast between the name and the character is intended for the ironic effect.

[8] *Wa-minhu summiyat al-maniyyatu sha'ub, ... wa-'ash'aba al-rajulu idha mata* ("And hence death was given the name *sha'ub*, ... and *'ash'aba al-rajulu* means 'the man died'"), *Lisan al-'arab*, s.v. "*sh-'-b*."

who is unjustly murdered.[9] In *al-Maraya*, Najib Mahfuz tells the story of a certain ʿAbd al-Rahman Shaʿban, a low ranking official, who was killed by the mob in the riots of 26 January 1950 in Cairo. This man blindly admired everything European and used to spend his free time in the company of European friends; he met his death when the club in which he was sitting with his friends was attacked and burned by a rioting mob.[10] It is typical of Najib Mahfuz that the pious martyr of *Awlad haretna*, the unfortunate victim in *al-Liss wa'l-kilab* and the rather dubious though good-natured character in *al-Maraya* share the name Shaʿban; in the eyes of Mahfuz they are all innocent victims.

The name of Saʿid's lover, the prostitute Nur ("light"), is clearly symbolic. Nur, however, reveals to Saʿid that this is not her real name; she comes from a village where her name was Shalabiyya (colloquial Arabic, originally Turkish, meaning "nice" or "pretty," used now mostly among the lower classes), but she has assumed the name Nur as her, so to speak, professional name (p. 129). There are various points of analogy, in correspondence or contrast, between name and character in this case. Nur, one of the so-called "daughters of the night" (*banat al-layl*), lights up Saʿid's dismal life with her selfless love and devotion.[11] Her name is thus a metaphor for her role in Saʿid's life. There is also a non-metaphoric light associated with Nur's person: while Saʿid is hiding in her apartment, he must put out the light whenever she leaves the house at night, so that the neighbors will not suspect that there is anyone there; only when Nur returns can they light the lamp (p. 104). The analogy and the irony here are very pointed; they are also perhaps a bit trite.

Is this all that Mahfuz had in mind when he chose this name? I think not. *Nur* is the key word in the famous "light verse" (*ayat al-nur*, Qur'an, 24:35). In this verse (for which the whole chapter is named "the light chapter," *surat al-nur*), "light" is God or, according to some exegetes, divine knowledge; the verse begins as follows: "Allah is the light of heaven and earth" (*allah nuru 'l-samawati wa'l-*

---

[9] *Awlad haretna*, pp. 383–85.

[10] *Al-Maraya*, pp. 252–60.

[11] *Banat al-layl* is a common Egyptian euphemism for prostitutes.

ardi). But is this not pushing the point too far? Is there any evidence that Najib Mahfuz had intended such a daring analogy?

In his short story "*Ṣūra*" ("A Picture"), Mahfuz tells us about a village girl who becomes a prostitute and is murdered by an angry lover.[12] Her name too is Shalabiyya, and as a prostitute she calls herself Durriyya. *Durriyya* (the feminine form of *durriyy*) means glittering or shining. This adjective occurs in the "light verse," the opening words of which have already been quoted here; the rest of the verse reads as follows: "His light is like a niche in which there is a lamp, the lamp is in a glass and the glass is like a shining star [*kawkab durriyy*]." To recapitulate, in our novel a girl called Shalabiyya is renamed Nur when she becomes a prostitute; in the short story "*Ṣūra*," another prostitute changes her name from Shalabiyya to Durriyya.

Irony, however, is not Mahfuz's only purpose in using a prostitute's name to evoke the "light verse." The verses preceding the "light verse" (Qur'an, 24:1–33) deal with the subject of sexual relations, the prohibition of fornication and the edict forbidding Muslims to force their slave-girls to prostitute themselves (v. 33). According to this verse, God will be forgiving and merciful to slave-girls who are coerced into prostitution. Mahfuz has often stated that, in his view, most prostitutes are forced into their wretched condition by harsh circumstances.[13]

Nur is one of a series of prostitute characters in Mahfuz's novels. We encounter Hamida in *Zuqaq al-midaqq*, Nafisa in *Bidaya wa-nihaya*, Riri in *al-Summan wa'l-kharif*. In the trilogy there are Warda/'Ayyusha and 'Atiyyah, as well as women who are not common prostitutes in brothels, like these two, but professional women of pleasure – the singers Jalila and Zubayda and the lute-player Zannuba. The personality of the prostitute and the social problem of prostitution have clearly occupied Mahfuz. In various interviews Mahfuz has expressed his opinion that prostitution is a social ill and that prostitutes, far from being moral delinquents, are primarily the

---

[12] In the collection *Khammarat al-qitt al-aswad*, 1968, pp. 231–43.

[13] Cf. Ahmad Abu Kaff "*al-Mar'a wa'l-jins fi adab Najib Mahfuz*," *al-Hilal*, (February 1970), p. 195; and Mahmud Fawzi, *Najib Mahfuz – za'im al-harafish* (Beirut, 1988), p. 144.

victims of an exploitative order. Nur is depicted in a way bound to elicit deep sympathy and compassion in the reader. Both her personal qualities – patience, and selfless love and devotion to Sa'id – and her symbolic role make her stand out as a very model of the "pure," kind-hearted prostitute. Not all Mahfuz's prostitute characters are stereotypes, however: not all are pure and kind-hearted. He makes it very clear that individual prostitutes are quite different from one another and are induced to practice their profession for a variety of reasons. Some are forced into their situation by poverty, like 'Atiyyah in the trilogy, a widow with two young children who must prostitute herself in order to put food on the table. Nafisa in *Bidaya wa-nihaya* becomes a prostitute for complex reasons resulting from her hopelessness and particular psychological make-up, as well as from the poverty of her family. Nur is meek and submissive; Hamida in *Zuqaq al-midaqq* is arrogant and defiant. Hamida becomes a prostitute from a desire to escape from her old impoverished neighborhood and live in luxury.

For all the differences in character and circumstances among these women, in Mahfuz's eyes they all are victims of the same perverted order. Prostitution is a form of slavery. Mahfuz expresses this idea in various forms. Thinking about 'Atiyyah, the prostitute whom he regularly sees, Kamal says, "She is a miserable picture of enslavement. . . ." And then, watching 'Atiyyah filling their glasses with liquor, he thinks, "In this house [the brothel] the bottle costs double its price; everything is expensive here, except for the woman, the human being" (*al-Sukkariyya*, p. 134). Earlier in the trilogy, when Sayyid Ahmad is rebuked by the Sufi shaykh for his promiscuity, he defends himself, saying, "Don't forget, Shaykh Mutawalli, that the professional women entertainers of today are the slave girls of yesterday whom God made available [to men] through buying and selling" (*Bayn al-Qasrayn*, p. 50). Zannuba, the ambitious lute player, who, as Sayyid Ahmad's mistress, is living for a while on a houseboat he has rented for her, is unhappy with her condition and would like him to marry her. When he questions her about her comings and goings she angrily retorts, "If living here means that you regard me as a slave, and that you make all sorts of accusations against me whenever you wish, then we'd better end our relationship" (*al-Sukkariyya*, p. 321).

In all of these examples, it is not only clear that Mahfuz looks upon prostitution as a form of slavery, but also that he condemns the institution of concubinage (held legal in Islamic law) as a form of prostitution.

Sana' is the name of Sa'id's daughter. It is his memory of her and the hope of getting her back which sustains him during his four years in prison. "His yearning for her shone [in his heart] as the clear sky after rain" (p. 8). However, when he is allowed to meet her upon his release from prison, Sana', by now six years old, does not recognize him and is frightened when he tries to kiss her. Her mother will not let him have custody of her. His hope of getting Sana' back is lost. *Sana'* means "a flash of light, radiance, splendor." Very commonly used in conjunction with lightning (*sana al-barq*) the word signifies a short spell of brightness in the dark which dazzles the eyes. This is based on Qur'an 24:43 – "the flash of His lightning [*sana barqihi*] all but snatches away the sight."

The name Sana' occurs again in Najib Mahfuz's *Tharthara fawq al-nil* ("Chatter on the Nile," 1966). The story takes place in a house-boat on the Nile, where a group of Egyptian intellectuals meet nightly to entertain themselves with drinking, drugs and sex. The main character, Anis Zaki, is a lonely man whose wife and only daughter died many years before. Sana', a young college student, is a newcomer to the group; she is brought to the boathouse by the actor Rajab al-Qadi, a "lady killer" in the films as well as in life, who is about to seduce the young girl and expose her to drugs and alcohol. Anis is deeply troubled by the thought of what will become of her. He feels that his concern for this girl is in fact a concern for his own daughter. He says to himself, "If my daughter were alive she would be Sana''s age" (*Tharthara*, p. 34). The name Sana' thus links Sa'id Mahran of *al-Liss wa'l-kilab* and Anis Zaki of *Tharthara fawq al-nil*. They are quite different in character: the former is a defiant rebel, the latter a lethargic introvert, but they share the predicament of loneliness and alienation.

Light and darkness have a special descriptive role throughout *al-Liss wa'l-kilab*. The novel opens with Sa'id's release from prison under the blazing sun of a July day in Cairo. It ends a few days later, when he is shot dead by the police in a cemetery in the dark of night. In between these two points various kinds of light are mentioned, natural and man-made: the stars at night, the pale of dawn, the red sky before dusk, the faint light in Nur's window overlooking the darkness of the cemetery, the shining lights of Ra'uf's villa. The contrast between light and darkness, and more precisely, the continuous contest between the two, is ever-present in this novel. Light, however, is not only the symbol of hope and love, as it is in the figures of Nur and Sana'; it is also depressingly unbearable, provocative, and at times violent. When Sa'id steps out of prison he finds himself in "streets upon which the sun weighs heavily" (p. 7). Sa'id thinks of Ra'uf's villa as "the mansion of lights and mirrors" (p. 48).

Sa'id usually finds shelter in the dark, but this shelter can very easily turn out to be unreliable. When Sa'id tries to burglarize Ra'uf's villa at night, he sneaks into the house under the cover of dark. But once inside he discovers that he cannot find his way around. "He saw darkness weighing heavily upon him like a nightmare and he thought of lighting a match for a second [to see his way], but suddenly he was overwhelmed by a dazzling light from all sides. Strong light slammed down upon him like a fatal blow" (p. 50).

Nur's light is true; Ra'uf's glamor is a false light. Challenging Ra'uf in his mind, Sa'id says, "If you had agreed that I could work as an editor on your paper, you bastard, I would have published our common memoirs there, and I would have extinguished your false light" (p. 115). Finally, when Sa'id attempts to hide from the police surrounding him in the cemetery, he finds himself helplessly exposed by floodlight: "Suddenly there was bright blinding light flooding the area in a circular movement. He closed his eyes and threw himself to the ground at the foot of the tombstone" (p. 172). It should be noted that Mahfuz, characteristically, does not assign a fixed symbolic role to either light or darkness; yet the continuous alternating movement between the two is of structural significance: it serves as a counterpoint to the plot.

CHAPTER 18

The Beggar

'Umar al-Hamzawi, the principal character in *al-Shahhadh* ("The Beggar"),[1] is one of a series of alienated heroes typical of Mahfuz's novels of the 1960s. Unlike the wretched Sa'id Mahran, the first of these characters, 'Umar is a successful Cairene lawyer. At the age of forty-five he is rich, professionally respected, apparently happily married and the father of two daughters; yet he feels exhausted and depressed. The doctor whom he consults finds nothing wrong with him physically and advises him to watch his diet and go on vacation with his family. He takes a holiday, but his condition does not improve. He is no longer interested in his wife of twenty years and is bored with his work. True, he is fond of his daughters, aged fourteen and four, and is especially attached to the elder. She resembles her mother at the same age, and reminds 'Umar of his passionate love for his wife twenty years earlier. He seems to have lost all sense of purpose in life, even the will to live. He calls this state his "illness."

In an attempt to regain his *joie de vivre*, he engages in affairs with women whom he finds easily in the night-clubs of Cairo. He leaves his home and pregnant wife and goes to live with a young dancer. This, too is of no help. He is obsessed with a desire to grasp "the meaning of life" and "the secret of being." While he is away from his family, his wife gives birth to a son. Hoping for a mystical experience, he retreats to a secluded hut on the outskirts of Cairo, on the

---

[1] Najib Mahfuz, *al-Shahhadh* (Cairo, 1965).

edge of the desert. There he is overtaken by wild hallucinations, but he does not experience that moment of divine bliss which he has been seeking. By the end of the story he is completely out of touch with reality.

Two characters in supporting roles are 'Umar's friends, Mustafa and 'Uthman. Twenty years before, when the three of them were law students in the same class, they were devoted to the idea of establishing a just society. The three were engaged at the time in illegal revolutionary activity, and were arrested. 'Umar and Mustafa were soon released, but 'Uthman was sentenced to many years in prison. 'Umar became a famous lawyer, Mustafa a popular radio and television personality. At the beginning of the novel 'Uthman is about to come out of prison, and, when he does so, 'Umar is already suffering from his "illness," but is not yet completely out of touch with reality. 'Umar is grateful to 'Uthman for not having implicated him and Mustafa in the investigation, and takes him as a partner into his law office, hoping that he will eventually take his place. 'Umar's daughter falls in love with 'Uthman, who has not lost any of his vitality or his Marxist faith and revolutionary zeal. At the close of the novel, 'Uthman is again arrested for his illegal political activity; 'Umar's daughter, now 'Uthman's wife, is expecting a child.

The names of 'Umar, the main character, and his two friends should be considered as a group and explored in conjunction with one another. The name 'Umar is the name of the second Caliph, 'Umar ibn al-Khattab. The Caliph 'Umar was known for his strong character and his single-mindedness and strictness in all matters, especially in judging the moral behavior of himself and others. He was also well known for his resolve. This is in sharp contrast to 'Umar of the novel.

'Umar's family name, al-Ḥamzawi – a fairly ordinary family name and the name of an alley in Cairo – has also some special meanings. Ḥamzawi is a *nisba* form derived from *ḥamza* ("lion"). The verb *ḥamaza* means, among other things, to be strong and courageous, as well as to be sharp, to burn the tongue. The classical Arabic dictionaries explain that *ḥamza* was applied as an epithet to the lion, because of the animal's power and courage. Ḥamza was the name of the Prophet's uncle, who was known for his great courage and who

died a martyr in the fight against the Meccan infidels in the battle of
Uhud (625 CE). Hence, this name also has historical connotations of
valor and power. Related to the other meaning of the verb ("to be
sharp," "to burn the tongue") is the phrase *hamm hāmiz*, meaning
intense or severe anxiety. In the case of 'Umar, his last name, Hamza-
wi alludes to all of these connotations: once he was courageous and
daring, now he is gripped by anxiety.

The journalist and television personality, Mustafa, has a name
which is the honorific of the Prophet himself: al-Mustafa, "the chosen one." In describing his vocation, Mustafa uses terms which
traditionally signify the vocation of the Prophet, except that he uses
them only to affirm that he has no meaningful message. He says,
"This is my mission [*risala*] in life, to entertain." *Risala* is the standard Islamic term signifying the prophetic vocation. In another
instance Mustafa says: "In our generation there is no divine revelation [*wahy*]" (p. 99). On his own admission, Mustafa has no message
other than entertainment and buffoonery, "*al-tasliya wa'l-tahrij*"
(p. 55). Speaking to Mustafa, 'Umar says, "You are an old hypocrite"
(*munafiq*). And again, "You are a hypocrite, and therefore you have
no right to know the secrets of the heart" (pp. 112, 116). It is ironic,
of course, that a man whose name is the epithet of the Prophet
should be addressed by the term *munafiq*, the very same pejorative
by which the Prophet referred to those who did not sincerely accept
his call and who, therefore, could not be trusted. 'Umar says to Mustafa, "you are a liar, like most people in your profession" (p. 22).

Mustafa describes his work as a journalist as "selling popcorn and
watermelon seeds," in Arabic *al-lubb wa'l-fishār* (pp. 20, 60).[2] This
in itself is a pun, for *lubb* (colloquial: *libb*), which here means watermelon seeds, also means "essence," "core," or "heart." *Fishār*, which
here means popcorn, is from the same root as the verb *fashar* which
means to brag (in Egyptian colloquial). *Fashshār* is a braggart, one
who invents tall tales. Thus, while deprecating his work as the sale of
popcorn and watermelon seeds, he is inadvertently describing himself
as "one who sells his soul and [spreads] tall tales."

Mustafa's family name is al-Minyawi, a *nisba* adjective usually in-

---

[2] Roasted watermelon seeds are eaten in Egypt as a popular snack food.

dicating a relationship to the Egyptian town of Minya. The name
Minyawi, however, could suggest another meaning: *munya* or *minya*
means "desire" or "wish," and *minyawi* can be construed as an adjective derived from it. Hence, "al-Minyawi" may mean "he who has
to do with wishes." Mustafa attempts to satisfy the wishes of his
friend 'Umar by finding him women from the cabarets of Cairo. As
editor of the theater and entertainment section of a magazine, he is
well connected in these circles. Mustafa acts in fact as a procurer for
his friend 'Umar. In this respect, Mustafa is 'Umar's Mephisto. It is
no coincidence that the first woman Mustafa introduces to 'Umar is
the singer Marguerite, a namesake of Faust's Margarete.

The other friend, 'Uthman, is named after the third Caliph.
'Uthman was an old man when he became Caliph, and while re-
nowned for his extreme piety, he is traditionally viewed as weak,
lethargic, and indecisive; he was killed by rebels who rose up against
him in the first "revolution" in the history of Islam. In our story,
'Uthman is the revolutionary *par excellence*. The second name of the
fictitious 'Uthman is Khalil, which means friend. 'Uthman Khalil has
proven his loyalty to his friends 'Umar and Mustafa by not revealing
anything about them to the police when he was caught. Khalil is the
Qur'anic epithet for Ibrahim (whom God saved). However, in Najib
Mahfuz's stories (as we have seen), Khalil is a name given to characters who do not enjoy God's protection and are not saved. Indeed, in
our story, 'Uthman Khalil is the "fall guy"; he is the only one of the
three to be caught by the police, and he served a long term in prison.
At the end of the novel he is again hunted and captured by the police.

Another character is the doctor whom 'Umar consults about his
"illness." Hamid Sabri, the doctor, was 'Umar's classmate in high
school, but the two men have not seen each other for many years.
Hamid was not a member of the group of three whose friendship
continued and deepened during their days in law-school and their
shared period of radical activism.

The name Ḥāmid is an active participle of the verb *ḥamida*, to
praise, specifically to praise God, to say *al-ḥamdu li'llah*, that is, to
express acceptance of God's will. In a secular sense, this widely-used
phrase expresses the acceptance of reality. Sabri, his family name – a
nisba from *sabr* ("patience," "perserverance"), suggests that the

bearer of this name is characterized by *sabr*. It should be recalled that *sabr*, which is highly praised in the Qur'an, is regarded by Najib Mahfuz as the most beneficial of human qualities – indeed the one quality which makes life endurable. Those who are devoid of it wreak havoc upon themselves and cause trouble to those close to them.[3] Hamid Sabri, unlike 'Umar, Mustafa and 'Uthman, does not search for "the absolute truth" or for "the meaning of life." He tells 'Umar that he has no time to inquire into the meaning of life, because he is constantly busy treating people who urgently need help (p. 12). When 'Umar repeats his question as to the meaning of life, Hamid answers, "To love life, that is the meaning" (p. 14).

His name, Hamid, also sets him apart from 'Umar, Mustafa and 'Uthman, because he, unlike them, is not named after a revered figure from the early days of Islam. His name does, however, contain a modern literary intertextual allusion: Hamid is the name of the hero and narrator of Muhammad Husayn Haykal's novel *Zaynab*, usually considered the first realistic Egyptian novel. There is no doubt that Mahfuz was familiar with Haykal's novel. There is, however, a particular reason for believing that Haykal's *Zaynab* was distinctly impressed on Mahfuz's memory: as I have already mentioned, Mahfuz's first published short story appeared in Haykal's weekly magazine *al-Siyasa*; the same page that carried his story also carried an advertisement announcing the publication of the third edition of Haykal's *Zaynab*.[4]

'Umar's wife's name is Zaynab, like that of the heroine of Haykal's book. This is a very popular name for Muslim women in Cairo. Zaynab, the Prophet's granddaughter, sister of Hasan and Husayn, is admired as a model of familial devotion. The mosque in Cairo which bears her name is held in deep reverence and is visited by many, especially by women who seek her blessing and intercession with her grandfather, the Prophet. 'Umar's wife Zaynab is the model wife and mother. When the story opens 'Umar is no longer in love with her; Zaynab has lost the youthful bloom which once captivated him. She is still dear to him as the mother of his children, but this is an am-

---

[3] This is a recurrent motif in *Bidaya wa-nihaya*, see e.g., pp. 19, 24, 37, 185, 203; cf. also *'Abath al-aqdar*, pp. 7–8.

[4] See *al-Siyasa*, Cairo, 22 July 1932, and above, p. 57.

bivalent feeling, for it reminds him of his own duties from which he would like to escape. This is how 'Umar sees her: "She stood like a *big statue* full of confidence and high principles" (my emphasis, p. 16). In a letter to his friend Mustafa, 'Umar writes, "I see dear Zaynab only as a *statue* representing the unity of family, constructiveness and work" (my emphasis, p. 32). Although 'Umar values Zaynab's steadfastness and "high principles," we cannot fail to hear in his words the sarcasm of one who has tired of his duties and now lacks both confidence and high principles. When 'Umar leaves the house, Zaynab courageously and quietly continues to take care of the family. She gives birth to 'Umar's son after he has abandoned her.

Mahfuz's use of the term "statue" (*timthal*) in relation to Zaynab is very significant because it points to the iconographic function of this figure, the model of motherhood. As the ideal mother, Zaynab resembles other female characters in Mahfuz's novels: Amina in the trilogy, the mother in *Bidaya wa-nihaya* (*The Beginning and the End*) and Saniyya al-Mahdi in *al-Baqi min al-zaman sa'a* (1982). In *Bidaya wa-nihaya* one of the sons compares his mother to Egypt the motherland. Saniyya al-Mahdi, it should be recalled, allegorically represents Egypt, and Zaynab is another such symbol.[5]

We learn that Zaynab was not the original name of 'Umar's wife. Before she married 'Umar, her name was Kamilya Fu'ad. She was a Christian, an Egyptian Copt, and upon marriage she changed her religion and her name (p. 53). Kamilya is of course the flower camellia; Fu'ad, the name of her father, means heart; so she is "camellia of the heart." This is Mahfuz's way of highlighting the romantic role she has played in 'Umar's life, for their marriage clearly was not arranged by their families, but was rather "an affair of the heart" which united 'Umar, a poor Muslim student, and Kamilya, the convent-school girl.

Her change of name from Kamilya to Zaynab is also of great significance: it expresses her conversion from Christianity to Islam. It should be pointed out that Saniyya al-Mahdi, the main female character in *al-Baqi min al-zaman sa'a*, also comes from a family of Coptic Christians who converted to Islam.[6] By attributing a Coptic

---

[5] See *Bidaya wa-nihaya*, p. 199, cf. al-Shaykh, *Mawaqif*, p. 102.

[6] Saniyya's grandfather converted to Islam. See *al-Baqi min al-zaman sa'a*, p. 8.

origin to these female characters who symbolically represent Egypt, Najib Mahfuz would appear to affirm that the Copts constitute an essential element in the Egyptian personality and that they have played a vital part in the formation of Egypt.

The choice of the name Kamilya would appear to have been motivated by a number of factors. First of all, and most obviously, it is the name of a flower. In this respect Kamilya resembles other female characters in Mahfuz's stories who have flower names. These are, notably: Zahra ("flower") in the novel *Miramar*, Qurunfila ("carnation") in the novel *al-Karnak*, and Randa ("laurel") in the novel *Yawma qutila 'l-za'im*. Significantly, all these women who are named after flowers share the symbolic or allegorical function of representing Egypt. It should also be noted that Qurunfila in *al-Karnak* has a young alter-ego, the student Zaynab. There is then a kind of chiastic parallelism between the heroines of *al-Shahhadh* and *al-Karnak*: Zaynab/Kamilya as a symbol for Egypt corresponds to Qurunfila/Zaynab.[7]

Secondly, the name Kamilya, too, is associated with Haykal's *Zaynab*. In this first realistic Egyptian novel, Zaynab is the name of the main female character, a *fallaha*. It is widely accepted among Egyptian literary experts that in his depiction of Zaynab's unfulfilled love and subsequent death by tuberculosis, Haykal was influenced by Alexandre Dumas's *La Dame aux camélias*. The first to point to a possible connection between Haykal's Zaynab and Dumas's "Lady of the Camellias" was the Egyptian writer Yahya Haqqi, a close friend of Mahfuz.[8] From one of Mahfuz's interviews we learn that the play

[7] It is interesting to note that the word *zaynab* has a botanical meaning. According to *Taj al-'arus* and *Lisan al-'arab*, *zaynab* signifies (among other things) a tree or bush (*shajar*) which is "beautiful to look at and has a pleasant scent [*jamil al-manzar tayyib al-ra'iha*]." Thus, Zaynab is in the same category as Zahra, Qurunfila, Kamilya and Randa not only with regard to their common allegorical function but also with regard to their lexical meaning. In the course of an interview in February 1990, Mahfuz told me that he was not familiar with the botanical meaning of the name Zaynab. However, it is nonetheless plausible that at some time he did see the *Lisan al-'arab* entry on *zaynab* and that this item of lexical information has since been relegated to his unconscious memory.

[8] Haykal himself notes the influence of French literature on *Zaynab* in his introduction to the third edition of the novel (published in 1932). The connection between Haykal's heroine Zaynab and Dumas's *La Dame aux camélias* was noted by Yahya Haqqi in *Fajr al-qissa al-misriyya* (Cairo, 1987), p. 50, and appears to have been generally accepted by

La Dame aux camélias had a special emotional significance for him.[9] Hence, the combination of these two names – Kamilya-become-Zaynab – in *al-Shahhadh*, is not mere coincidence; it bears out the inter-textual relationship between Mahfuz's Zaynab and Haykal's Zaynab.

On the allegorical level, in evoking *La Dame aux camélias* (the French novel that influenced the first Egyptian novel), precisely through the name of a character symbolically representing Egypt, Mahfuz alludes to the influence of European culture on modern Egyptian culture and to the existence of a vital Western component in modern Egyptian life.

Zaynab's youthful bloom, with which 'Umar was once infatuated and which she has since lost, is re-created in their daughter, fourteen-year-old Buthayna, who is in various ways her mother's alter ego. Her name, Buthayna, evokes romantic notions, since Buthayna was the beloved of the ancient poet Jamil (d. 701), famous for his poems of chaste and idealized love, dedicated to her. Jamil's unfulfilled love for Buthayna has thus become the byword for pure love. His kind of love is usually contrasted to the sensual love celebrated in the poems of his contemporary 'Umar ibn abi Rabi'a. 'Umar al-Hamzawi's daughter Buthayna also writes love poems; the subject of her poems is not love for an actual person but her love for "the ultimate goal of everything," or, in 'Umar's words, "the secret of being." Reading her poems, 'Umar says to her, "This is real poetry. . . . It is beautiful poetry." This last phrase in Arabic is *shi'r jamil*, a double entendre evoking the name of the famous poet.

Since 'Umar's affair with Marguerite is interrupted, almost before it begins, by her sudden trip abroad, 'Umar finds another woman in

---

Egyptian literary historians. See, e.g., Badr, *Tatawwur al-riwaya al-'arabiyya al-haditha fi misr* (Cairo, 1968), p. 330, and Ahmad Haykal, *Tatawwur al-adab al-hadith fi misr* (Cairo, 1968), p. 200.

[9] Mahfuz told Jadhibiyya Sidqi that he had cried bitterly three times in his life: "the day Sa'd Zaghlul died, the day my father died and the day I learned that Manfaluti had been dead for a long time. I had devoured all his writings and I had planned to meet him." He then added, "There was a fourth time. In 1932, when Rose al-Yusuf organized a charity theatrical performance . . . in which she played the leading role in *La Dame aux camélias*. Her performance was so remarkable that it moved me to tears" (*Sabah al-khayr*, 31 October 1957).

another cabaret. She is the dancer Warda ("rose" or "flower"). 'Umar lives with her for some time, and feels, at least for a short while, that he is like "Adam in paradise" (*Adam fi 'l-janna*, p. 111). Warda is a dancer like a number of Mahfuz's heroines, notably Qurunfila in *al-Karnak* and the female character from an early story, "A Dancer from Bardis," as well as the female character in the short story "*Rawd al-faraj.*"[10]

The name Warda gives the author the opportunity for a number of puns based on the two uses of this word, a common noun and a name. For example, when 'Umar's passion for Warda has burned out, and he is already drawn to other women, he thinks to himself "How is it that Warda was plucked out from [my] mind as though she were an artificial flower?" (p. 119).[11] In another instance, there is a whole paragraph which plays on the meaning of the name Warda. The owner of the cabaret where Warda used to dance pays a visit to 'Umar in his law office. 'Umar suspects that he has come to complain that Warda has not shown up for work since 'Umar established his relationship with her. 'Umar says ironically, "You really came from the ends of the earth because of Warda." This is a pun; it also means "because of one flower." The owner of the cabaret answers "My dear great lawyer, you know that my garden is full of flowers." "Well then," answers 'Umar, "let's not say even one word about Warda" (p. 100).

The image of Adam in paradise that occurs to 'Umar as a simile for his joy in his love nest with Warda recalls another instance where the term *janna* (Arabic meaning "garden" or "paradise") is used (p. 65). 'Umar uses it – this time sarcastically – with reference to the gardens of the cabarets to which he is guided by his friend Mustafa. "Lucky you," says 'Umar to Mustafa, "you seem to be an expert on these forbidden gardens."[12] The sarcasm is all the more biting since it is addressed to a person bearing the Prophet's name Mustafa, and while

---

[10] The story "*Raqisa min bardis*" ("A Dancer from Bardis") appeared in *al-Majalla al-jadida*, Cairo, 29 April 1936. The story "*Rawd al-faraj*," originally published in *al-Riwaya* (Cairo, 15 December 1938), is included in *Hams al-junun*, pp. 113–28.

[11] Arabic: *wa-lakin kayfa 'qtuli'at warda min nafsihi ka-annaha zahra sina'iyya?*

[12] Arabic: ... *bi-hadhihi 'l-jannat al-muharrama.*

'Umar is probably unaware of this particular ironic twist hidden in his own words, the author did certainly intend it. Mahfuz's use of the term *janna* (or *jannāt* in the plural form) with reference to cabaret gardens has another implication: it mocks the traditional Islamic picture of paradise – a garden where the blessed can enjoy without limit the pleasures of wine and sex.[13]

The name of 'Umar's newborn son is Samīr. He was named by his mother, perhaps with Buthayna's help. *Samīr* means "companion," and especially signifies a person participating in an evening conversation or a party with a group of friends. The name Samir has, therefore, the connotation of congeniality and, in our story, when chosen for her son by a woman abandoned by her husband, the name serves as a reminder of what she is missing – a companion. Upon hearing from his daughter that his new son is named Samir, 'Umar thinks to himself, "May his name protect him from world-weariness [*idhan, fal-yahmihi 'smuhu min al-dajar*]" (p. 142). World-weariness (*dajar*) is in fact the malady of the mind that bedevils 'Umar.[14]

There remains the name of the novel, *al-Shahhadh*, "the beggar," which refers to 'Umar. This warrants some explanation. 'Umar, as we have seen, is a rich lawyer; even when he abandons his home to become a recluse, he is certainly not a beggar. Why, then, this title? A key to this question may be found in the words of Mustafa, "There is no revelation in our generation. The likes of us have no choice but to go begging" (p. 99). Begging is of course meant metaphorically: begging for an answer to the existential problems.

It should be recalled here that in another work by Najib Mahfuz, the short play "*Yumitu wa-yuhyi*," one of the characters is a blind beggar (*shahhadh*), precisely the same term. The beggar in that play

---

[13] It is noteworthy that Tawfiq al-Hakim's short story "*Tarid al-firdaws*" ("The Man Who Was Expelled from Paradise," in his collection *al-Majmu'a al-ula*, Cairo, 1949, pp. 47–86) is based on the juxtaposition of Paradise, as seen by Muslims, and "Paradise," a Cairene bar.

[14] The verb *dajira* (from which the verbal noun *dajar* is derived) means to be annoyed, exasperated, displeased; also to be weary of (someone or something). The contrast *samir* ("companion") versus world-weariness or boredom (*dajar*) occurs in *al-Sukkariya*. Yasin, sitting idly in a café, sees his brother Kamal passing by; he thinks, "Kamal is the best companion when you are world-weary [*Kamal khayr samir 'inda 'l-dajar*]." *Al-Sukkariyya*, p. 66.

represents, according to my interpretation, the forlorn and confused Egyptian intellectual.[15] It has this meaning, too, in the title of the novel with which we are dealing.[16]

Beggar, *shahhadh* in Arabic, is *darwish* in Persian, and this Persian word is the standard term used to designate a Sufi, that is a Muslim mystic.[17] The Sufi "beggar" (*darwish*) renounces all wordly concerns and possessions to become totally engaged in an unceasing quest for the ultimate truth. It is precisely this Sufi connotation of "beggar" which Najib Mahfuz had in mind when he named this novel *al-Shahhadh*. The novel is indeed suffused with Sufi terminology. It is easy to understand why: 'Umar is searching for the meaning of life and aspiring to experience mystical bliss. At one point, alone in the desert at night, he feels great joy and relief from all anxiety. He would like this sensation to last forever, and longs to relive this moment. He fails miserably.

'Umar's two friends, Mustafa and 'Uthman, represent two aspects of his own personality which he has suppressed. Mustafa has pursued creative writing, whereas 'Umar has given up poetry; 'Uthman has remained a revolutionary in search of Utopia, a dream which 'Umar has long since abandoned. Both Mustafa and 'Uthman fail, each in his own way. Mustafa, who at one time believed in art (p. 22), has become disillusioned with it and now maintains that art has no role other than to supply entertainment to the masses; he deprecates himself as being a "vendor of popcorn and watermelon seeds." 'Uthman's unending struggle for utopia is by definition doomed to failure. 'Umar's quest for the meaning of life and the secret of all being ends in hallucination and madness.

All three were students of law. The Arabic word signifying law studies, *huquq*, is of great significance. *Huquq* is the plural form of *haqq*, meaning "that which is right," "reality," "truth"; it is also one of "the beautiful names," that is, an epithet of Allah. Indeed, *al-Haqq*, "the real one" or "the one and only reality" is the Sufis'

[15] Cf. above, the image of the blind beggar in the play "*Yumitu wa-yuhyi*," pp. 140–41.

[16] Beggars have a metaphorical function also in the symbolic story "*al-Hawi khatafa 'l-tabaq*" ("The Sorcerer Snatched the Plate"), from the collection, *Taht al-mizalla*.

[17] The standard Arabic equivalent of the Persian *darwish* in the particular Sufi sense is *faqir* (literally, "a poor man"), but *shahhadh* is a fairly close lexical equivalent.

preferred name for God. In our novel, all of the three who were students of law (*huquq*) fail, whereas Hamid Sabri, who practices medicine (*tibb*), finds satisfaction in life. The contrast suggested by Mahfuz is not between the practice of law and medicine as such but, rather, between *huquq* as "absolute truths" or "absolute rights" and *tibb* which means "remedy." It is a contrast between the inevitably hopeless quest for the unattainable on one hand, and the pragmatic attempt to alleviate human suffering on the other.

In the light of the contrast between *huquq* and *tibb*, we can more fully appreciate the significance of the different provenance of the names of the four male characters. The three whose names evoke the early days of Islam (and whose personalities stand in stark contrast to their historical namesakes) are frustrated in their quest for absolute truths; Hamid, whose name recalls the first realistic Egyptian novel, does not look for metaphysical truth and finds contentment and self-realization in his work which, by definition, consists in striving pragmatically to relieve the sufferings of fellow human beings and to ameliorate their condition.

The *problematique* of names, i.e., the set of questions concerning names and their relationship to reality, is not only implicit in Najib Mahfuz's choice of names for his characters, but also looms large in various instances in the words of the characters themselves.

Mustafa says to 'Umar, "My son 'Umar, whom I regrettably named after you, is a petulant adolescent" (p. 111). Evidently, Mustafa named his son 'Umar after his friend partly as a token of friendship, but more importantly because he took it to be a propitious name in view of his friend's success at the time. Now that 'Umar has lost his way in life, Mustafa regrets his choice of the name. This instance makes it clear that the same name may signify quite different things even to the same person at two different points of time. Here, it simultaneously attests to and ridicules a common practice in the choice of personal names. On another level, Mustafa's words touch on one particular aspect of the question of name and identity, that is, the relation between a person's name, which is normally not altered, and his personality, which does change.

Mustafa's regret at having named his son after 'Umar clearly as-

sumes recognition of the palpable change in 'Umar's personality
which might be viewed as amounting to a change of identity. His wife
says to him, "Admit it, you are no longer you" (p. 49). His friend
'Uthman, who has not seen him for years, says to him, using exactly
the same words, "You are no longer you" (p. 153).

The precarious nature of the connection between name and reality
becomes keenly manifest when we examine people's reputations, that
is, their public "names." It is not surprising, therefore, that the issue
of reputation figures in the novel. Mustafa, who has given up his
former high artistic aspirations, says, "Let's be content with having a
popular name [al-ism al-mahbub, literally: a well-liked name] and a lot
of money" (p. 45). One of 'Umar's clients says to him in admiration,
"You are fully versed in the details of the case in an amazing degree, as
befits your great name [bi-daraja mudhhila haqiqa bi-'smika al-
kabir]..."(p. 50).

The philosophical problem of name and reality is not confined, of
course, to personal names, nor is Mahfuz's interest in it. His preoccupation with the problematic nature of names and of naming,
proper nouns and common nouns alike, is apparent in various instances in al-Shahhadh.

'Uthman, 'Umar's friend who has recently come out of jail, stresses
on a number of occasions the relative nature of the meaning of words
and their intrinsic ambiguity. When 'Umar's wife explains to her
daughter that 'Uthman served time in prison because he was "a political hero," he retorts, "Hero or criminal are [in the category of]
ambiguous names" (p. 154). What 'Uthman is saying is that one
man's hero is another man's criminal. To make his point 'Uthman
uses the Arabic technical term "ambiguous names" (Arabic: asma' al-
addād, literally: "names signifying opposite concepts") which Arab
classical philologists have coined to characterize words signifying
two opposite things, e.g., jalal meaning both "something great" and
"something trifling," mawla signifying both "master" and "client",
nidd signifying "opposite" or "adversary" as well as "equivalent".
There are numerous classical compilations of Arabic words of this
kind. 'Uthman (speaking in fact for the author) extends the applica-
tion of the technical term addād beyond its more or less limited
classical inventory.

Speaking about his life in prison, 'Uthman says to 'Umar, "A day is like a year in its loathsomeness and a year like a day in its worthlessness" (p. 145). Since 'Umar views the world as a prison (p. 5), this equivocality of "day" and "year" is as pertinent to his present experience as it was to 'Uthman's while he was in prison. Thus, even words which are ostensibly unambiguous and fixed in meaning are not truly unequivocal, because the things that they are intended to name are experienced or perceived differently under different circumstances.

Words cannot be trusted; that is at least the opinion expressed by Warda in one of her conversations with 'Umar. When Warda asks 'Umar whether his "interest" in her will last until the coming winter, he answers "It is not [just] interest as you said, but ... " At this point, when 'Umar is apparently going to declare his love for her, Warda interrupts him and says, "Don't give it a name, let it name itself, that would be better." 'Umar compliments her on this "witty" statement, but she continues, "I do not trust words, because I am originally an actress." 'Umar interjects, "And a lady in every sense of the word" (p. 86). Needless to say, this statement by 'Umar more than vindicates Warda's refusal to trust words. By the same token, it underscores the general problem of the relationship between names and reality.

PART FIVE

THE MASKS OF REALITY, THE ENIGMA OF NAMES

CHAPTER 19

Names and Rememberance

> We set to recalling those enwrapped by oblivion:
> Safwan al-Nadi and Zahrana Karim, Ra'fat Basha al-
> Zayn and Zubayda Hanim 'Iffat, Ihsan, Yusry Basha
> al-Hilwani and 'Afifa Hanim Nur al-Din, 'Ubayd
> Basha al-Armalawi and Insaf Hanim al-Qilli, Qadri
> Sulayman and Fathiyya 'Asal, and dozens of col-
> leagues and freinds.
>
> Najib Mahfuz, *Qushtumor*

It is evident that personal names are of great significance to Najib Mahfuz. Two of his novels are in fact constructed as lexicons of names. *Al-Maraya* ("Mirrors," 1972), a collection of fifty-five profiles of fictitious characters based largely on real life, represents the concerns and attitudes of Cairene intellectuals during the Nasser era, especially in the years following the 1967 war. The profiles are arranged alphabetically. The author calls this book a novel (*riwaya*); most critics, however, would not admit this definition for the book, and, indeed, there seems to be little in it to warrant such an appellation. What the characters in this book have in common is that they all live in the memory of the narrator-author; it is the mind of the narrator that integrates the many profiles into one literary work.

Apparently, the point Mahfuz wanted to make in calling *al-Maraya* a novel was that a novel did not have to be constructed along the lines established in the Western tradition of the genre, which he himself has admirably employed in most of his books. The organizing principle of al-Maraya – short narratives arranged in alphabetical order of the characters' personal names – is that of medieval Arabic biographical dictionaries.

Alphabetical order of personal names is also the structural principle of Mahfuz's novel Hadith al-sabah wa'l-masa' ("Morning and Evening Tales," 1987). This book, also defined by the author as "a novel," draws a picture of the political and cultural history of Egypt from the end of the eighteenth century to the present, through the stories of two families. However, the story is not told chronologically or genealogically, family by family, but rather character by character, according to the alphabetical order of their names – sixty-seven name-entries altogether.[1] As a result the materials are intermingled both chronologically and genealogically, and Mahfuz leaves it up to the reader to rearrange them in his mind.

Family names are the organizing principle of the story "Sabah al-ward" ("Morning of blossom," i.e., "Good morning," published 1987) in a collection bearing the same title. The fifteen chapters of "Sabah al-ward" are Mahfuz's fictionalized memoirs of his friends and their families in the 'Abbasiyya quarter. Each chapter recounts the story of one family, and bears that family's name as its title.

It is interesting to note in the context of our discussion that in each of the three above-mentioned works, both the life experience of the narrator-author and his fictionalized history of Egypt take shape around personal names. Private memories of one's life and national history revolve around names; hence, consciousness and identity, individual and collective alike, depend on the remembrance of names. To forget the names of people one has known is, therefore, to lose one's grip on reality, and, in some sense, part of one's identity. Mahfuz puts this idea in high relief in the figure of Mutawalli 'Abd al-Samad, the local "holy man" in the trilogy. The stages of his physical and mental deterioration are marked off by his increasing in-

---

[1] As though to emphasize the dictionary-like arrangement of this "novel," the author uses the names of the letters of the alphabet (harf al-alif, harf al-ba', etc.) as headings to introduce the name or names beginning with that letter.

ability to remember the names of the people he once knew.[2] Viewed conversely, those whose names are no longer remembered might never have existed. This notion had a powerful influenke on Mahfuz from his earliest years: it reinforced his resolve to write and publish so that his name would not be forgotten.[3]

[2] See above, pp. 221–22.
[3] See above, pp. 34–35.

CHAPTER 20

Mahfuz's Enigmatic Name

> Najib Mahfuz's name did him harm.
> Dr. Adham Rajab

Mahfuz's preoccupation with names would seem to be closely connected to his personal experience with his own name. Najib Mahfuz, as I have already mentioned, was named after the obstetrician who delivered him.[1] It was this dual name (comprising the first name and the surname of the doctor) that Najib Mahfuz received as his given name. His full name, i.e., his given name and his father's name, is Najib Mahfuz 'Abd al-'Aziz. We may safely assume that Mahfuz, as a child, heard from his mother the story of his birth and of his being named after the doctor who had saved both his life and hers.[2] From Mahfuz's personal perspective, the circumstances that led to the choice of his name are undoubtedly extraordinary and memorable. Hence, the name Najib Mahfuz must have always had a very special meaning for him, but this meaning, by its very nature, is covert, known only to those who are familiar with the story behind

---

[1] See above, p. 25. In an interview in February 1990 Najib Mahfuz confirmed to me that he was named after Dr. Najib Mahfuz, the famous Egyptian obstetrician who, as Mahfuz put it, "apparently helped mother in one of the cases."

[2] Kamal, the main character in the trilogy, who, according to Najib Mahfuz, represents his personality more closely than any of his other characters, recalls on his nineteenth birthday that he heard from his mother that his birth had been difficult and had followed a very painful labor lasting two days (*Qasr al-shawq*, p. 424).

it. It is also a name that can (and, as we shall presently see, did) lead people to make various wrong assumptions. For one thing, the second component of Najib Mahfuz's name is neither his father's name nor a surname, as one would normally expect, but part of his given name. Another potentially confusing feature of this name is that it is not distinctively Muslim. This is not surprising, as the obstetrician Dr. Najib Mahfuz was an Egyptian Copt. However, *Najib Mahfuz* is not a distinctively Coptic name either; the two names of which it consists can be used by Copts and Muslims alike. It is, so to speak, religiously ambiguous.[3]

In an interview in 1970, Mahfuz's long-time friend Dr. Adham Rajab recounted a story previously known only to a very small number of people:

> Najib Mahfuz's name did him harm; he was denied a [government] scholarship to study in France because of it. But I cannot elaborate upon this, because it is a very sensitive matter. His full name is, in fact, Najib Mahfuz 'Abd al-'Aziz al-Sabilji, but he used to sign his official papers and his documents "Najib Mahfuz" only.[4] And because of his name he lost the chance of his life, that is, as far as the past is concerned. But I thank God for that, because probably, if Najib Mahfuz had gone on this scholarship [for the study] of philosophy ... he might have returned a philosophy professor and perhaps his interest would have been diverted from literature.[5]

Commenting on this, Mahfuz adds:

> Rather, I lost two scholarships, not one: one to study philosophy and another to study the French language. My name was indeed the cause. Dr. Adham was reluctant to explain the cause, but I see no reason for embarrassment as it is a thing of the

[3] On religiously ambiguous names and on the meaning of the words *najib* and *mahfūz*, see above, p. 161.

[4] Mahfuz explained that "al-Sabilji" is not really his family name but a humorous nickname invented by one of his friends when Mahfuz told them that one of his grandfathers had been the headmaster of a Qur'an school which had a public drinking-fountain (*sabil*) attached to it. See interview in *al-Musawwar* (21 October 1988), p. 16.

[5] Adham Rajab, "*Safahat majhula min hayat Najib Mahfuz*," *al-Hilal* (February 1970), pp. 96–97, and see above, p. 38.

past. The story is that the Palace was persecuting the Copts, because it considered them to be the mainstay of the Wafd. My name appeared doubtful to them, and they [that is the committee] suspected that I was Copt. I came out second and the first was a Copt, so they said, "One Copt is enough." They took the first and the third and passed me over.[6]

We cannot ascertain whether or not it was the name Najib Mahfuz or, more precisely, the "religious ambiguity" of the name that induced the committee to deny him the scholarship to go abroad, but Najib Mahfuz's conjecture as to the reason for the committee's decision is quite plausible. Be that as it may, it is clear that he saw this decision as resulting from the way his name was construed by the committee.

The decision not to send him abroad had far-reaching consequences for Najib Mahfuz's life and literary career. He told an interviewer that had he received the philosophy scholarship, it might have changed his life (for it would presumably have diverted him from his career as a novelist). However, "the scholarship for the [French] language would undoubtedly have benefited me [in my career as a writer]. I would have learned French thoroughly and would have returned to teach in the university instead of becoming a civil servant. I would have used my stay in Paris to study literature and art.[7]

The "religious ambiguity" of his name would have been removed if Najib Mahfuz had given his name in full: Najib Mahfuz 'Abd al-'Aziz, with his father's name attached to his own, in the customary manner. He obviously did not. For reasons which he has never fully explained, Najib Mahfuz has virtually eliminated his father's name from his own; he never used the name 'Abd al-'Aziz in any of his published works nor even – as far as we can tell from the aforementioned account of his candidacy for a government scholarship – in official

---

[6] Rajab, "*Safahat Majhula...*," *al-Hilal*, pp. 96–97.

[7] Jamal Al-Ghitani, *Najib Mahfuz yatadhakkar* (Beirut, 1980), pp. 93–94. It should be noted that the account of the committee's passing over Mahfuz – as presented by Ghitani, who apparently copied it from Mahfuz's story in *al-Hilal* some ten years before – is somewhat confused. The version given by Ghitani, that both first and third places were taken by Coptic students, makes no sense and is obviously a mistake.

documents.[8] Mahfuz once mentioned that he considered the "tripartite name" (*al-ism al-thulathi*) too long. Although this may sound reasonable, it does not really explain the elimination of his father's name, for if his sole purpose had been to use a dual rather than a tripartite name, this could have been accomplished by using one of his names (either Najib or Mahfuz) plus his father's name. I would suggest three additional reasons for his omission of his father's name which are not mutually exclusive, nor do they negate Mahfuz's own explanation – that is, his preference for a shorter name.

Firstly, this omission heralds Najib Mahfuz's rejection of paternal authority and his assertion of personal autonomy. It should be remembered that Mahfuz is a severe critic of the patriarchal order; his negative view of it is revealed in his description of family life in the trilogy.[9] In an ideologically pregnant chapter of this novel, Mahfuz's alter ego Kamal announces his rejection of his father's dominance, while affirming his love for him (*Qasr al-shawq*, p. 412). One of the elementary external signs of the patriarchal order is the appending of the father's name to that of the son.

Secondly, the very meaning of the name 'Abd al-'Aziz ("servant of the Mighty One") contradicts the attribute that Mahfuz values most highly, freedom. Furthermore, this name – "servant of the Mighty One" – represents precisely the kind of religious attitude that is obnoxious to him. Mahfuz, through his character Kamal, rejects the attributes of God that signify His unlimited power and dominance. In the aforementioned chapter, even while declaring his emancipation from his father's rule, Kamal reveals his changed view of God: "I sift the attributes of God to cleanse Him of tyranny, arbitrary power, coercion, dictatorship and all other human impulses" (ibid.).

The similarity and the connection between the tyranny of the father and the tyranny of religion are frequently suggested and occasionally spelled out in Mahfuz's works. Commenting on the ab-

---

[8] The notion that "Mahfuz's full – and less known – name appeared in his early works, and that he later adopted a shorter name, omitting 'Abd al-'Aziz," as claimed by S. Somekh, *The Changing Rhythm: A Study of Najib Mahfuz's Novels* (Leiden, 1973), p. 36, n. 1, is mistaken; in all of Mahfuz's published stories and articles of the 1930s his name appears as Najib Mahfuz. Mahfuz's tripartite name, i.e., his own name followed by his father's and grandfather's names, is Najib Mahfuz 'Abd al-'Aziz Ibrahim.

[9] See above, p. 198.

solute rule exercised by the father over his family in the trilogy, Mahfuz says, "Everything in this house yields blindly to a supreme will that has unlimited power similar to the power of religion" (*Bayn al-qasrayn*, p. 272).

Thirdly, the "religious ambiguity" of the name Najib Mahfuz may well have suited his view of the Egyptian collective identity according to which all Egyptians – Muslims and Christians – are Egyptian first and foremost. Mahfuz, therefore, felt a strong aversion to any form of religious discrimination.

In summary, Najib Mahfuz's own name must have alerted him to the paradox of the personal name: it can be highly informative (if one finds the clue to the story behind it), but it can also be mischievously misleading. Hence, it is both correct and incorrect, both meaningful and meaningless.

CHAPTER 21

Names and Language

> He taught Adam the names of all things and then set
> them before the angels: "Tell me the names of these, if
> what you say be true."
>
> Qur'an, 2:31

> They are but names which you and your fathers have
> invented; God has vested no power in them.
>
> Qur'an, 53:23

Najib Mahfuz is well aware that the paradoxical quality of names is not peculiar to personal names, but is characteristic of the names of things in general; indeed, it is the bedeviling nature of language itself.[1] Mahfuz repeatedly alludes, in a variety of subtle ways, to the intricate relationship between words and reality. The same word may have different, even contradictory meanings, which vary according to context, the intention of the speaker, and the understanding of the person addressed. Thus, for example, when Kamal's closest friend tells him, "You are a perfect example of a conservative," Kamal thinks, "What does he mean by this? Is it a compliment or an insult?"[2]

---

[1] It should be noted that the Arabic word *ism* ("name") signifies both proper and common nouns. Hence it can be translated as either "name" or "noun."

[2] *Madḥ am dhamm*, literally "praise or derogation."

In the course of further conversation, the same friend tells Kamal: "You were born to be a teacher." Kamal again asks himself: "Is this a compliment or an insult?"[3]

In a conversation between a group of students, when the progressive Ahmad states his belief that women are equal to men, his brother, a member of the Muslim Brotherhood, replies, "I don't know whether it's a compliment or an insult to tell women that they are like us."[4]

Jalila, the famous singer and former mistress of Sayyid Ahmad, asks the same question in the course of bawdy repartee at a late-night party on a houseboat. One of Sayyid Ahmad's friends teases him about his son Kamal's article on Darwin in which he claims that man is descended from the ape. Zubayda (Sayyid Ahmad's present mistress) asks: "From the ape?" Then, as if on further reflection, she says, "Perhaps he's thinking of his own origins." Sayyid Ahmad cautions her, "Kamal [in his article] also shows that woman is descended from the lioness." Lioness, *labwa*, in Egyptian colloquial Arabic, signifies "a highly-sexed woman." A friend tells him, "One day your son will grow up and leave home, then he'll realize that mankind is descended from Adam and Eve." Sayyid Ahmad rejoins, "Or I'll bring him here so he can see that man is descended from the dog." Indicating Sayyid Ahmad, another member of the company asks Zubayda, "You know him better than we do, what animal is he descended from?" Smiling, she says, "From the ass." Jalila asks, "Is that an insult or a compliment?" (This remark alludes to the size of the male ass's organ). Sayyid Ahmad retorts, "The actual truth is inside the speaker."[5] Sayyid Ahmad's response is, of course, a reference to the fact that "the speaker" in this case is his mistress, but Mahfuz is also making a serious observation here, namely, that, invariably, only the speaker knows exactly what he intends.

As different people may define the same word in different ways, the degree of appropriateness of any word to what it is intended to signify will always be a matter of opinion. The problem of the ap-

---

[3] *Qasr al-shawq*, pp. 202–3.

[4] *Al-Sukkariyya*, p. 159.

[5] *Qasr al-shawq*, pp. 436–37; *al-ma'na fi batn al-qa'il*, literally "the meaning is in the speaker's inside."

propriateness of words is reflected in 'Uthman's remark to 'Umar (in *al-Shahhadh*): "We will never reach a truth worthy of the name, except by intelligence, science and work."[6] Likewise, Sawsan, the communist, talking to Ahmad of the writer's role in society, asserts: "A writer worthy of the name should be in the vanguard of political struggle."[7] Kamal, ever assailed by doubts as to the meaning of life, comforts himself: "I may be truly in agony, but I am alive, a living human being, and one must pay a price for any human life worthy of the name."[8]

In many cases the name used may be felt to be inappropriate. When Amina brings the bedridden Sayyid Ahmad his evening portion of the bland diet which is all he is now permitted to eat, she asks him, "Shall I serve you dinner?" Sayyid Ahmad answers, bitterly, "Dinner? Do you still give this the name 'dinner'? Set down the bowl of yogurt."[9]

'Abd al-Mun'im's mentor, the shaykh who leads a group of the Muslim Brotherhood, explains to his disciples, "We are Muslims in name only. We should become Muslims in fact."[10] In another quite different context we find the same distinction between the nominal and the actual: in the novel *Bidaya wa-nihaya*, when Bahiyya refuses to kiss her fiancé, he rebukes her, "So this is love in name only."[11]

The same object may be designated by more than one name. For example, the agonized Kamal thinks, "*'A'ida* and *pain* are two [different] words signifying the same thing."[12] In *Bidaya wa-nihaya* we find much the same concept expressed in similar terms. Hasanayn, looking forward to meeting his fiancée at sunset, reflects, "In my mind, Bahiyya and the cool of early evening are one and the same thing."[13] Sayyid Ahmad, when planning an evening with his friends and their mistresses, announces that he himself will join the party but will con-

---

[6] *Al-Shahhadh*, p. 162.   [7] *Al-Sukkariyya*, p. 249.

[8] Ibid., p. 18.   [9] Ibid., p. 241.   [10] Ibid., p. 99.

[11] *Bidaya wa-nihaya*, p. 108. The trilogy provides many similar examples: Khadija's complaint that she must discipline her sons because "their father exists in name only" (*al-ab ghayr mawjud illa bi'l-ism*), *Qasr al-shawq*, p. 49; Khadija's son's comment on Italy's entering the war: "Perhaps these nominal raids will turn into actual raids" (*rubbama tahawwalat hadhihi al-gharat al-ismiyya ila gharat fi'liyya*), *al-Sukkariyya*, p. 213.

[12] *Qasr al-shawq*, p. 291.

[13] *Bidaya wa-nihaya*, p. 105.

fine his pleasures to "enjoying the company of his friends and the cordial atmosphere." Unconvinced, his friend Muhammad 'Iffat replies: "Call it what you will, its names are many, but the act is one [and the same]."[14]

Usually, the name survives all the changes undergone by the person who bears it; in some cases, indeed, the name is all that remains. When, in old age, Sayyid Ahmad recalls his past, he remembers "the people of whom nothing remained but their names: Zubayda, Jalila, Haniyya."[15] Likewise, 'A'isha, Kamal's beautiful sister, in middle age becomes an ailing, depressed woman (after she has lost her husband and all her children) "and nothing survived of her old self except the name."[16] Sayyid Ahmad reflects, when he realizes that his former mistresses no longer attract him: "Zubayda is no longer Zubayda and Jalila is no longer Jalila."[17]

However, the bond which unites a name and the person who bears it is neither immutable nor necessary. Sometimes people do change their names, and this may reflect a change of appearance or social status, though not a change of heart. In *Kifah Tiba*, the Pharaoh says, "What do names mean? Yesterday I was called Isfinis and today I am called Ahmas, but I am the same person with the same feelings."[18]

In some cases words are treated as if possessed of a power of their own. Kamal, as a child, is in the habit of reciting to his mother those portions of the Qur'an which he has learned that day in school. One day he starts reciting *Surat al-jinn* ("The Chapter of the Demons"). His mother had always warned him never to utter either one of the two names denoting "demon" (*jinn, shaytan*). Yet now he finds himself pronoucing the dangerous word "*jinn*," much to his mother's horror. She immediately prays for God's protection.[19]

---

[14] *Qasr al-shawq*, p. 104.

[15] *Al-Sukkariyya*, p. 238.

[16] Ibid., p. 233.

[17] *Qasr al-shawq*, p. 92. Cf. Kamal's remark to his friend Riyad Qaldes, when the latter tells him that he is about to get married: "You will then be a different Riyad Qaldes" (*al-Sukkariyya*, p. 283).

[18] *Kifah Tiba*, p. 201. Cf. above, p. 213, the prostitute 'Ayyusha who changes her name to Warda, and Nur (pp. 231–32) in *al-Liss wa'l-kilab*, formerly Shalabiyya. Also Zaynab in *al-Shahhadh*, who, before her conversion to Islam, was called Kamilya, pp. 241–42.

[19] *Bayn al-qasrayn*, p. 76.

Kamal, as a child, repeatedly hears it mentioned that the next-door neighbor Muhammad Ridwan is paralyzed, and he asks his mother what the word means. His horrified mother hastens to "beg God's protection to ward off the evil of the word he uttered."[20] Sometimes the mere utterance of a name may have a powerful effect: when Sayyid Ahmad tries to persuade Zubayda to become his mistress – after he has tired of Jalila – Zubayda tells him that she has heard all about him. Sayyid Ahmad asks her, "Who told you about me?" Zubayda replies, "Jalila." Mahfuz adds: "The name startled him, as though it were a person coming to rebuke him."[21] Although in the above examples the power of words stems from two distinct sources – in one case from a common belief in the magical power of the word, in the other from personal memories associated with a particular name – the effect of both shows that a word may attain the power of an actual being.

Mahfuz himself is a believer in the power of words as a social and historical force. Kamal remarks, in the course of a political debate with his friends, "You belittle the significance of words, as if they were of no importance. But, in fact, in the final analysis, the greatest events in human history originate in words. A great speech contains hope, strength and truth."[22] In *Miramar*, the aging journalist 'Amir Wajdi, who, like Kamal, represents Mahfuz's own views, tells the young engineer, "Young man, nations are awakened by words, not by engineers or economists."[23]

Two brief scenes in the trilogy reveal Mahfuz's abiding interest in the evolution and psychology of language. When Sayyid Ahmad learns that his wife has independently introduced their daughter to a prospective suitor, "he gave her a stern look and began to snarl and growl and murmur and grumble, as though his anger had carried him back to the stage of expressing himself by sounds, a stage through which his early ancestors had passed."[24] When Yasin tires of his wife, he says, "I am tired of [her] very beauty, it's like a new word which

[20] Ibid., p. 152.
[21] Ibid., p. 107.
[22] *Qasr al-shawq*, p. 170.
[23] *Miramar*, p. 218.
[24] *Bayn al-qasrayn*, p. 352.

dazzles you at first, but then, as you keep using it, it becomes just like 'dog,' 'worm,' 'lesson,' and other insignificant things, it loses its novelty and sweet taste, you may even forget its meaning; and then it will become just another unfamiliar word without meaning or purpose. But, if someone else encounters it in your composition, he may perhaps marvel at your ingenuity, while you will marvel at his lack of understanding."[25]

In some contexts words lose their meaning. When Sayyid Ahmad nostalgically recalls the "glorious past," Kamal says to him, "Every age has its merits and faults." Sayyid Ahmad retorts, "That's just empty words."[26]

In 1935 Mahfuz published an article presenting a brief and very general review of the various approaches to the problem of language: philosophical, psychological and linguistic.[27] In the first part of the article, he summarizes, in a few lines, Plato's dialogue, *Cratylus*, which deals with the nature of names: "Plato dealt with the problem of language in the dialogue *Cratylus* and presented the two conflicting views on this problem. One view is that of Democritus [*sic*],[28] which holds language to be a matter of convention and arbitrary invention; hence [according to this view], there is no objection to your changing the names [of things] as you wish and fitting them to whatever things you wish. The second view is that of Cratylus, the student of Heraclitus, which holds that there is a natural connection between the name and that which is named; the name expresses the nature of the thing so that he who knows the name knows the thing itself."

Mahfuz notes (correctly) that Plato rejects the first view (i.e., that names are merely signs accepted by convention) and that "at the same time, Plato does not espouse the opinion of Cratylus that he who knows the names also knows the true natures of the things [designated by them]."

[25] Ibid., pp. 385–86.   [26] *Al-Sukkariyya*, p. 240.

[27] "*Al-Lugha*," *al-Majalla al-jadida* (Cairo, August 1935), pp. 65–71.

[28] The view presented by Mahfuz as that of Democritus is, in fact, presented by Hermogenes. I do not know the origin of this apparent mistake, but it seems that Mahfuz's remarks on this matter are based on some secondary source, probably lecture notes which he took when he studied philosophy at the university.

It should be recalled that Plato's *Cratylus* begins with an inquiry into the question of the "correctness" of personal names, that is, the question of whether or not personal names truly represent the persons bearing the names, but this inquiry develops into a discussion of the relationship between names and reality in general – the core problem of the philosophy of language. Mahfuz, who as an undergraduate studied philosophy at the university in the hope of discovering "the secret of being," gave up the systematic study of philosophy and the hope of thereby attaining absolute metaphysical truth, in order to become a novelist who in his stories would explore the true nature of things. His article on language makes it quite clear that when he embarked on his literary enterprise he was fully aware that the writer's tool – language – is no less fluid and ambiguous than reality itself.

"Things change through [ever changing] circumstances just as words change because of the new meanings they acquire."[29] This line, which occurs at the beginning of one of the chapters of the trilogy, discloses Mahfuz's awareness that language is no more constant than reality. Time and again Mahfuz returns to the elusive quality of language. He seems to envisage a dynamic dialectical relationship between things and names (words), the latter constantly acquiring new meanings as a result of the changes which occur in the things to which they refer. Mahfuz's artistic undertaking is, therefore, twofold: to explore and describe reality by means of words and to examine the appropriateness (or, to use Plato's expression, the correctness) of words by juxtaposing them with the reality they are presumed to designate. Mahfuz's preoccupation with personal names, which may well have been born out of his experience with his own name, assumed a philosophical bent as a result of his interest in the philosophy of language. The intriguing relationships between persons and their names in Mahfuz's fictional world thus illustrate a larger issue: the tense and precarious relationship between language and reality.

---

[29] *Qasr al-shawq*, p. 339 (chap. 31).

CHAPTER 22

Mahfuz as Allegorist

The Sage has said: "A word fitly spoken is like apples of gold in settings of silver." [Prov. 25:11]. Hear now an elucidation of the thought
that he has set forth. . . . A saying uttered with a view to two meanings
is like an apple of gold overlaid with silver filigree work having
very small holes. Now see how marvellously this dictum describes a
well-constructed parable. For he says that in a saying that has two
meanings – that is, an external and an internal one – the external
meaning ought to be as beautiful as silver, while its internal meaning
ought to be more beautiful than the external one, the former being in
comparison to the latter as gold is to silver. Its external meaning also
ought to contain in it something that indicates to someone considering
it what is to be found in its internal meaning, as happens in the case of
an apple of gold overlaid with silver filigree-work having very small
holes. When looked at from a distance or with imperfect attention, it
is deemed to be an apple of silver; but when a keen-sighted observer
looks at it with full attention, its interior becomes clear to him and he
knows that it is of gold.

Maimonides, *The Guide of the Perplexed*[1]

Kamal, Mahfuz's alter ego in the trilogy, as a senior in high school
who intends to be a novelist, discusses with his friends the question
of religious observance and reveals that he has lost his religious faith.

[1] Maimonides, *The Guide of the Perplexed*, trans. S. Pines (Chicago, 1963), pp. 11–12.

His friends ask him whether he intends to fast in Ramadan (the Muslim month of fasting). He informs them that he will not fast, but neither will he tell his parents, in order to avoid hurting them: "I see no reason to cause pain to those I love." (Kamal's answer here is characteristic of Mahfuz himself, who instinctively avoids confrontation.) One of Kamal's friends then asks him how he thinks he can ever be a writer, if he cannot face telling people things they do not want to hear. Kamal does not answer but, pondering the question, an idea occurs to him: "*Kalila wa-Dimna* [– that is the solution]."[2] This is a somewhat enigmatic statement which requires explication: *Kalila wa-Dimna*, a famous eighth-century didactic work, intended for the moral edification of princes, is an allegory in which the characters are animals. And, indeed, allegory would seem to be an essential feature of Mahfuz's literary enterprise: his words always have more than one level of meaning. This quality in his work is not merely the reflection of some unconscious mental process, but rather the result of a deliberate effort to convey covert messages under the surface story.

The young Najib Mahfuz would, therefore, appear to have had allegory in mind as a stratagem even before he started to publish his stories, and he had certainly adopted it as a literary mode by the time he wrote the trilogy. With this approach, Mahfuz was able to function as a writer and a social critic under the oppressive political conditions of the monarchy and, later, of the Nasser regime in the 1950s and 1960s.

It would, however, be a mistake to believe that allegory for Mahfuz was merely a device for escaping harassment by the authorities, or even, more generally, a convenient way of avoiding embarrassing social confrontations. Allegory is Mahfuz's way of reading reality, which, he believes, cannot be fully observed, let alone understood. Ambiguity fascinates him as much as it bedevils him. Allegory, which contains more than one level of meaning, and which may imply more than one kind of reality, offered him a way of dealing with the problems which concerned him, without forcing him to propose unequivocal answers, which he did not possess.

---

[2] *Qasr al-shawq*, p. 381.

Mahfuz's predilection for allegory has been colored by his study of Sufism (Islamic mysticism) under Mustafa 'Abd al-Raziq.[3] In Sufism, everything external (*zahir*) has an internal aspect (*batin*) and everything internal, in turn, contains an inner core which is its real essence (*haqiqa*). For the Sufi, things are therefore not what they appear to be; hence, ambiguous phrases and oxymorons are the very staple of Sufi diction. Mahfuz is certainly no Sufi, but Sufism's allegorical interpretation of reality and treatment of words suits him well.

Mahfuz's allegorical approach is perhaps among the reasons for his use of literary rather than colloquial Arabic, even in dialogue, because literary Arabic lends itself to allegory far better than the colloquial.[4] If Mahfuz were a proponent of pan-Arabism, one could possibly construe his avoidance of the Egyptian colloquial as an implicit political statement in favor of the elimination of everything which distinguishes Egyptians from other speakers of Arabic, and an adherance to that by which all Arabs are united. But Mahfuz has never been a supporter of pan-Arab nationalism; on the contrary, he has always firmly upheld the idea of a distinct Egyptian nationalism.

The high prestige of literary Arabic and its capacity to enhance readership in other Arab countries would not have been enough to induce Mahfuz to avoid the use of Egyptian dialect even in dialogue. True, there is also the artistic consideration of having the same character use only one type of language for the words in his mouth and for the thoughts in his head, rather than having him alternate between two quite different kinds of language. However, this artistic consideration must be weighed against another, equally important: rendering dialogue in literary Arabic involves an act of translation by which one is likely to lose some of the local atmosphere and tone.

The deeper reason for Mahfuz's very conspicuous adherence to literary Arabic would therefore seem to lie in a particular quality of the "eloquent" Arabic, namely, the notorious ambiguity of its vocabulary. This peculiarity of literary Arabic, reflecting many centuries of semantic development, is regarded by some as a shortcoming. For Mahfuz it is a boon; it provides him with the ideal artistic tool. Liter-

---

[3] See above, p. 31.

[4] On Mahfuz's preference for literary Arabic, see above, pp. 13–14.

ary Arabic furnishes Mahfuz with ample opportunites for allegory. By using it throughout his works, he can draw on the wealth of literary and cultural associations inherent in literary Arabic but absent from the colloquial. This medium enables him to weave a narrative fabric whose texture suggests more than what is represented merely in the structure of the story. Thus, Mahfuz uses a multivocal instrument to deal with a multi-faceted reality.

CHAPTER 23

Mahfuz and the Secret of Being

> The life which he was about to abandon by suicide
> became a purpose in itself, ... and knowledge, which
> he once thought to be a goal, now became a means for
> enjoying life by perceiving its affairs and discovering
> its hidden beauty.
>
> Najib Mahfuz, *"Fatra min al-shabab"*

As an adolescent, Mahfuz was possessed by a desire to grasp the ultimate meaning of life, which in interviews in later years he came to refer to as *sirr al-wujud* ("the secret of being"). This "secret of being" is identical with "the truth" (*al-haqiqa*) which is the object of Kamal's search in the trilogy.[1] Kamal tells his friend Husayn Shaddad, who plans to travel round the world, "My first object is the pursuit of truth: what is God, what is man, what is the spirit, what is matter? Only philosophy, as I have just recently realized, encompasses all of these in one shining logical whole. This is what I desire with all my heart to know. Indeed, this is the real journey, beside which your trip around the world is not such an important matter. Just imagine, I'll be able to find satisfactory answers to all these questions."[2]

Kamal's desire to study philosophy – the ambition of an intellectu-

---

[1] The Arabic word *haqiqa* may be translated as "truth," "reality," or "fact."
[2] *Qasr al-shawq*, p. 222.

ally alert mind – develops into an obsessive passion, as a result of a
series of crises which devastate his inner world. Darwinism has shattered his religious belief; he realizes that his faith in his father's power
and exalted social status is an illusion, and that his beloved 'A'ida,
whom he has worshipped as a heavenly being, is only a selfish, flirta-
tious and insincere young girl. In Kamal's mind (and undoubtedly
also in Mahfuz's), the two autocracies – his father's domination of
the family and God's domination of the world – are parallel and inter-related; so, too, are their declines. When he realizes that his father
is not the important man he has believed him to be, he reflects, "You
are not the only one whose image has changed: God himself is no
longer the God I used to worship."[3]

The truth he now seeks must fill the void created by the collapse of
the mainstays of his inner world – God, patriarchal authority and
Platonic love – and give new meaning to his life. Some of the expressions Kamal uses when speaking of this sought-after truth show that
it has assumed divine qualities in his mind: "In his heart [Kamal]
promises his mother to devote his life to spreading the light of God,
for is this not the light of truth? It certainly is. Thus, liberated from
religion, he will draw nearer to God than when he believed in
Him. . . . Thus, the paths leading to God will open before him, the
paths of knowledge, goodness and beauty."[4]

The emotional energy which Kamal once invested in his love for
'A'ida is now directed towards his search for truth. Truth has become
his new beloved: "The yearnings are intense, but the nature of the
beloved is now unknown. [The unknown beloved] has consented to
grant his lover only some of his *beautiful names*, and thus he is
[called] Truth and the Joy of Life and the Light of Knowledge."[5] The
"beautiful names" referred to here clearly allude to the "beautiful
names" by which Allah is known to his believers.[6] Here Mahfuz deliberately emphasizes the similarity between Kamal's philosophic
quest and that of a religious mystic. Reaffirming to himself the importance of the quest he has undertaken, Kamal reflects: "My

[3] *Qasr al-shawq*, p. 412
[4] Ibid., p. 375.
[5] Ibid., p. 425, my emphasis.
[6] On Allah's "beautiful names," see above, p. 166.

aspiration ... is a thirst that can be quenched only by truth, and to attain it I am prepared for every sacrifice, save life itself."[7]

However, as we know, Mahfuz – unlike his alter ego Kamal – later abandoned the study of philosophy in order to devote himself to literature. This change of direction, as he himself has recounted, stemmed not only from the attraction which literature held for him, but also from his realization that philosophy had failed to provide the truth he so passionately sought.[8] He understood that absolute, all-encompassing philosophical truth is a dream. Truth, he came to recognize, does not reside in one philosophical system, but is in fact reality itself. "Truth" and "reality" are in Arabic both denoted by the same word, *al-haqiqa*; and so, although Mahfuz changed the nature of his search, the name of his object remained the same. From this point on he devoted himself to literature, in an unrelenting effort to reveal the innumerable faces of reality.

The unmasking of the truth is a recurrent motif in Mahfuz's novels. The interplay between attempted concealment and eventual exposure provides a counterpoint to plot and sub-plot throughout the trilogy. Several examples will illustrate this point:

At 'A'ida's wedding party, Kamal observes the rich and aristocratic guests and thinks, "Look at them closely, so as to see what goes on behind the masks of their faces."[9]

Yasin keeps his marriage to Zannuba, his father's former mistress, a secret from his family. His father eventually learns the truth from one of his friends, who tells him, "I thought it better to reveal the truth to you, so as to spare you an embarrassing surprise."[10] The angry Sayyid Ahmad summons Yasin and demands an explanation for his behavior. Irritated by his son's "false varnish of contrition," he shouts, "Remove this mask. Stop this hypocrisy."[11]

When the two brothers, Kamal and Yasin, accidentally meet in a brothel, Yasin exclaims, "This is a happy night, Thursday the 30th of October 1926, a happy night indeed. It should be celebrated every year as the night two brothers revealed themselves to each other."[12]

Kamal, who is certain that his love for 'A'ida is a secret known only to the two of them, is shocked to hear from his friend Isma'il that his

---

[7] *Qasr al-shawq*, pp. 426–27.   [8] See above, p. 32.   [9] *Qasr al-shawq*, p. 350.
[10] Ibid., p. 359.   [11] Ibid., p. 363.   [12] *Qasr al-shawq*, p. 396.

affections are common knowledge; 'A'ida herself has "revealed" the secret to all her friends.[13]

But some masks are never removed: Yasin is never to learn that his wife Zannuba was at one time his father's mistress; Sayyid Ahmad is not aware that Yasin knows of his affair with Zubayda and has secretly observed him with her. No one, except the reader and the actors themselves, knows that Sayyid Ahmad and Yasin have each had an affair with Umm Maryam. Thus, though many secrets are exposed, many remain concealed, and absolute certainty is always beyond human reach. Kamal wonders, "Is there [a distinction between] real and unreal? What is the relationship between reality and what takes place in our head?"[14]

Mahfuz's continuous pursuit of the truth is curiously analogous to the Sufi quest. The teachings of Sufism, which, as we have seen, informed Mahfuz's use of allegory, would appear also to have influenced his view of reality. In Sufism, every external phenomenon possesses an internal aspect; hence, observed phenomena, like words, must constantly be unmasked and decoded.

Even after Mahfuz abandoned the study of philosophy in order to become a writer, he retained his interest in it. In an interview in 1962 he said: "In general, there is no escape from philosophy. Take away the philosophic substratum from a literary work and it will have no real value."[15] In the same interview he explained that philosophy combines with literature in a number of ways:

> It may enter into a literary work through the contents. I mean that the work expresses a philosophical idea so that it is primarily a philosophical work. Take for example Camus's novels *L'Étranger* and *La Peste* and Sartre's plays, in contemporary existentialist literature; *Faust*, in pre-modern literature; and *Risalat al-ghufran* and *Hayy ibn Yaqzan*, in medieval Arabic literature.
>
> [Or] the work may have characters who are in the habit of philosophizing, and this [quality] becomes clear from the dialogue, e.g., Aldous Huxley's *Point Counter Point*.

[13] Ibid., p. 353.
[14] Ibid., p. 401.
[15] In a panel discussion conducted by Faruq Shusha, *al-Ādāb* (Beirut, March 1962).

Or philosophy may enter in another way.... It may be reflected in the underlying structure of the work, that is, in the plot itself. As we follow the events of the story and the fortunes of the characters, we may find that the author intends to say that character and destiny are shaped by environment. This would express [the author's] belief in a materialistic philosophy which maintains that man is the product of his environment.

Or we may find a series of accidents causing certain misfortunes, such as the accidental events in [the novels of] Thomas Hardy, which reflect his fatalistic philosophy. In such cases philosophy seeps into the work through its general structure.

There is a fourth way in which philosophy may enter [a literary work]: the author may be influenced by his own philosophical training. In such a case, philosophy influences the work indirectly, yet it enriches it in a palpable way.

In his explanation of the four ways in which philosophy intertwines with literature, Mahfuz is in fact explaining how philosophy is blended into his own work.

Mahfuz's own philosophy is expressed in his works in a great variety of ways. Some of his stories are moral parables which deal allegorically with philosophical questions. In his novels, there is usually at least one character who is given to philosophical speculation. In a number of novels and short stories, Mahfuz expresses his conviction that man should not sacrifice everyday human concerns to an endless search for an implicitly unattainable ultimate truth. An obsessive quest for the ultimate inevitably results in self-destruction. Such is the fate of 'Umar in *al-Shahhadh* (*The Beggar*) and of Sabir in *al-Tariq* (*The Search*).[16] The essential assumption of Mahfuz's philosophical outlook is that no certainty exists – except death, which awaits us all. Paradoxically, however, man must disregard this one certainty in order to live, act and preserve his sanity.[17] The affirmation of life's value underlies all Mahfuz's work, from his first story "*Fatra min al-shabab*" (1932) – in which the hero's awakening to the beauty of life and nature enables him to overcome the

---

[16] See above, pp. 28, 236–37, 246–47.

[17] This idea is allegorically expressed in the story "*Didd majhul*" ("An Unknown Adversary") in the collection *Dunya 'llah*.

temptation to commit suicide – to *Afrah al-qubba* (1981), in which the hero resists a similar temptation. "Life is beautiful despite all the conflicts," says the heroine in the allegorical story *"Ruh tabib al-qulub"* ("The Spirit of the Healer of Hearts"), who advises the hero to find work and get married.[18]

Kamal's quest for the truth is doomed to failure, and his life is barren. Yasin, criticizing Kamal's endless search, speaks also for Mahfuz: "You avoid all everyday preoccupations, so as not to be distracted from your search for 'the truth.' However, it is in these preoccupations that truth is to be found. In the library you will never learn what life is. Truth is in the home and in the street."[19] Kamal himself, in a moment of illumination, says: "It is perhaps a mistake to look for a meaning in this world, when our primary task is to create this meaning."[20] This, indeed, would seem to be the quintessence of Mahfuz's philosophy.

Mahfuz has been observing Egyptian society and commenting on it for more than sixty years now. His critique has often been severe, but it has always been full of empathy. An eminent Egyptian critic said of Mahfuz a few years ago: "He has a love affair with Egypt as no other writer has had before or after him."[21] He then summed up, "Even if you read hundreds of books on Egyptian history and politics, you cannot understand Egypt unless you read Najib Mahfuz. Najib Mahfuz gives you the real taste of Egypt. He puts the keys to understanding the Egyptian personality into your hands, and then leads you into the hidden chambers of the authentic Egyptian spirit."

[18] See M. Milson, "Religion and Revolution in an Allegory by Najib Mahfuz: A Study of *Ruh tabib al-qulub*," in Miriam Rosen-Ayalon (ed.), *Studies in Memory of Gaston Wiet* (Jerusalem, 1977). Cf. also M. Milson, "Naǧib Mahfuz and the Quest for Meaning," *Arabica* 17 (1970), p. 184.

[19] *Al-Sukkariyya*, p. 35.

[20] Ibid., p. 257.

[21] Raja' al-Naqqash, *"Najib Mahfuz wa'l-mishwar al-tawil min al-Husayn ila Stockholm,"* *al-Musawwar* (Cairo, 21 October 1988), p. 36.

Bibliography

Najib Mahfuz's Works

With the exception of *Awlad haretna*, all Mahfuz's books listed below were published by Sa'id Jawda al-Sahhar's publishing house, Maktabat Misr. Mahfuz's first book, *Misr al-qadima* (a translation of Baikie's *Ancient Egypt*) originally appeared in 1932 as a special issue of the magazine *al-Majalla al-jadida*.

The original publication year of each book is given immediately after the title. Where the references in my work are not to the original printing, I indicate in brackets the edition I used.

Misr al-qadima (Ancient Egypt), 1932 [1988].
'Abath al-aqdar (Fate's Play), 1939 [1988].
Radubis, 1943 [1988].
Kifah Tiba (The Struggle of Thebes), 1944 [1988].
Khan al-Khalili, 1945 [6th print., 1965].
Al-Qahira al-jadida (The New Cairo), 1946 [8th print., 1971].
Hams al-junun (The Whisper of Madness), 1947 or 1948. The date given in the publisher's lists, 1938, is erroneous. [5th print., 1966].
Zuqaq al-midaqq, 1947 [n.d., probably 1988]. Trans. Trevor Le Gassick, *Midaq Alley*. Beirut: Khayat, 1966. Reprint. London: Heinemann, 1975; Washington, D.C.: Three Continents Press, 1974.
Al-Sarab (Mirage), 1948 [11th print., 1982].
Bidaya wa-nihaya, 1949 [7th print., 1967]. Trans. Ramses Awad, *The Beginning and the End*. New York: Doubleday, 1989.
Bayn al-qasrayn, 1956 [6th print., 1966]. Trans. William M. Hutchins and Olive E. Kenny, *Palace Walk*. New York: Doubleday, 1991.
Qasr al-shawq, 1957 [6th print., 1966]. Trans. William M. Hutchins, Lorne M. Kenny and Olive E. Kenny, *Palace of Desire*. New York: Doubleday, 1991.

Al-Sukkariyya, 1957 [5th print., 1964]. Trans. William Maynard Hutchins and Angele Botros Samaan, *Sugar Street*. New York: Doubleday, 1992.

Al-Liss wa'l-kilab, 1961 [3rd print., 1964]. Trans. Trevor Le Gassick and Mustafa Badawi and revised by John Rodenbeck, *The Thief and the Dogs*. New York: Doubleday, 1989.

Al-Summan wa'l-kharif, 1962 [2nd print., 1964]. Trans. Roger Allen, *Autumn Quail*. Cairo: American University in Cairo Press, 1985; London: Doubleday, 1991.

Dunya 'llah (God's World), 1963.

Al-Tariq, 1964 [2nd print., 1965]. Trans. Mohamed Islam, edited by Magdi Wahba, *The Search*. Cairo: American University in Cairo Press, 1987; London: Doubleday, 1991.

Bayt sayyi' al-sum'a (A House of Ill Repute), 1965 [2nd print., 1966].

Al-Shahhadh, 1965 [2nd print., 1966]. Trans. Kristin Walker Henry and Nariman Khales Naili al-Warraki, *The Beggar*. Cairo: American University in Cairo Press, 1986; London: Doubleday, 1990.

Tharthara fawq al-nil, 1966 [n.d.] Trans. Frances Liardet, *Adrift on the Nile*. Cairo: The American University in Cairo Press, 1993.

Miramar, 1967. Trans. Fatma Moussa-Mahmoud, *Miramar*. London: Heinemann, 1978.

Awlad haretna, 1967. Beirut: Dar al-Adab. Trans. Philip Stewart, *Children of Gebelawi*. London: Heinemann, 1981; Washington, D.C.: Three Continents Press, 1981.

Khammarat al-qitt al-aswad (The Black Cat Tavern), 1968.

Taht al-mizalla (In the Bus Shelter), 1969.

Hikaya bila bidaya wala nihaya (A Tale without Beginning or End), 1971.

Shahr al-'asal (Honeymoon), 1971.

Al-Maraya, 1972. Trans. Roger Allen, *Mirrors*. Minneapolis: Bibliotheca Islamica, 1977.

Al-Hubb taht al-matar (Love in the Rain), 1973.

Al-Jarima (The Crime), 1973.

Al-Karnak, 1974. In *Three Egyptian Contemporary Novels* trans. Saad El-Gabalawy. Fredricton, New Brunswick: York Press, 1984.

Hikayat haretna, 1975. Trans. Soad Sobhy, Essam Fattouh and James Kenneson, *Fountain and Tomb*. Washington, D.C.: Three Continents Press, 1988.

Qalb al-layl (The Heart of the Night), 1975.

Hadrat al-muhtaram, 1975. Trans. Rasheed El-Enany, *Respected Sir*. London: Quartet Books, 1986.

Malhamat al-harafish, 1977. Trans. Catherine Cobham, *The Harafish*. New

York: Doubleday, 1994.

Al-Hubb fawq hadbat al-haram (Love on Top of the Pyramid), 1979 [3rd print., 1984].

Al-Shaytan ya'iz (Satan Preaches), 1979.

'Asr al-hubb (The Age of Love), 1980.

Afrah al-qubba, 1981. Trans. Olive Kenny, revised by Mursi Saad El Din and John Rodenbeck, *Wedding Song*. New York: Doubleday, 1989.

Layali alf layla (The Nights of a Thousand Nights), 1982. Trans. Denys Johnson-Davies, *Arabian Nights and Days*. New York: Doubleday, 1995.

Ra'aytu fima yara al-na'im (I Saw in a Dream), 1982.

Al-Baqi min al-zaman sa'a (You Have One Hour Left), 1982.

Amam al-'arsh (Before the Throne), 1983.

Rihlat Ibn Fattuma, 1983. Trans. Denys Johnson-Davies, *The Journey of Ibn Fattouma*. London: Doubleday, 1992.

Al-Tanzim al-sirri (The Secret Organization), 1984.

Al-'A'ish fi 'l-haqiqa (He Who Lives in the Truth), 1985.

Yawm qutila 'l-za'im, 1985. Trans. Malak Hashim, *The Day the Leader Was Killed*. Cairo: General Egyptian Book Organization, 1989.

Hadith al-sabah wa'l-masa' (Morning and Evening Tales), 1987.

Sabah al-ward (Morning of Blossom, i.e., "Good Morning"), 1987.

Qushtumor, 1988.

Al-Fajr al-kadhib (False Dawn), 1989.

Asda' al-sira al-dhatiyya, n.d. [1995]. Trans. Denys Johnson-Davies, *Echoes of an Autobiography*. New York: Doubleday, 1995.

Al-Qarar al-akhir (The Final Decision), 1996.

Essays

Hawl al-din wa'l-Dimuqratiyya (On Religion and Democracy), 1990.

Hawl al-thaqafa wa'l-ta'lim (On Culture and Education), 1990.

Hawl al-shabab wa'l-hurriyya (On Youth and Freedom), 1990.

Hawl al-tadayyun wa'l-tatarruf (On Religiosity and Extremism), 1996.

Hawl al-'adl wa'l-'adala (On Justice and Equity), 1996.

Hawl al-taharrur wa'l-taqaddum (On Liberation and Progress), 1996.

Hawl al-'ilm wa'l-'amal (On Science and Work), 1996.

Hawl al-'arab wa'l-'uruba (On the Arabs and Arabism), 1996.

All eight titles are edited by Fathi al-'Ashri.

Works in Arabic

'Abd al-Hayy, 'Abd al-Tawwab. *'Asir hayati.* Cairo: al-Dar al-Qawmiyya li'l-Tiba'a, 1966. Interview with Najib Mahfuz, 126–34; orig. pub. in *al-'Idha'a*, 21 December 1957.

al-Ma'arri, Abu al-'Ala'. *Risalat al-ghufran.* Edited by 'A'isha 'Abd al-Rahman 4th printing. Cairo: Dar al-Ma'arif.

Abu 'Awf, 'Abd al-Rahman. *Al-Ru'a al-mutaghayyira fi riwayat Najib Mahfuz.* Cairo: al-Hay'a al-Misriyya al-'Amma li'l-Kitab, 1991.

———. *"Misdaqiyyat shahadat Najib Mahfuz 'ala marhalatay 'Abd al-Nasir wa'l-Sadat." Majallat al-mawqif al-'arabi* 78 (October 1986), pp. 126–29.

Abu Kaff, Ahmad. *"Al-Mar'a wa'l-jins fi adab Najib Mahfuz." Al-Hilal,* February 1970.

'Afifi, Muhammad. *"Najib Mahfuz rajul al-sa'a"* (Najib Mahfuz: The Man of the Watch). *Al-Hilal* 2 (February 1970), pp. 136–41.

Amin, Ahmad. *Qamus al-'adat wa'l taqalid w'al ta'abir al-misriyya.* Cairo: Matba'at Lajnat al-Ta'lif w'al-Tarjama, 1953.

'Amir, Ibrahim. *"Najib Mahfuz siyasiyyan." Al-Hilal,* Cairo, February 1970, pp. 26–37.

al-'Aqqad, 'Abbas Mahmud. *Fi bayti.* Cairo: Dar al-Ma'arif, *Iqra'* Series, August 1945.

'Asfur, Jabir. *"Nuqqad Najib Mahfuz,"* in *Najib Mahfuz: Ibda' nisf qarn.* ed. Ghali Shukri. Beirut and Cairo: Dar al-Shuruq, 1989, pp. 225–63. An abridged translation of this article appears in Michael Beard and Adnan Haydar (eds.), *Naguib Mahfouz: From Regional Fame to Global Recognition.*

al-Aswad, Fadil, ed. *Al-Rajul wa'l-qimma.* Cairo: Al-Hai'a al-Misriyya al-'Amma li'l-Kitab, 1989.

'Awad, Luwis. *"Al-Liss wa'l-kilab,"* in *Najib Mahfuz: Ibda' nisf qarn,* ed. Ghali Shukri. Beirut and Cairo: Dar al-Shuruq, 1989, pp. 101–106. Orig. pub. in 'Awad's *Dirasat fi'l naqd wa'l adab,* Cairo, 1967.

———. *Awraq al-'umr.* Cairo: Maktabat Madbuli, 1989.

'Awda, Muhammad. *Al-Wa'y al-mafqud.* Cairo: Al-Qahira li'l Thaqafa al-'Arabiyya, 1975.

Badr, 'Abd al-Muhsin Taha. *Al-Ru'ya wa'l-ada: Najib Mahfuz.* 3rd printing. Cairo: Dar al-Ma'arif, 1984 [1978].

———. *Tatawwur al-riwaya al-'arabiyya al-haditha fi misr.* 2nd printing. Cairo: Dar al-Ma'arif, 1968.

al-Baydawi, Abu Sa'id. *Anwar al-tanzil wa-asrar al-ta'wil.*

al-Damiri, Muhammad b. Musa Kamal al-Din. *Kitab hayat al- hayawan al-kubra*. Cairo: Matba'at Muhammad 'Ali Subayh, 1353 AH (1933).

Dawwara, Fu'ad. *Najib Mahfuz min al-qawmiyya ila al-'alamiyya*. Cairo: Al-Hay'a al-Misriyya al-'Amma li'l-kitab, 1989. Contains interview pub. Jan. 1963 in *al-Katib*, "*Rihlat al-khamsin ma'a 'l-qira'a wa'l- kitaba*," pp. 209–36; and interview pub. in *al-Kawakib* 22 (29 December 1981 and 5 January 1982), "*Fi 'id miladihi al-sab'in*," pp. 251–293.

Dayf, Shawqi. *Al-Adab al-'arabi al-mu'asir fi misr*. 2nd ed. Cairo: Dar al-Ma'arif, 1961.

Fawzi, Mahmud. *Najib Mahfuz – za'im al-harafish*. Beirut: Dar al-Jil, 1989. An interview with Mahfuz.

al-Ghitani, Jamal. *Najib Mahfuz yatadhakkar*. Beirut: Dar al-Masira, 1980. A series of edited interviews, apparently with additional, unacknowledged material.

Hafiz, Sabri, ed. *Atahaddath ilaykum*. Beirut: Dar al-'Awda, 1977. A collection of ten interviews 1957–1973.

al-Hakim, Tawfiq. *Taht shams al-fikr*. Cairo: Lajnat al-Ta'lif wa'l-Tarjama wa'l-Nashr, 1938.

Hamrush, Ahmad. Interview. *Al-jumhuriyya*, 2 January 1960.

Haqqi, Yahya. *Fajr al-qissa al-misriyya*. 2nd printing. Cairo: Al-Hay'a al-Misriyya al-'Amma li'l-Kitab, 1987.

Haykal, Ahmad. *Al-Adab al-qasasi wa'l-masrahi fi misr*. 3rd printing. Cairo: Dar al-Ma'arif, 1979.

———. *Tatawwur al-adab al-hadith fi misr*. Cairo: Dar al-Ma'arif, 1968.

Husayn, Taha. *Min adabina al-mu'asir*. 2nd printing. Cairo: Matba'at Misr, 1959 [1958].

———. *Min hadith al-shi'r wa'l-nathr*. Cairo, Matba'at al-Sawi, 1936.

'Id, Raja'. *Qira'a fi adab Najib Mahfuz: Ru'ya naqdiyya*. Alexandria: Munsha'at al-Ma'arif, 1989.

Karim, Samih. "*Najib Mahfuz wa-thawrat 1919*." *Al-Katib*, April, 1969.

Khuri, Ilyas. "*Bayn al-riwaya wa-naqidiha*" in his collection *al-Dhakira al-mafquda*. Beirut: Mu'assasat al-Abhath al-'Arabiyya, 1982.

Kisa'i, Muhammad ben 'Abdallah. *Qisas al-anbiya'*. Ed. I. Eisenberg. Leiden: E. J. Brill, 1922–1923.

Musa, Salama. *Al-Adab li'l-sha'b*. Cairo: Mu'assasat al-Khanji, 1971.

———. *Mukhtarat Salama Musa*. Cairo: Al-Matba'a al-'Asriyya, 1924.

al-Nahhas, Hashim. *Najib Mahfuz 'ala al-shasha*. Cairo: al-Hay'a al-Misriyya al-'Amma li'l-Kitab, 1975.

Najm, Muhammad Yusuf. *Al-Qissa fi 'l-adab al-'arabi al-hadith – 1870–1914*. 2nd ed. Beirut: al-Maktaba al-Ahliyya, 1961.

———. *"Faharis al-adab al-'arabi al-hadith."* *Al-Abhath*, Beirut, March 1963.

al-Naqqash, Amina. *"Hiwar ma'a Najib Mahfuz."* *Afaq 'arabiyya*, February, 1976.

al-Naqqash, Raja'. *"Bayn al-wafdiyya wa'l-marxiyya,"* *al-Hilal*, February 1970.

Raghib, Nabil. *Qadiyyat al-shakl al-fanni 'ind Najib Mahfuz*. Cairo: Al-Hay'a al-Misriyya al-'Amma li'l-Kitab, 1975.

al-Ra'i, 'Ali. *"Thulathiyyat bayn al-qasrayn,"* in *Dirasat fi 'l-riwaya al-misriyya*. Cairo, 1964.

Rajab, Adham. *"Safahat majhula min hayat Najib Mahfuz."* *Al-Hilal*, Cairo, February 1970.

———. *"Khitabat bi-khatt Najib Mahfuz."* *October*, 11 December 1988, pp. 39–46.

Sarraj, 'Abdallah Bin 'Ali al-Tusi. *Kitab al-luma'*. Ed. R.A. Nicholson. Leiden: E.J. Brill and London, Luzac & Co., 1914.

Shalash, 'Ali. *Najib Mahfuz: al-Tariq wa'l-sada*. Beirut; Dar al-Ādāb, 1990.

al-Sharif, 'Ai'da. *"Dhikrayat wa-hadith ma'a Najib Mahfuz."* *Al-Ādāb*, March 1967, pp. 26–29.

al-Shaykh, Ibrahim. *Mawaqif ijtima'iyya wa-siyasiyya fi adab Najib Mahfuz*. 3rd printing. Cairo, 1987.

Shukri, Ghali. Interview with Mahfuz. *"Najib Mahfuz yatahaddath 'an fannihi al-riwa'i."* *Hiwar* 3 (March- April 1963), pp. 65–74.

———. *Thawrat al-fikr fi adabina al-hadith*. Cairo: Maktabat al-Anglo al-Misriyya, 1965.

———. *Al-Muntami: Dirasa fi adab Najib Mahfuz*. 2nd rev. ed. Cairo: Dar al-Ma'arif, 1969.

———. *"Nobel yafuz bi-ja'izat Najib Mahfuz."* *Al-Ahram*, 19 October 1988.

———. Interview in *al Watan al-'arabi* 46 (29 January 1988), pp. 42–47.

———. Interview in *al-Watan al-'arabi* 48 (12 February 1988), pp. 42–46.

———. *Najib Mahfuz: Ibda' nisf qarn*. Beirut and Cairo: Dar al-Shuruq, 1989.

al-Suyuti, Jalal-al-Din. *Lubab al-nuqul fi asbab al-nuzul*.

al-Tabari, Abu Ja'far Muhammad b. Jarir b. Rastum. *Dala'il al-imama*. Najaf, 1963/1383.

al-Tahtawi, Rifa'a Rafi'. *Takhlis al-ibriz fi talkhis bariz* [based on the second edition of Bulaq, 1265 AH] in Mahmud Fahmi Hijazi, *Usul al-fikr al-'arabi al-hadith 'ind al-Tahtawi*. Cairo: al-Hay'a al-Misriyya al-'Amma li'l-Kitab, 1974.

Tarabishi, George. *Allah fi rihlat Najib Mahfuz al-ramziyya*. 3rd printing. Beirut: Dar al-Tali'a, 1980.

Taymur, Mahmud. *Al-Shaykh Jum'a wa-aqasis 'ukhra*. 2nd ed. Cairo: Al-

Matba'a al-Salafiyya, 1927.
al-Tirmidhi, Muhammad Bin 'Isa Abu 'Isa. *Sunan*, Vol. 8. Homs, 1967.
Tlas, Mustafa, and 'Adi Nadim. *Mu'jam al-asma' al-'arabiyya*. Damascus: Dar Tlas, 1985.
'Ukasha, Tharwat. *Mudhakkirati fi 'l-siyasa wa'l-thaqafa*. Cairo [1987–1988].
Wadi, Taha 'Imran. *Dirasat fi naqd al-riwaya*. Cairo: al-Hay'a al-Misriyya al-'Amma li'l-Kitab, 1989.
al-Zabidi, Muhammad Murtada. *Taj al-'arus min jawahir al-qamus*, vol. 17, ed. Mustafa Hijazi. Kuwait: Matba'at Hukumat al-Kuwait, 1397 AH (1977).

Works in English and Other Languages

Abdel-Malek, Anwar. *Egypt: Military Society*. New York: Random House, 1968.
Abu-Haidar, Jareer. "Awlad Haratina by Najib Mahfuz: An Event in the Arab World." *Journal of Arabic Literature* 16 (1985), pp. 119–31.
Abu-Lughod, Janet L. *Cairo: 1001 Years of the City Victorious*. Princeton: Princeton University Press, 1971.
Allen, Roger. *The Arabic Novel: An Historical and Critical Introduction*. Syracuse: Syracuse University Press, 1982.
———. "*Mirrors* by Najib Mahfuz," in *Critical Perspectives on Naguib Mahfouz*, ed. Trevor Le Gassick. Washington, 1991, pp. 131–50. Orig. pub. in *The Muslim World* 62, no. 2 (April 1972), pp. 115–25, and 63, no. 1 (Jan. 1973), pp. 15–27.
Beard, Michael, and Haydar Adnan, eds. *Naguib Mahfouz: From Regional Fame to Global Recognition*. Syracuse: Syracuse University Press, 1993.
Cachia, Pierre. *An Overview of Modern Arabic Literature*. Edinburgh: Edinburgh University Press, 1990.
———. *Taha Husayn: His Place in the Egyptian Literary Renaissance*. London: Luzac & Co., 1956.
Dekmejian, R. Hrair. *Egypt under Nasser: A Study in Political Dynamics*. Albany: State University of New York Press, 1971.
El-Enany, Rasheed. *Naguib Mahfouz: The Pursuit of Meaning*. London and New York: Routledge, 1993.
Ewen, Joseph. *Ha-Demut ba-sipporet* (Character in Narrative). Tel Aviv: Sifriyat Po'alim, 1980. Hebrew.
Fletcher, Angus. *Allegory*. Ithaca and London: Cornell University Press, 1964.
Forster, E. M. *Alexandria: A History and a Guide*. Alexandria: Whitehead Morris Limited, 1922.

Gershoni, Israel, and James P. Jankowski. *Egypt, Islam and the Arabs*. New York: Oxford University Press, 1986.

Ghanayim, Mahmud. "Microcosm and Macrocosm in Najib Mahfuz's *al-Baqi min al-Zaman Sa'ah*," in *Writer, Culture, Text: Studies in Modern Arabic Literature*, edited by A. Elad. Fredericton, N.B., Canada: York Press, 1993.

Gibb, H. A. R. *Arabic Literature*. Oxford: Oxford University Press, 1963.

———. *Studies on the Civilization of Islam*. Boston: Beacon Press, 1962.

Gordon, Elizabeth Hope. *The Naming of Characters in the Works of Charles Dickens*. University of Nebraska Studies in Language, Literature and Criticism, 1. Lincoln, Nebraska: University of Nebraska Press, 1917.

Hamon, Philippe. "Pour un statut sémiologique du personnage," in R. Barthes et al., *Poétique du récit*. Paris: Editions du Seuil, 1977.

Hinds, Martin, and El-Said Badawi. *A Dictionary of Egyptian Arabic*. Beirut: Librairie du Liban, 1986.

Hourani, Albert. *Arabic Thought in the Liberal Age: 1798–1939*. London: Oxford University Press, 1962.

Kilpatrick, Hilary. *The Modern Egyptian Novel: A Study in Social Criticism*. London: The Ithaca Press, 1974.

King, Joan Wucher. *Historical Dictionary of Egypt*. Cairo: The American University Press, 1984.

Le Bon, Gustave. *Psychologie du socialisme*. Paris: F. Alcan, 1898.

Levi-Strauss, Claude. "The Structural Study of Myth," in *Reader in Comparative Religion: An Anthropological Approach*. eds. William A. Lessa and Evon Z. Vogt. 3rd edition. New York: Harper and Row, 1972.

Lewis, Bernard. *Race and Color in Islam*. New York: Harper and Row, 1971.

Lodge, David. *The Art of Fiction*. London: Penguin Books, 1992.

Mahmoud, Mohamed. "The Unchanging Hero in a Changing World: Najib Mahfuz's *al-Liss wa'l-kilab (The Thief and the Dogs)*," in *Critical Perspectives on Naguib Mahfouz*, ed. Trevor le Gassick. Washington: Three Continents Press, 1991. Orig. pub. *Journal of Arabic Literature* 15 (1984), pp. 58–75.

Mehrez, Samia. "Respected Sir," in *Naguib Mahfouz: From Regional Fame to Global Recognition*. eds. M. Beard and A. Haydar. New York: Syracuse University Press, 1993, pp. 61–80.

Milson, Menahem. "An Allegory on the Social and Cultural Crisis in Egypt: *Walid al-'Ana'* by Najib Mahfuz." *International Journal of Middle East Studies* 3 (1972), p. 324–47.

———. "Nagib Mahfuz and the Quest for Meaning." *Arabica* 17 (1970).

———. "Religion and Revolution in an Allegory by Najib Mahfuz: A Study of *Ruh tabib al-qulub*," in *Studies in Memory of Gaston Wiet* ed. Miriam Rosen-Ayalon. Jerusalem: Institute of Asian and African Studies, The Hebrew University of Jerusalem, 1977.

Moreh, Shmuel. *Modern Arabic Poetry 1800–1970.* Leiden: E. J. Brill, 1976.

———. *Studies in Modern Arabic Prose and Poetry.* Leiden: E. J. Brill, 1988.

Moussa-Mahmoud, Fatma. "Depth of Vision: The Fiction of Naguib Mahfouz." *Third World Quarterly* 2, no. 2 (April 1989).

Parker, Richard, Robin Sabin, and Caroline Williams. *Islamic Monuments in Cairo: A Practical Guide.* 3rd ed. Cairo: The American University Press, 1985.

Peled, Mattityahu. *Religion, My Own: The Literary Works of Najib Mahfuz.* New Brunswick and London: Transaction Books, 1983.

———. "Yasin the Gate-Crasher." *Middle Eastern Studies* 9, no. 3 (October 1973), pp. 341–47.

Philipp, Thomas. *Ǧurǧi Zaidān: His Life and Thought.* Wiesbaden: F. Steiner, 1979.

Pines, S. *The Guide of the Perplexed.* Chicago: University of Chicago Press, 1963.

Rimmon-Kenan, Shlomith. *Narrative Fiction: Contemporary Poetics.* London and New York: Routledge, 1989 [1983].

Rudnyckyj, J. B. "Function of Proper Names," in *Stil- und Formprobleme in der Literatur.* Vorträge des VII. Kongresses der Internationalen Vereinigung für moderne Sprachen und Literaturen in Heidelberg. Heidelberg: C. Winter, 1959.

Safran, Nadav. *Egypt in Search of Political Community.* Cambridge: Harvard University Press, 1961.

Schimmel, Annemarie. *Islamic Names.* Edinburgh: Edinburgh University Press, 1989.

Semah, David. *Four Egyptian Literary Critics.* Leiden: E. J. Brill, 1974.

Snir, Reuven. "The Arab-Israeli Conflict as Reflected in the Writings of Najib Mahfuz." *Abr-Nahrain* 27 (1989), pp. 120–53.

Somekh, Sasson. *The Changing Rhythm: A Study of Najib Mahfuz's Novels.* Leiden: E. J. Brill, 1973.

Smith, Charles D. *Islam and the Search for Social Order in Modern Egypt: A Biography of Muhammad Husayn Haykal.* Albany: State University of New York, 1983.

Stagh, Marina. *The Limits of Freedom of Speech: Prose Literature and Prose Writers in Egypt under Nasser and Sadat.* Acta Universitatis Stockholmiensis, Stockholm Oriental Series 14. Stockholm: Almquist & Wiksell International, 1993.

Vatikiotis, P. J. *The History of Egypt.* 3rd ed. Baltimore: Johns Hopkins University Press, 1985.

Weaver, Mary Anne. "The Novelist and the Sheikh." *The New Yorker*, 30 January 1995, pp. 52–69.

Wellek, Rene, and Austin Warren. *Theory of Literature.* New York: Harcourt, Brace & World, 1956.

Whitman, Jon. *Allegory: The Dynamics of an Ancient and Medieval Technique.* Oxford: Oxford University Press, 1987.

Index